The Greatest Brush

Love, Tragedy and Redemption

of Artist

Frank Duveneck

By

JAMES OTT

Library of Congress Cataloging-in-Publication Data

Names: Ott, James, author.
Title: The greatest brush : love, tragedy and redemption of artist
Frank Duveneck / By James Ott.
Description: Boston : Branden Books, 2016. | Includes index. | Description based on print version record and CIP data provided by publisher; resource not viewed.
Identifiers: LCCN 2015046006 (print) | LCCN 2015045360 (ebook) | ISBN
    9780828326117 (E-Book) | ISBN 9780828326094 (pbk. : alk. paper)
Subjects: LCSH: Duveneck, Frank, 1848-1919. | Painters--United
    States--Biography.
Classification: LCC ND237.D85 (print) | LCC ND237.D85 O88
2016 (ebook) | DDC
    759.13--dc23
LC record available at http://lccn.loc.gov/2015046006

ISBN 9780828326094 Paperback
ISBN 9780828326117 E-Book

Branden Books
PO Box 812094
Wellesley MA 02482

www.brandenbooks.com

__Dedication__

To Charlotte

Verba volant, scripta manent

Words fly, written word stays

Theme

This is a story about a great painter and artist, his dedication to his craft, his rejection of fame and his ultimate personal triumphs. The Benedictines trained young Frank Duveneck and directed him to studies in nineteenth century Europe. He tasted Bohemianism and became an important artist who came in contact with the nineteenth century's most talented individuals. He married an artist, a textile heiress from Boston whose death demoralized him. He turned to teaching, adapted his natural abilities to other genre and trends, and became a legendary figure as an artist, teacher and founder of American art. The Cincinnati Art Museum will be one of the major institutions commemorating the centenary of his death in 2019.

Contents

Frank Duveneck
Painter, Sculptor, Muralist and Teacher

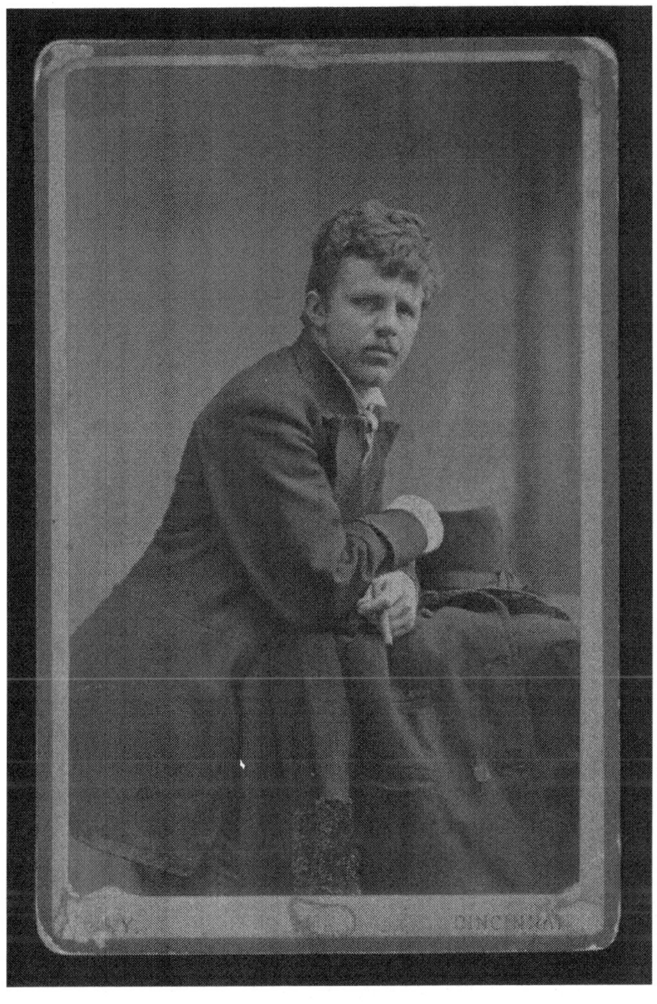

Frank Duveneck, 1877/J. Landy, photographer, Frank and Elizabeth Boott Duveneck papers, Archives of American Art, Smithsonian Institution

Foreward

In 1979 I was driving my mentor, R.H. Ives Gammell, back to the Fenway Studios from his daily lunch at the Tavern Club in Boston. In an effort to shed light on this or that aspect of painting, he often quizzed me while riding in the car. "What three painters relied mostly on an understanding of three dimensional planes to express form?" he asked. Well, I knew Franz Hals had to be among them. I suspected John Singer Sargent, and much to his surprise, I correctly guessed the third— Frank Duveneck.

Mr. Gammell, then 87 years old, had been to the opera with Sargent while a young artist in Boston. He was also a friend and student of Boston painter Joseph DeCamp around World War I. DeCamp, born in Cincinnati, had been one of the "Duveneck Boys," traveling through Italy with his slightly older and already famous friend. In just this way begins the cross pollination so critical to the development of any art and demonstrates how the appreciation and respect painters have for each other is often transmitted from one generation to the next. That I would eventually become much more familiar with Duveneck seemed destined from that point on.

In 1986 I moved to Cincinnati and found the instructional gold mine that Frank Duveneck had left as his legacy to the Cincinnati Art Museum. He had bought back many of his own works from their original owners only to give them to the museum, a fact which made my visits there seem very much a gift to me from him personally. For, as all young painters dedicated to representational art do, we struggle mightily. And here on the walls were paintings that, with concentrated study, could point the way.

Painting was, and largely still is, an art of observation. In fact, it's been suggested that genius has more to do with one's powers of observation than with any other trait. Open to and moved by visual phenomena, we are struck by the beauty, poetry and poignancy of the visible world. Our strongest desire is to share that joy and excitement with others. But any young painter, with the idea that doing so is as easy as mindlessly copying what you see before you on canvas, is quickly disabused of that notion. Nature has its laws, and learning them is the cornerstone of how we can effectively represent three-dimensional space on a two-dimensional surface. At his best, no one has done this better than Frank Duveneck.

Here in Cincinnati, his former students themselves went on to teach at the Cincinnati Art Academy. , They held the banner high through the better part of the early to the middle of the twentieth century. But eventually, the tidal wave that was Modernism eclipsed Duveneck's reputation, and he was largely forgotten. There were a few hold outs, chief among them a handful of painters in Boston and New York who knew what he had achieved was considerable—and rare. The occasional article was published. In 1965 there was one written by a former student, Henry C. Loughmiller, entitled, "I Studied with Frank Duveneck." Painters Herman and Bessie Wessel, married in Duveneck's Gloucester cottage in 1917, carried on the esthetic tradition of their master in Cincinnati into the early 1970s, when Bessie followed Herman (who had passed in 1969) into art history in 1973.

So what can Frank Duveneck teach the aspiring young artist today? A technical analysis of his work should begin with his uncanny ability to indicate maximum form and volume with an extraordinary economy of means. Every brush stroke is loaded with purpose and resolve. Nothing is superfluous. There is great confidence in the work, made manifest in the exceptional vitality and vigor of his execution. In his best work, we see a mastery of all the facets of the painter's craft. As a young student he started strong in the Munich style and grew dramatically out of that auspicious beginning toward landscapes in the area around Polling Germany, which sparkle with a joyful handling of paint. His Venetian etchings, at times confused by some with Whistler's because of their exquisite quality, show a fine sense of design and composition. While in Italy, he assimilated a lighter, more colorful sensibility for a time. This was followed by a highly polished phase in the French man-

11

ner. After his beloved wife died, Duveneck turned increasingly to landscape. The brilliant pieces he painted in the American Impressionist style in Gloucester and Rockport are exceptional examples of the genre. As if that weren't enough, toward the end of his life he executed the extraordinary murals for the Cathedral of the Basilica in Covington, Kentucky, in honor of his mother. He changed, experimented, tried new approaches and appears to have through it all freely shared his discoveries, knowledge and experience with any promising and sincere student of painting in a most generous and kindly way.

Returning to Boston, the city in which Duveneck had considerable early success, his pupil, Joseph DeCamp, was to develop a fine career backed in large part on the formidable technical equipment he had gained from his association with the master. The young Ives Gammell eventually encountered DeCamp, and in many ways found in him his artistic salvation. Years later, in 1945, Mr. Gammell goes on to write for many what was a seminal book called The Twilight of Painting - An Analysis of Recent Trends to Serve in a Period of Reconstruction. At the height of the iconoclastic purging of anything that smacked of Realism, he thus made his prediction; after a period of reassessment by succeeding generations, young art students would once again be hungry for the knowledge of how to make representational paintings. As a fourteen year old in Sandusky, Ohio I encountered this book, and it quite simply changed my life. It eventually led me to study under its author as a high school graduate, and still further, to a profound appreciation of Mr. Duveneck's life and oeuvre.

As anyone who has taken the time to look into the rebirth of landscape, figure and portrait painting in this country and abroad in the last twenty years can attest, this day has surely come. As painters across the globe continue to rebuild the art of representational painting from its near demise in the mid-twentieth century, they are increasingly rediscovering the work of this monumentally gifted artist, Frank Duveneck. But perhaps equal to his great contribution to the art of painting was the shining example he gives us of kindness and generosity that still reverberates even today.

Carl Samson
Wessel Studio
Eden Park, Cincinnati, Ohio

Carl Samson is a portrait artist and former Chairman of the Governing Board of the American Society of Portrait Artists.

Prelude

Nearly a century has passed since the dramatic ending of the multifaceted life of artist Frank Duveneck, a prize-winning American painter in nineteenth century Europe and a founder of art education in the United States. While studying in Europe he tended toward Bohemianism and launched himself as a wholly independent character: obstinate, lovable, brash at times yet always courteous. He was the single-minded good guy, always intent in his quest to obtain what he wanted. He achieved fame early in his career and maintained a renown that extended through much of his life. Approaching his last day, January 3, 1919, ill from throat cancer and unable to speak, he signaled in an inimitable way with nursing religious women attending him in hospital that he wished to return to the Roman Catholic Church. The final hours were as dramatic as Lord Flyte's in Evelyn Waugh's masterpiece, *Brideshead Revisited.*

A host of permanent legacies abound from this artist, a precocious youth skillful with the brush who attained early stardom on the Continent. The bounty of his secular art works is showcased today at the Cincinnati Art Museum--one of America's oldest founded in 1881, and can be found in the leading institutions in this country. Some of his handiwork appears in scattered trendy exhibitions of American and European artists.

Duveneck produced a second harvest, that of religious icons and decorations in churches and abbeys in eastern United States and Canada. Most famous is a mural painted in the first decade of the twentieth century in the Cathedral Basilica of the Assumption in Covington, Kentucky. The basilica stands only a few city blocks from where he was reared and where he returned as a wealthy and lonely middle-aged widower, a successful artist and already an admired teacher. On his return home, all of Cincinnati held him in high regard as a true cosmopolitan; but he was a loveable old shoe to his close friends.

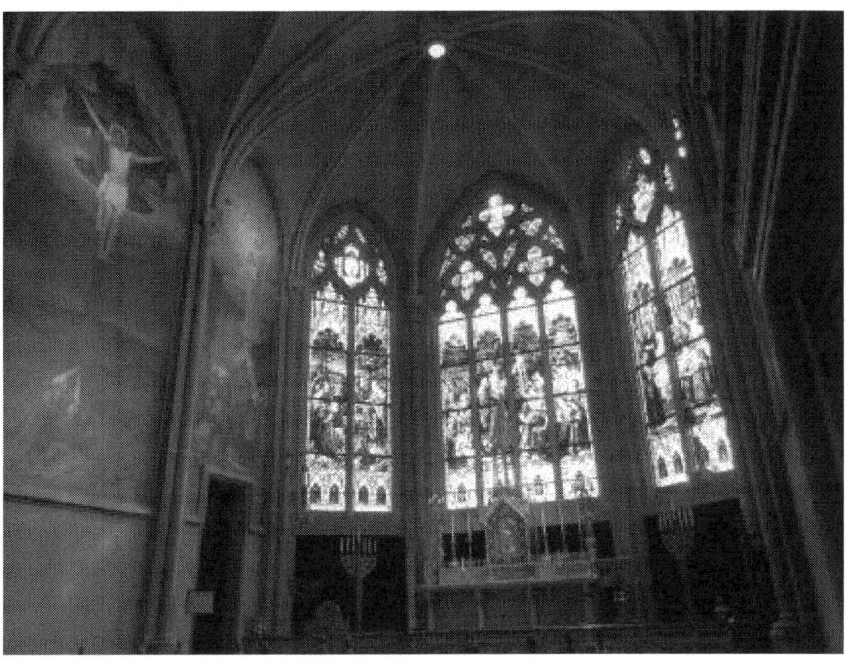

Two panels of Duveneck's mural in the Blessed Sacrament Chapel of the Cathedral Basilica of the Assumption, Covington

The artist's mural does not leap out at visitors to the cathedral basilica. Stained glass windows capture their attention as they, *Stories in Glass*[1], fashioned by artisans of Franz Mayer of Munich, Inc., wrap around the nave and the sanctuary of this French Gothic structure. Shafts of light on sunny days stream into the interior of the basilica, a boutique facsimile of the burial place of France's kings, Paris's Saint Denis. Catholics in the Covington Diocese built the basilica, starting in the late 1890s, dedicating the addition of a façade based on Notre Dame in 1910, and have renovated it twice. When visitors move around in it today, they naturally come across the Blessed Sacrament Chapel in a south wing. There, the

15

long wall comes alive with Duveneck's stunning series of images depicting important Catholic beliefs.

The artist dedicated the mural to his mother, Katherine Siemers Duveneck. In the central panel a woman who could easily pass for her prays imploringly at the foot of the Cross. To the right an Old Testament temple priest presides at an offering of bread and wine. His vestments precisely follow their description in *Exodus 28* and in other biblical passages. The panel to the left portrays a bishop, surrounded by priests, deacons and an acolyte, raising the monstrance containing the host, the Body of Christ, for the faithful. This action is shown taking place in the very cathedral church where the murals are displayed.

More than even this mural, the artist's secular works on permanent exhibition at the Cincinnati museum perpetuate the legend. The paintings share the spotlight with other key holdings of the museum, an assembly of classical structures on a plateau near Mount Adams, the *haut monde* residential area. A one-time vineyard, Mount Adams later served immigrants and then transformed into an art colony around the reputable Rookwood Pottery. Entering the Schmidlapp Wing, the main gallery building, visitors walk through a lobby to a long hall where ultra-significant highlighted items, *Icons of the Collection*, taken from the museum's 60,000 objects, are on display. One of these is a Duveneck painting *The Whistling Boy* completed in Munich when he was twenty-four years old, one of his best known works.

Proceeding through the Great Hall visitors arrive at the Cincinnati Wing, opened in 2003. They are treated to art works that bear Cincinnati labels, pottery, furniture, sculpture and paintings. Across the hall and dominating that part of the museum, many of Duveneck's works of art are exhibited in a large room. Several interesting paintings, neat in execution and complete in arresting detail, by his wife, Elizabeth Otis Lyman Boott Duveneck, a New England textile heiress and American expatriate, hang shoulder-to-shoulder with his. Her death in Paris, two years to the day of their marriage, left him numb with grief and obligated to a fifteen-month-old son. The sense of loss lingered, regarded by some as the final factor that stifled him from a strongly aggressive pursuit of his talents.

The depth of Duveneck's love and admiration for Elizabeth can be seen readily in a painted plaster copy of her sarcophagus. Created in Cincinnati with counsel from a friend and sculptor, Clement John Barnhorn, the dark effigy, though masterfully done, offers at first a funereal sensation. On closer look, Elizabeth's angelic features are formed with grace and serenity that only talent and great love can bestow. The bronze original sits above her grave in Allori Cemetery in Florence, the city where she spent most of her life. A bronze and gold leaf version sits in Gallery 700 at the Metropolitan Museum of Art in New York City. A magnificent effigy in marble, the best mode to view the refined face, is part of the Duveneck collection of the Museum of Fine Arts in Boston, which extends to several paintings, a sample of his etchings and woodcuts. The Boston museum also owns one of Elizabeth's paintings.

The Cincinnati museum has in its temperature-controlled storage area a sketchbook containing some fifty-seven pieces by Elizabeth Boott, keen, accurate and sometimes playful pen and ink and pencil sketches of people and scenes in Europe. Dated 1870-72 and titled *Florence*, the sketches cover scenes in Florence, Liverpool, Leghorn, and areas of France and Switzerland. In that time period Lizzie was in Europe after taking instructions from William Morris Hunt in Boston. A steady progression may be seen in increasingly detailed work, prudent care in the use of shading and in compositional skills that ultimately led to her work in oils and watercolors.

Elizabeth's story and that of her New England family are obscured in the art world, but they are among the riches of the total Duveneck chronicle. Her maiden name lives on in The Boott Cotton Mills Complex, a large component of the Lowell National Historical Park in Lowell, Massachusetts. Founded in 1835 by her great, great uncle ancestor, Kirk Boott, the Boott Mills brought the

17

industrial revolution to the United States, and it played a key part in the New England textile industry. Elizabeth's father, Francis, extended the franchise when he married into the Lyman family, mill owners as well and one of the most respected families of Boston. The financial prosperity of the mills enabled Francis and Elizabeth Boott to live as expatriates absorbing the culture of Europe. The textile industry thrived throughout the nineteenth century, declined after each of the two world wars, and the last mill closed in 1958.

The Duveneck legend merges with popular culture in Cincinnati. In recent years the Keystone restaurant in Covington has offered a corned beef and pastrami sandwich with sauerkraut in his name. It is a favorite of Polly Campbell, food writer and restaurant critic for *The Cincinnati Enquirer*. The Over the Rhine brewing company (OTR) has produced a Dortmunder style lager named Duveneck.

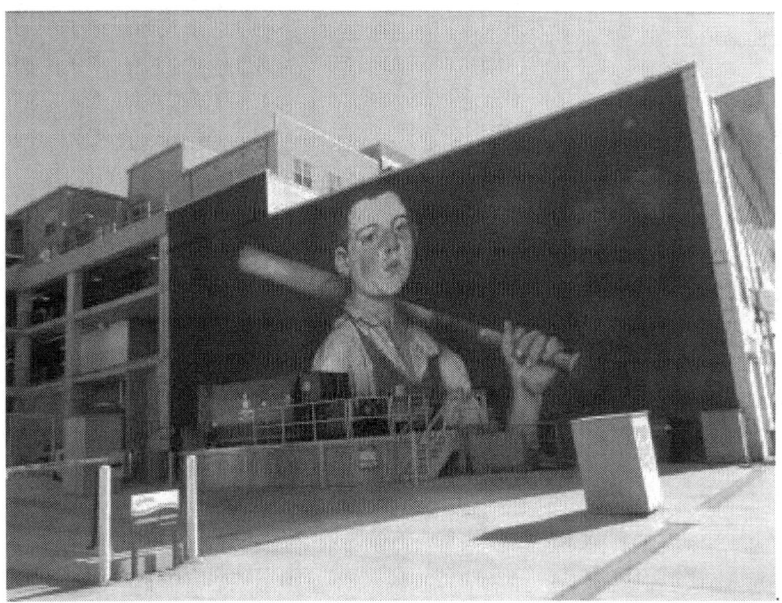

A play on Duveneck's The Cobbler's Apprentice in the Banks, Cincinnati

The legend becomes all the more graphic. As crowds move down major sloping streets going to a Cincinnati Reds game at the Great American Ball Park along the Ohio River, they are confronted by a huge mural on the wall of a building in the new Banks area. It is a clever play on the artist's painting, *The Cobbler's Apprentice.* Instead of exhaling smoke and concentrating on the lift he gets from his cigar in the original painting, the boy stares out and carries a baseball bat over his left shoulder.[2] The original painting, the gift of Mr. and Mrs. Charles Phelps Taft, hangs in the Taft Museum less than a mile away, one of the oldest buildings in the city and a former Taft residence.

The Cincinnati Art Museum employs the legend for fund raising at a gala each June. Members of the Duveneck Society meet monthly in a quest to learn more about art and the famous local painter. Each Memorial Day, members of the Cincinnati Art Club, gather at the site of his burial in Mother of God Cemetery in Covington to pay homage to the painter. Local artists and admirers, such as Carl Samson, former chairman of the Governing Board of the American Society of Portrait Artists, prepare texts that are read aloud in commemoration.

Another key physical remnant of his legacy, the Duveneck house at 1232 Greenup Street in Covington, authenticates the origin of this talented artist in a community of German immigrants under tutelage of nuns, monks and artists connected with the Order of St. Benedict. The frame home sits on a narrow lot, which stood adjacent to a small beer garden operated by the painter's father, Squire, who also served as a justice of the peace. Today, a building that formerly housed a hardware store sits on the beer garden space, and is designated to serve as a center for art in the community. In 2015 the Duveneck House was placed on the National Registry of Historic Places.

The house has no pretensions, much like the Duvenecks themselves. It began as a one-story building, a second level added later as the family grew in size. In his later years when Frank lived there

19

with a half-brother, Charlie Duveneck, and his half-sister, the youngest of the female siblings and a favorite named Mollie, the former beer garden was transformed into a private flower garden. The house itself has contributed to adding spice to the family story. By happenstance one day several decades ago, a young workman happened on a loose red brick in an attic staircase. Behind it, he found a cigar box containing personal letters and other items that revealed intimate secrets and recorded details of a family crisis. More of this sensational discovery is available in Chapter Nine.

Duveneck's own personality and his years of teaching helped to forge his legendary status. His students adored him, revered him as a master, yet found him an extremely private man, separated from them, even standoffish to some in later years. Throughout his life, his actions reveal him as always being himself, an authentic personality easy going with others, no matter how far different in background they may be. The written record also demonstrates that he tolerated arrogance from people of achievement such as the writer Henry James, a friend of his wife's, and other New Englanders who considered themselves, educated and cultured Americans, his betters, though, they, too, recognized his genius. While a private man, he enjoyed his select friends among artists and ordinary people in his hometown, and many local story tellers say that he loved too much his beer and tobacco.

Duveneck was wealthy from his wife's inheritance. Observers of his daily routine would not have suspected his affluence. He lived ordinarily, taking street cars daily from his home in Covington to the art academy where he taught in a heavy stone Romanesque Revival building, now a part of the Cincinnati museum. Each year he got away to Boston where he played father to his beloved son, reared there by the boy's mother's relations.

First recognized by American critics in Boston, Duveneck, though known widely there, is not a focal point of celebration today. If given any consideration, he is secondary when compared to well-known and successful New England-related American artists John

Singer Sargent, Winslow Homer or Whistler who painted vigorously through their adult lives and achieved lasting renown. However, only thirty miles to the north of Boston, Duveneck is regarded as a pivotal figure in the development of the still-thriving art colony around Gloucester. He first painted in the fishing and resort community in 1890 and spent summers there virtually every year after the turn of the century working and relaxing at the shore.

In Gloucester the Cape Ann Museum, pays homage to the artist on its web site and in its exhibition halls where a few of his paintings of Gloucester harbor are displayed. The museum concentrates its collection on the maritime world and features modern and contemporary local artists. A book of the cape's art history gives credit to his important role as an establishing figure, a beacon to artists who worked and settled there to paint its fisher folk, quaint villages and its many wave-lashed coves.

Once a phenomenon in Europe after extraordinary successes and prizes in Munich as a student in the 1870s, considered by some experts to be his finest period, today he is regarded as a minor Bavarian painter.[3] A German company, Kunstdrucke & Gemalde, has produced posters of several Duveneck paintings. A dozen or so companies offer copies of his paintings, rendered by hand of contemporary artists, for prices ranging from less than a hundred dollars to several hundred, depending on the size of the finished work and possibly the complexity.

The art epicenter of Florence has not forgotten its illustrious Americans of the nineteenth century. In 2012 (March 3-July 15) an exhibit at the Palazzo Strozzi heralded the Duvenecks and their art. A broad range of works by Frank and Lizzie were important parts of the exhibit including *The Bridges*, an oil painting on canvas, executed by Frank Duveneck in 1880, lent by the St. Louis Art Museum, and a water color of *Villa Castellani*, completed by wife, Lizzie, in 1886, the year of their marriage. The work now resides in the National Museum of Women in the Arts in Washington, D.C.

The family legacy of the Duvenecks continues in the peninsula region south of San Francisco. There, Frank Duveneck Jr., and his wife, Josephine Whitney Duveneck, acquired a working farm, Hidden Villa, in the Los Altos hills west of Palo Alto. The family prospered and shared its 2,500-acre estate with the community. Dedicated to the principles of social justice, the family transformed Hidden Villa into a constant safe haven for refugees. These included those who escaped Nazi oppression, Japanese-Americans dislocated by government edict during World War II, and field workers representing the farm movement led by Cesar Chavez. In happier times Hidden Villa served as a lively summer camp especially for disadvantaged children. The spirit of compassion that underlay these activities continues today through programs operated under a nonprofit trust. In response to this outpouring of love and concern for humanity, for the dedication to education in general and the family's long regard for the environment, the community named a school, Duveneck Elementary, after Frank Jr. and Josephine.

There's little wonder that Duveneck, the artist, the teacher, the man, still astonishes, perplexes and mystifies critics and enthusiasts nearly a century after his death. Tales about him provide often conflicting images. His talents with the brush broke new ground, but he was thought at times lazy; he turned down many invitations throughout his life, apparently deigning them too much bother; he was a religious person who strayed into a Bohemian life style in art-centered Munich, yet he is one who returned to the Faith and presented it to the world in a famous mural. Set apart from other children of immigrants by his God-given talent, he was a strong personality. Yet he emerged as a fairly standard version of a single-minded, if not bull-headed and otherwise modest German-American who in his youth forged ahead against odds and became somebody. Artist and art historian R.H. Ives Gammell wrote that Duveneck's reputation has never declined even as the art world has twisted and turned.

In America, this young genius, son of pioneer immigrants, husband to a wealthy and talented American expatriate, a father of American art education, deserves more than a footnote in art history. Guided by his religious mentors, he flourished as an artist and found success abroad. He was on close terms with the famous in his chosen field, with writers and intelligentsia of that time and place. His life *was* extraordinary and deserves to be told, wrote William Dean Howells, the American author, in a note to Cincinnati museum officials after the painter's death. Howells, a former editor of *The Atlantic* and a novelist, shared one aspect of Duveneck's life with his readers, referring to the painter and his students in Florence as the Inglehart Boys in his book, *Indian Summer*.

Howells was right; Duveneck's was an extraordinary life. He was *sui generis* as a man and as an artist. His relationships, with his family, his teachers, his Church, his wife's family, other artists and students, provide valuable insights into the character of this man who was, and is, America's gift to the world of art.

Stories in Glass, The Windows of the Cathedral Basilica of the Assumption, Covington, Kentucky, by Msgr. William F. Cleves, Copyright, 2009 Cathedral Foundation, Inc.

[2] *The Cobbler's Apprentice Plays Ball*, a mural on the wall at 120 E. Freedom Way, Cincinnati, Ohio, Tim Parsley, lead artist, and Artworks, Cincinnati.

[3] Letter from Frederick Yeiser, arts connoisseur and former book editor of *The Cincinnati Enquirer*, a resident of Vienna, Austria, in his retirement

Chapter One

Beginnings of Romance

Venice, summer, 1878

Entering the Venetian studio of the artist Frank Duveneck in the company of a visiting Boston friend, winsome and wealthy Elizabeth Lyman Boott was making what she described as a pilgrimage. She owned a painting of his purchased in 1875 from an exhibit at the Boston Art Club and, an earnest student of art and an eager practitioner, she was anxious to learn more about Duveneck and his celebrated painting technique. She liked what she saw in the artist, known as the Viking for his bushy blond hair; but was disappointed that he could illustrate his craft by showing her and her friend, Miss Lucy Ellis, only one portrait and several studies.

She wrote to a Boston acquaintance:

"He is a remarkable looking young man, and a gentleman. He has a fine head and a keen eye and the perceptions strongly developed."

Standing by an easel casually dressed, Duveneck looked very much the artist. His blue eyes commanded attention over a blunt nose. His jaw sloped toward a strong, almost square chin, and his blond mustache drooped around his mouth. The artist carried his weight well, like a healthy American of German extraction. Not a big shouldered man, his head was a trifle larger than it should have been, and he stood a sturdy five feet, nine inches tall.

Lean and graceful, wearing high-quality clothes of European design, Miss Boott made a deep impression on the painter. She was about his age, thirty years or so. She carried herself in a dignified way. As she looked up to him and peppered him with a few quick questions, Duveneck knew she was intelligent and had a vast knowledge of art. He was drawn to her Grecian face and bright eyes as she dabbled in genteel conversation of a cultivated Victorian woman.

He told a future student that she "had the only perfect nose" he had ever seen on a woman.* It is an odd compliment but perhaps typical of him.

More than likely Duveneck knew of this smartly dressed woman by reputation. Not that it meant that much to him, he understood that she and her father, Francis, were eminent, moneyed American expatriates in Europe with high Boston family connections, the Otises, the Lymans, the Lowells and the Cabots.

Francis Boott had made a name for himself for his work in music. She was known as an accomplished student of art, a linguist and a woman of great appeal.

Certainly Miss Boott and Miss Ellis were aware of Duveneck. He was the new thunderbolt of the tumultuous art world, redefining itself again after the invention of photography was capturing much of the straight pictorial segment of the artistic domain. Paintings from his first Munich period (1870-74) displayed in the Boston exhibit had caught the eye of then critic and later novelist Henry James, long-time friend of the Boott family and a weighty figure among admirers of the woman known as Lizzie to her family and friends. Duveneck, Lizzie and James were to play significant roles in each other's lives through the decade of the 1880s.

Duveneck had been in Venice for a year, in a new venture, working with artist friends from the Royal Academy of Fine Arts in Munich, William Merritt Chase and fellow Cincinnatian, John Twachtman. Duveneck was learning the modern medium of etching with help from a student-friend, Otto Bacher, and from the master, James Abbott McNeill Whistler. An etching by Duveneck of the Riva degli Schiavoni in Venice depicts the boardwalk alive with fishermen and Venetians of all kinds, alone and in groups, a couple here and there, a cluster of padres, attired in cassocks and cappello romano hats, walking forward against a line of moored sailing vessels.

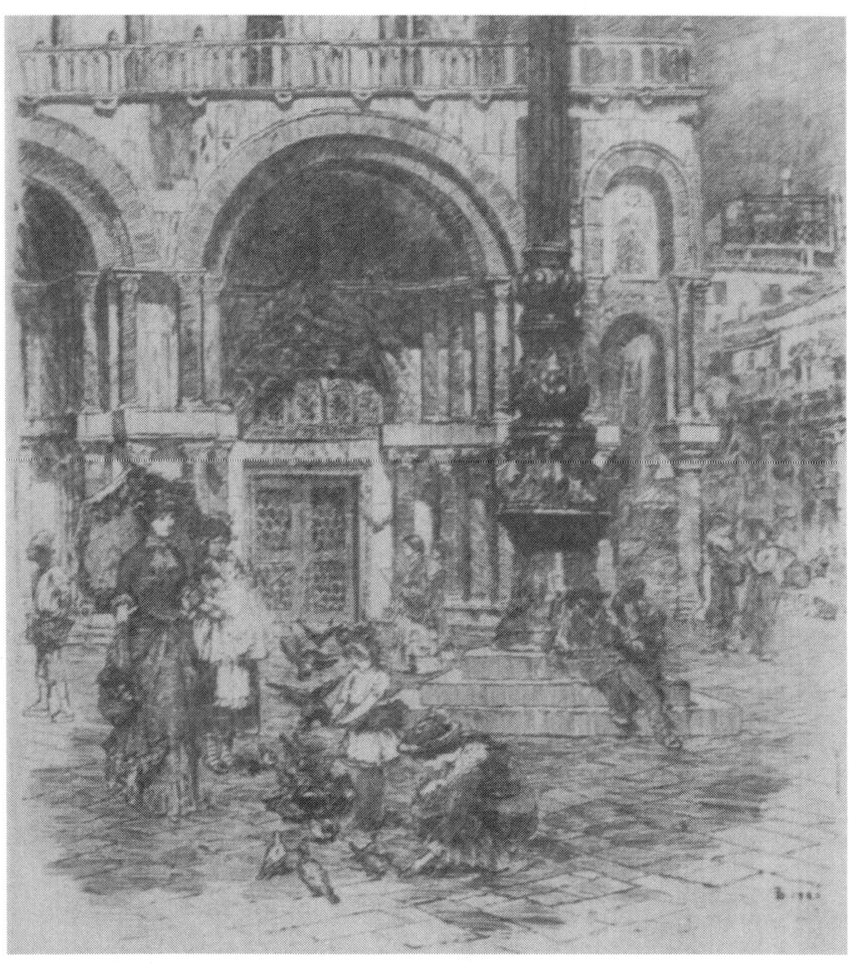

An etching of a Venetian scene by Duveneck

It was a view Lizzie Boott could see from Duveneck's studio located on the fourth floor of the Casa Kirsch. He later presented the etching to Miss Boott inscribed "with many good wishes."

In the artist's studio Lizzie and Miss Ellis chatted as they discreetly inquired into details of the life of this interesting Midwestern American artist. Duveneck readily offered where he came from, the town of Covington, in Kentucky across the Ohio River from Cincinnati. He told them he learned the fundamentals of art from church decorators trained in Germany and was educated at a Benedictine-operated parish school not far from his home. During his teenage years he learned the basics of art and decorated churches in eastern United States and in French Canada.

He may have even told his visitors that as a young man he considered becoming a priest. After all, the Benedictines had exerted a powerful influence over his home region. The clergy, nuns and monks, well-educated and energetic, filled with the fuel of Faith, had spread out from East Coast monasteries, fostering a wave of education and spiritual development for the growing populace of natives and immigrants. It was they, the Benedictines, one of the four major orders of the Roman Catholic Church, who supported Duveneck by arranging for his first trip abroad in 1870 to study at the Munich Art Academy. His studies had embarked him on a new life beyond church decoration as an artist.

Lizzie looked him over carefully as Duveneck responded casually.

She wrote of him later, using superlatives.

"He is a child of Nature, but a natural gentleman. He seems to have led the queerest, most vagrant sort of life among monks and nuns and convents in America, and rough art students here."

In her keen assessment of Duveneck she captured something of his character.

"He is the frankest, kindest-hearted of mortals and the least likely to make his way in the world. He is rather lazy, I fancy, and besides never looks at all to the main chance, so I suppose he will always be out at elbow as he seems to be now."

She was attracted to him, there's little doubt about that, and he reciprocated. He didn't want her to leave his studio, and he tried to continue the conversation uncharacteristically as he was always a bit shy with sophisticated women, even at the end of his third decade. Lizzie surprised him by expressing interest in becoming his student. Women in art classes, even in Europe, were "scarcer than hen's teeth," he thought to himself in the idiom of his native area. Yet he didn't want to lose this attractive and talented prospect as a student or a friend, and perhaps an intimate one.

They talked more about art and artists. She was aware of his circle of friends, Twachtman, and Chase. Duveneck remained close to these graduates of his Munich school, so much so that the older Walter Shirlaw (1838-1909), Chase (1849-1916) and Duveneck (1848-1919) were known as "father, son and holy ghost." While she was visiting, Duveneck must have mentioned that fellow American Whistler was working in Venice, if she didn't know already. One can easily see how Lizzie Boott the artist, intrigued by Duveneck, his painting technique and his influence, would have accepted all this information as interesting if not fascinating. During their exchange, she would have remarked that she had studied with William Morris Hunt in Boston and with Hunt's famed teacher, Thomas Couture in Paris. No doubt, Duveneck was delighted to learn that in her possession was his *Portrait of William Adams*, acquired at a Boston exhibition three years earlier. On this personal note, the relationship began to blossom.

Love of Art Unites

Any observer on that day in the Venetian studio could see that the contrast between him and Lizzie went beyond her personal wealth and his poverty. Their families and societal conditions of their lives differed significantly. She was the daughter of Boston Brahmins. Her father, Francis Boott, descended from comparatively recent English ancestors who had married into the old New England families, founded the textile industry there and launched the American industrial age. The Boott Mills in Lowell, Massachu-

28

setts, was among the first companies in the United States that hired women on a large scale. In the early days at the mill, "workers lived in houses within a brick quadrangle which included the mill itself, the company church and a school. The whole life of the employees was centered there. They labored 14 hours a day, six days a week," a slice of England in America that was later decried as exploitive.[1]

As for Lizzie Boott's father, Francis, a great nephew of the mill founder, Kirk Boott, the mill was a resource that supported his privileged life style. Something of a rebel who preferred the study of music to other more practical Brahmin pursuits, such as law or the church, he had married well to Elizabeth Otis Lyman and was living independently when the first of several family crises intervened. In 1844 Elizabeth Lyman Boott bore a son but he unfortunately died at only several months old, the first disappointment for the young family. Two years later, however, despite lung trouble, possibly tuberculosis, she gave birth to a daughter christened Elizabeth Otis Lyman Boott, always called Lizzie, who was to become the painter's wife. The second family crisis occurred when the respiratory-troubled mother succumbed to her ailments when Lizzie was 18 months old. Traumatized by this loss Francis Boott took the bold and unusual step of removing the toddler from Boston to Europe. He was wealthy by inheriting his wife's Lyman fortune and could afford it. He also had an independent streak. Ultrasensitive to his daughter's needs, he hired a nurse for Lizzie who was to stay with her for her entire life, while he began exclusively mentoring her education in language, art and music, a nineteenth century home schooling heavy on culture.

Lizzie spent her childhood and most of her teenage years on the Continent until after her eighteenth birthday when she returned to her native place and to other members of her family in America. She had studied French, Italian and Latin and lived a gracious life in Florence dedicated to self-development, education and art. Lizzie's sketchbook from her childhood contains drawing portraits of Robert Browning, the painter Arnold Henry Savage Landor, Amer-

29

ican novelist Nathaniel Hawthorne, and Thomas Adolphus Trollope, historian and novelist, the older brother of the incomparable Anthony Trollope, author of *Barchester Towers,* and some fifty novels.

In New England the Bootts knew everyone who counted highly: the famous James's, the critic and writer Henry and the psychologist and philosopher-to-be William; philosopher and writer Ralph Waldo Emerson; and authors Hawthorne and William Dean Howells. Not to mention the Lymans, the Otises and the Cabots, the Lowells, et cetera.

Circumstances differed completely in Duveneck's life hewed by a native talent, formed by basics of Benedictine learning, and expert tutelage in the craft of art. He was the eldest son of pioneer Midwesterners who had emigrated from the northern German duchy of Oldenburg. His instruction had come as an apprentice to the religious artists in medieval-like tradition. Young Frank demonstrated his knack by painting commercial signs before he ventured as a teenager into church and altar decoration. He had the support of his family who lived in a frame house on Grunopp Strasse [current Greenup Street] in Covington. His father, Joseph Duveneck, better known as Squire, served as a justice of the peace, operated a brewery and hosted a beer garden next to his home. His mother, Katharine (nee Siemers) Duveneck was renowned in the community for an epic journey out of the wilderness of northern Ohio, a distance of more than one hundred miles, after the death of both her parents. At the age of ten years she and her year-older sister, arrived ragged and exhausted in Covington where they sought out family friends. Katharine took up as a servant in the household of local painter James Beard, who was to become an early influence for young Duveneck.

Such personal family differences, at this moment in Venice, meant little to Lizzie. She was all too aware of classic divisions of people due to social standing, nobility, poverty, power and money, name, family and tradition. For her, Duveneck's talent made up for any lack of sophistication and qualified him as a person of interest. He had a charming and simple manner derived from his character and his upbringing by a warm and supportive family and Church. She described him as polite, a trait not always associated with artists and certainly not with Whistler.

In Lizzie's estimation, talent and good manners were highly important qualities. Besides, Duveneck cut a handsome figure and carried himself with manly bearing. Naturally, he was not perfect. He caroused in beer halls with his students, the Duveneck Boys, and was known by other artists as a fun companion and story teller. And, he had a way with women generally. He was liked. As she looked him over standing there in his studio, it was clear that opposites attract. In her case, love would conquer all.

Lizzie and Frank Duveneck each ranked as a desirable person in the whole of society. People wanted to know them better. The James's mother, Mary Walsh James, thought that her son, William, was at one point in love with Lizzie. Her son, Henry James, the writer, older than Lizzie by three years, showed much personal interest. Some friends in Boston considered Lizzie and Henry a possible match, maturing growths from the same cultural flower pot. The elusive Henry and forthright Lizzie corresponded for more than two decades. The author was fraternally friendly with Lizzie's father and stood among Lizzie's American friends who later strongly opposed any close personal ties to Duveneck. Typical of a writer, James situated two novels, *Roderick Hudson* and *The Portrait of a Lady*, at a place he knew well, the Villa Castellani where the Bootts were to reside on Bellosguardo hill overlooking Florence. So desirable were they that he amply based characters on Lizzie and her father, in several novels including *Portrait* and *The Golden Bowl*, though radically revising them as he did with many of his inspirations.

O*n a Roll in Venice*

While on his Venetian sojourn, Frank Duveneck was finding a taste of the good life. He was a frequent guest at soirees held by Mrs. Arthur (Katherine) De Kay Bronson of New York City who had acquired Casa Alvisi and annexed a part of the ancient palace, the Palazzo Guistiniani-Recanti, for parties.

As Henry James snobbishly wrote,

"She [Mrs. Bronson] sat for twenty years at the wide mouth, as it were, of the Grand Canal, holding out her hand, with endless good-nature, patience, charity, to all decently accredited petitioners, the incessant troop of those either bewilderedly making or fondly renewing acquaintance with the dazzling city."

James named Mrs. Bronson the genial *padrona*[2] with good reason. She was infused with power in another important way. She was the sister of Richard Watson Gilder, Richard Watson American poet and journalist, who became an influential editor of *The Century Magazine* and served as a prime mover for arts and letters.

During this Venetian period, a very likeable trait in Duveneck evidenced itself, his lack of pretense among the wealthy and powerful, never ashamed of his Germanic heritage and Midwestern upbringing no matter where he walked. It is what it is, he seemed to say; take it or leave it, a straight-forward and open-minded attitude, neither haughty nor subservient.

A later memoir of Elizabeth Robins Pennell, the journalist and wife of the etcher Joseph Pennell, described Duveneck at this time as "large, fair, golden haired with long drooping golden mustache of a type apt to suggest indolence and indifference. As he lolled against the red velvet cushions smoking his Cavour, enjoying the talk of others as much as his own or more—for he had the talent of eloquent silence when he chose to cultivate it—his eyes half shut, smiling with casual benevolence, he may have looked to a stranger incapable of action and as if he did not know whether he was alone or not, and cared less."[3]

When Elizabeth Pennell made this observation Duveneck was probably lounging in one of the three Venetian night clubs, namely Florian's, the Quadri or the Caffe Orientale, which never closed. The Orientale was defined by T.A. Trollope in a book of etchings by Pennell as "a specialty" of Venetian life. "Men of pleasure know that they shall find their peers there and gaze at the stream of life, as it flows past them, for hours together." It was a place where beauties of Italy communed with the fashionable.[4]

The Duveneck Boys often encountered the Pennells, he the artist and master etcher, she the writer, who reported from Europe for periodicals including Gilders' *Century Magazine*. Elizabeth Robins specialized in writing about food and art. She met Duveneck in Venice that summer and learned that the painter was, in effect, the toast of the town.

Duveneck, she wrote:

"told us that he slept in the Casa Kirsch, dined at the Antica Panada, and drank coffee at the Orientale, which was as much as to say that we might too if we liked. And of course we liked, for it is a great compliment when a man in Venice, or any Italian town, especially if he is of the importance and distinction to which Duveneck had already attained, makes you free to join him at dinner and over after-dinner coffee. It is more than a compliment, it launches you in Venice as to be presented at court launches you in London."[5]

Duveneck had a corner in a shabby low-ceilinged room of the Orientale where he held court that was never dull. "Nobody whoever sat there with us could have complained of dullness so long as Duveneck presided at our table."

Mrs. Pennell broke her own rule of not writing about a living person in her comments about Duveneck in Venice in her 1915 book. "I might not write at all about our nights in Venice as to leave him out of them, he who held them together and fashioned them into what they were."

After a night on the town, the Duveneck Boys frequently and gallantly escorted Mrs. Pennell to her lodgings.

Beyond Duveneck, the outstanding personality for the Boys for that summer in Venice was no less than James Abbott McNeill Whistler, the Lowell, Massachusetts-born painter and etcher, the embodiment of the "Art for Art's Sake" school. He was a sometimes reckless character who, in contrast with Duveneck's easy-going personality, had a reputation as a rebellious, restive and intractable artist and a first-rate innovative painter. A group of the Boys encountered Whistler while walking one day. A companion of the painter's on the walk introduced each of the Boys and to each he remarked:

"Whistler is charmed," and shook hands.

He became fast friends with the band of young artists. "Whistler sometimes played shamelessly on their idolatry. He borrowed money and paints from the boys, and made free use of the high quality printer's ink and portable press [Otto] Bacher had brought from Germany."[6]

And, he enthralled the Duveneck entourage with stories of life in London and his recent legal wrangle with the Oxford Slade professor of art John Ruskin, the leading critic of the Victorian era. Ruskin had found his *Nocturne in Black and Gold: The Falling* Rocket an abomination, with these words:

"I have seen, and heard, much of Cockney impudence before now; but never expected to hear a coxcomb ask two hundred guineas for flinging a pot of paint in the public's face."

Whistler had taken umbrage at the remark, filed a libel suit against Ruskin, and won his case. The courtroom victory was Pyrrhic. Compensation for his suffering was minimal. Distracted by it all, he produced less in the way of art work and was left stony broke. He filed for bankruptcy protection, which prompted the sale of assets, his so-named White House residence in London and an auction of art works.

At forty-four years old and in financial ruin, Whistler arrived in Venice in September, 1879, "the most famous pauper in the world." It was a place he had wanted to visit for over twenty–five years, he explained to all. At first he had rooms in a palazzo but in short order joined the Duveneck Boys at the Casa Jankovitz.

The young etcher Otto Bacher fell in with Whistler. Bacher recalled those days as exciting if not adventurous. The painter, he told Elizabeth Pennell, climbed to the top of the interior dome of the Scuola Grande di San Rocco to see Tintoretto's paintings close at hand. Mrs. Bronson later told Elizabeth Pennell that Whistler "used to say Venice was an impossible place to sit down and sketch in—he always felt 'there was something still better around the corner.'"

And, there was another side of their lives for some of them that summer in Venice. There were the inevitable affairs with women, life models and their landladies. One of the boys was so enamored that he brought his Venetian model with him on the fall return to Florence and kept her in his room. Duveneck himself became attached to a girl, another model, and the Boys wouldn't dare make a play for her out of respect for him.

"Duveneck, his friends said, never had any trouble with women. They loved him."[7]

Mrs. Pennell's memoir refers to Duveneck at this time as the "most procrastinating of mortals" but inspired, nevertheless, to produce his series of Venetian etchings. He was living the high life at this time after a string of successes and achievements as a student and practicing artist. And now he had Whistler as an associate of sorts, and that was to bring about a bit of trouble.

Glamorous Miss Blood

When Lizzie Boott visited the Venetian studio, she wasn't the only woman in the artist's life. There was the unnamed model, of course, and he had charmed a famous beauty, Gertrude Elizabeth Blood, later Lady Colin Campbell, an acquaintance of Lizzie's who, like her, was to become one of Duveneck's female art students.

Miss Blood is forever linked to the Duveneck story and not because of a steamy love affair, or the famous divorce case involving her and her husband some years later. She and the painter could have been romantically close, but there's no record to support the contention. She was his student in Florence, that's all we know, and a cheering sight to all men for her beauty.

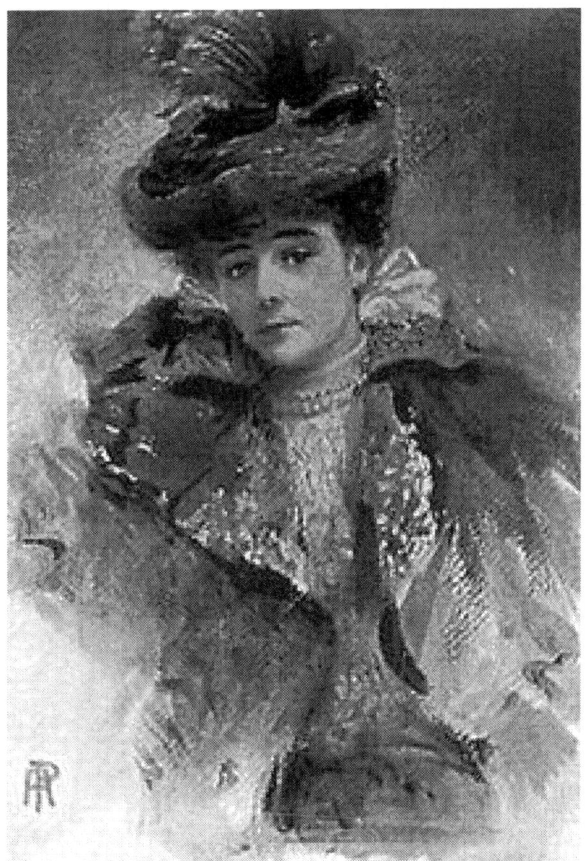

Lady Colin Campbell by Percy Anderson

The ties to Duveneck have their origin in her considerable interest in the artist's Venetian etchings. In Miss Blood's case, this interest launched a confusing episode over authorship of the Duveneck sketches in Victorian London. With the best intentions she dispatched them to London for a display at the Painter-Etchers' Exhibition, undoubtedly with Duveneck's approval. This simple act of loyalty by Miss

Blood caused "A Storm in an Aesthetic Teapot," according to a period magazine, and left the Duveneck helpless to quell it while Miss Blood, a breezy young woman on the rise, was probably enjoying her role as *agent provocateur.*

The etchings, clearly signed by Duveneck, appeared in the Painter-Etchers' exhibition at the Hanover Gallery, but still, confusion reigned over the authorship of the works.

In his autobiography, *The Gentle Art of Making Enemies,* Whistler wrote:

"The Painter-Etchers appear to have suspected for a moment that the works were really Mr. Whistler's..."

A threesome of art enthusiasts including of all people, Whistler's brother-in-law, Dr. Seymour Haden, suspected a hoax was being perpetrated by Whistler himself. They said he had submitted the sketches to the Painter-Etchers under an assumed name, *Duveneck's,* to avoid a contractual restriction placed on him at another outlet in London. They said Whistler wanted to improve his cash position by fraudulently presenting sketches under Duveneck's name at the Painter-Etchers at the Hanover while, under the name of Whistler presenting other sketches at the gallery on New Bond Street sponsored by the Fine Art Society.

The threesome didn't have any evidence on which to build their case of fraud. While visiting the second gallery in New Bond Street, Haden asked a gallery assistant, ostensibly for comparison purposes, to see the Venetian plates etched by Whistler on exhibit there. In a conversation among the trio and the talkative gallery assistant, it was disclosed that Whistler had an exclusive showing and sales contract with the Fine Art Society. The disclosure heightened the suspicion that the Duveneck etchings, similar in style to works by Whistler were actually Whistler's.

If he had exhibited at both outlets, Whistler could have evaded restrictions under his exclusive exhibition and sales contract with the

Fine Art Society and use the Painter-Etchers' exhibit to broaden the marketing of his works. Whistler said he learned that the trio of critics believed in this charge of duplicity and they cited a Fine Art Society source. In his autobiography Whistler referred to the odd exchange and misapprehension as one of the "squabbles which amuse everybody."

Artists and lovers of art recounted the story of an attempted hoax, however. A tempest in a teapot, surely, and no one was harmed, but the unfounded suspicion that Whistler was behind a hoax was spread and interpreted and re-interpreted as only artists can. Most artists love attention, Whistler certainly did; but given Frank Duveneck's personality, he likely thought the mistake a patchwork of nothing.

The dustup over the authorship of the etchings raised up in the popular consciousness in London society the name of Gertrude Elizabeth Blood, twenty-three years old in 1880. In this pre-feminist Victorian age, but perhaps in any age, the dark-eyed beauty, born in Dublin to a family of the Protestant Ascendancy, was received graciously, her beauty a living asset and source of widespread attraction. She was a hit especially in the artsy community, dramatically painted by Boldoni and John Singer Sargent. She commissioned Duveneck to do her portrait, which he prosaically titled *Portrait of Miss Blood (Woman in a Satin Gown)*. In it her figure emerges from a black background, her full oval face and skin in its whiteness nearly merging with the sheer, pearl-like glistening of her attire.

At this time Miss Blood was on the rise, a fair prospect for an eligible bachelor. Her friendship with Duveneck resulted in an invitation to join her with her family in England. A photograph of him taken at a country house presents him wearing correct accessories, a beret and a bow tie, and a smile that seems to say, "Look at me, I've arrived."

Naturally, Duveneck, just being himself in this high English Victorian society, was headed for a fall. It would be a *faux pas* slightly more critical than being found fingering for the wrong fork at table. He was relatively unsophisticated compared to his European and American acquaintances and friends. Furthermore, he was poor, accustomed to dining at modest establishments in the search for good, solid food at low prices, not in high-class dining rooms. An incident in England demonstrates his lack of training. He was in demand for his talent, and having received an invitation from a celebrity-conscious duchess, he accepted and found himself among a large and brilliant cast. As they sat at table, the food service was unexpectedly delayed. The artist was observed to sink into a darkish quiet during this time and he absent mindedly picked up his plate from the table and polished it with his napkin. At the end of the table, the hostess observed Duveneck's actions and suspecting the plate soiled, sent a footman to investigate. In the meantime Duveneck had snapped back from his slump into the real world and offered this explanation: He was so sorry; he had so often dined in low establishments that he always made a point of giving his restaurant plate a needed scrub and shine.**

Lady Campbell's Case

On a similar country house jaunt with a family friend in Scotland, Miss Blood,   the new star, made a fateful choice. Duveneck by this time was clearly out of the picture for Miss Blood—if he ever had a chance in the first place—as she had come across a solid prospect. She wasted no time. In the span of three days, she first met and then managed to become engaged to Sir Colin Campbell, the sickly son of the eighth Duke of Argyll.

Immediately, the duke's family expressed opposition to the marriage due to their assessment of differences of station. But it came off in spite of that assessment on July 21, 1881, creating Lady Colin Campbell, and what became an intolerable union. The marriage was not consummated for many months as Sir Colin's ailments needed attention and repair. His sickness, it was later alleged, came from venereal disease. He rallied for a time and it's fairly certain that he infected her from their connubial relations. She fell ill, and the marriage began crashing on the rocks. In 1884, a British court granted her a judicial separation on grounds of cruelty. Obtaining a divorce was another matter. ***

The divorce case lasted two years (1884-86). The press covered it extensively, Duveneck a likely avid reader of the legal circus. In making a case against Gertrude, the wily barrister for the defense smeared her character, alleging affairs with at least four prominent men, among them, the fire chief of London and George Spencer Churchill, older brother of Randolph Churchill and uncle of Winston Spencer Churchill, then a boy. Strangely, her appeal for divorce was denied. The negative court ruling is regarded as a prime example of the Victorian Age's double standard that absolved men from responsibility in immoral conduct while women, easily convicted, suffered ostracism from polite society.

Gertrude was not without resources. She exploited her newly found celebrity and turned to journalism. There she found acclaim, welcomed as a martyr in literary and artistic circles. In a twist of fate she became a confidante of Whistler's, despite any differences that could have arisen between them over the authorship of the etchings. Duveneck naturally had faded from her life, leaving to us only the dust of an issue over the London etchings and a realistic portrait by him of a famous woman.

'Her Fate, Her Destiny'

These few developments occurred during the tumultuous first years of the decade of the 1880s, a time of trial, blissful happiness and heartbreak for Frank Duveneck and Lizzie Boott. Their courtship was to face its own heavy obstacles from family and friends. As they conversed that day in Duveneck's Venetian studio, seeds of mutual love and respect germinated for a young and talented artist and an extraordinary beautiful and talented woman. They must have known they would meet again and carry on their love affair.

41

Duveneck's feelings are unexpressed, but in the wake of this first meeting Lizzie realized that the painter was to be "her fate—her destiny."[8]

---

*Interview with Aileen McCarthy, a former student, by the author

**Article by William C. Bozman, *The Cincinnati Enquirer*, Undated

****Love Well the Hour*, by Anne Jordan, Life of Lady Colin Campbell (1857-1911), Matador (2010) ISBN 9781 848766112

[1]*Life on Two Levels, An Autobiography,* Josephine Whitney Duveneck, Trust for Hidden Villa, Los Altos Hills, CA, p. 99

[2] *Italian Hours,* Henry James, with Illustrations in Color by Joseph Pennell, Houghton Mifflin Company, Boston and New York, 1909, p.110

[3]*Frank Duveneck, Painter-Teacher,* Josephine W. Duveneck, John Howell—Books, San Francisco, CA, 1970, quotation from journalist Elizabeth Robins Pennell, p. 95

[4]*Venice, the City by the Sea*, Pennell, Joseph [1857-1926]

[5]*The Two Worlds of Frank Duveneck*, Mahonri Sharp Young, *The American Art Journal*, Kennedy Galleries, Inc., Vol. 1, No. 1 (Spring, 1969), p. 99, and *Nights: Rome & Venice in the Aesthetic Eighties*, Elizabeth Robins Pennell and Joseph Pennell, Archives.com, pp.83-86

[6]*Whistler, A life for Art's Sake*, Daniel E. Sutherland, Yale University Press, New Haven, 2014, p.173

[7]*The Life of James McNeill Whistler*, E.R. and J. Pennell, J.B. Lippincott Co., London, 1908, p. 264.

[8]*Duveneck and Henry James: A Study in Contrasts*, Mahonri Sharp Young, *Apollo*, 1970, p. 212, and *Nights: Rome & Venice in the Aesthetic Eighties*, Elizabeth Robins Pennell and Joseph Pennell, Archives.com, pp. 83-86

Chapter Two

The Feeling Is Mutual

Munich, summer 1879

Seated upright at the easel in her rented studio, Elizabeth Boott carefully applied paint to canvas, and looked intently at it. No man could forget such a wonderful face nor ignore the fine manner of this lean elegant woman. Frank Duveneck, the admiring teacher, makes that observation from his lonely chair, but hides it. He couldn't believe his luck in attracting such a student. Everyone called her, Lizzie. In a short matter of time, so did he.

Old Man or *Der Herr Professor* to his youthful male students, the husky artist walked to Lizzie's easel, smiled a little—he couldn't help himself—and wielded a brush daubed with black paint mixed with vermilion, sketching a head on her canvas. The figure took shape as a flower would bloom.

She boasted to friends in Boston:

"It is wonderful to see him sling the paint."

Duveneck may have appeared to have been slapdash as he worked. He laid on the flesh color with a large flat brush and, by all accounts, worked eagerly. The eyes of his subjects were a specialty. In one of his rare brags, in high contrast to the impression of a haphazard approach to his painting, he said he spent a week on the keen and mischievous orbs of the "Whistling Boy," one of his famous works.

Lizzie sat there amazed. She had only met Duveneck, the American phenomenon, a few months earlier in Venice and discussed studying with him. She had relayed her plan to her "Papa," Francis Boott, heir to a New England textile fortune. They each loved fine and wonderful things and cherished talent; and he agreed she

43

should study under the young master, if they could persuade him to serve her as teacher and if, of course, he passed muster from the father.

Duveneck was already a painter of importance in Europe. He had made his mark during his studies in Munich in the early 1870s. He returned to America in 1873-74 and gained notoriety in Boston for his Munich paintings. On his return to Europe in 1875, his second and lengthy tour, he initially worked in Venice where he had met Lizzie and her friend, Lucy Ellis. Munich served as the home base for his school, however. And it was to Munich that the Bootts early that summer of 1879 had traveled to meet the painter from their residence in Florence.

As a cabbie reined in his horse in front of Duveneck's studio, they spotted the artist in the act of closing the main door to his Munich studio. They dismounted, paid the fare and hurried towards him as he collected an easel, brushes and a box of paints after locking the door. The painter was about to endure "a drastic encounter with New England culture," according to daughter-in-law Josephine Whitney Duveneck, author of the painter's privately printed 1970 biography. He wasn't heading just for lunch either. He was closing down the studio for the season and was planning to join his students for summer classes in the Bavarian village of Polling.

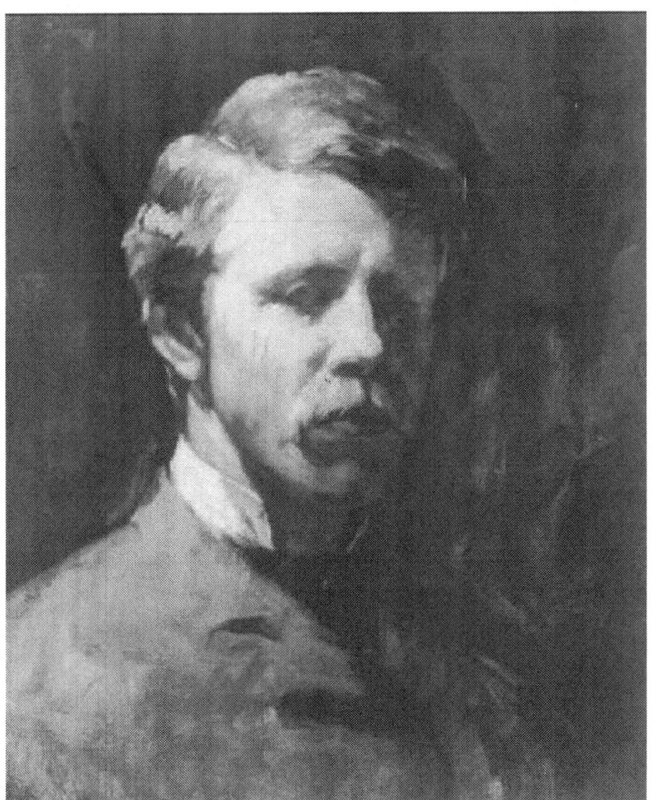

Self-portrait by Duveneck
-Courtesy of the Kenton County Public Library, Covington, Ky.

Mr. Boott introduced himself and his daughter. They hardly needed to, propriety called for it. Duveneck recognized them, and there was a burst of bonhomie from each of them. He was delighted to see her and listened intently to her as she explained her mission. Would he accept her as his student? Duveneck was apologetic. He had his commitments to the students, the Boys. The Bootts expressed dismay at their not having written. "Papa" looked over the painter carefully as his daughter talked, his busy mind probing with the question: What kind of man is he? And he answered his own question quickly: He was an artist and looked every bit like one, from his loose attire and the paint on his hands. He was certainly different from them, dressed spiffily in current fashion.

45

Lizzie was calm and smiling all this time, but then a look of distress came over her, an indication of her sincere concern, as she began to question whether the long trip had been worthwhile. Duveneck stood there among his artist tools perplexed at what to do. He began to give the problem some thought as the Bootts continued to talk.

Seeing her again was a pleasure. Clearly, he was anxious to serve her as teacher; but how and when? Decorum prevented her from joining the male cadre at Polling. What to do? It took less than a minute before Duveneck blurted out a solution. Would she rent a studio of her own in Munich? While he would be away during the week he pledged to make scheduled visits to the city and monitor the progress of her work. Clearly he didn't want to lose this beautiful and talented prospect either as a student or as a friend, and perhaps, who knows, an intimate one.

During the week, Duveneck told his visitors, he would be working with his students at Polling where he had rented an abandoned monastery. He said his students at that very moment were setting up in former monks' cells complete with beds and equipping with easels, brushes and paints, absent *prie-dieus*. The former monastery was already transforming as the earnest students had decorated the white-washed walls with sketches and pictures in a nineteenth century version of graffiti.

Polling and that former monastery would be no place for a woman, Duveneck thought, and father Francis Boott would rush to agree. Lizzie could set up a studio in Munich, which he would visit regularly. They agreed to this arrangement, which caused Lizzie to smile with happiness. Frank was pleased with the prospect, too, and the father, *well*, satisfied for the time being. The arrangement, however, was not welcome to Lizzie's friend, Henry James.

He wrote to her in June that he was delighted she had secured a place in Munich. But he expressed regret she was not studying with an instructor with high fame. Still, he said he was comforted by the notion that Duveneck would open her eyes to some new ideas.

James never quite got over Lizzie's choice of a teacher. All the while James was living in London over the ensuing years he deflated the Munich experience and urged her to come to England to paint.[1] It's not entirely clear what was in his mind for Lizzie beyond taking up her career in London.

The Relationship Grows

Decisions made quickly that day in Munich launched an alliance that would make an impression on the lives of many who knew Frank Duveneck, especially Lizzie Boott and her father. In setting herself up in Munich and renting a studio she was achieving her goal to study painting techniques of the young master. While she would be receiving instruction, her father, ever the faithful companion and mentor, could absorb at least for a time the pleasures of Munich, which for an all-too-brief a period was serving as a capital of the European art world. The city and its art schools, home to six thousand artists, had developed into a study center for the comparatively recent rise of Realism in painting. Duveneck had fit right in. Some of his finest works had been painted in Munich on his first tour, 1870-1874. He learned to love and respect the good, warm and welcoming people, and understand their solid character, religious bent and the strength of family there; and he appreciated the wide streets of Munich and the bountiful gardens. It was a place where art students could enjoy themselves and get away with it if no harm were done.

Lizzie had been recommended to pursue her studies in Munich, that's why she was so eager. She had devoted two summers in Paris with the historical and genre painter, Thomas Couture, winner of the Prix de Rome in 1837 and painter of *Romans in the Decadence of the Empire*, 1847. In a letter from her friend, Henry James, the author had described Couture as "a vulgar, little fat and dirty old man." Somewhat in contrast to that harsh view, she found him an admirable teacher, but she may have been looking for a new instructor if only because Couture would not be available. He would die that year, 1879.

Moreover, Lizzie's father had consulted the American painter William Merritt Chase, an associate of Duveneck's and his close friend besides, who told him that Munich was the best place for study. While in the city Lizzie saw an exhibition of works by the art academy's scholars. She found the paintings uniformly excellent and, writing in her typically honest fashion, said the scholars' works rather paled in comparison with Duveneck's. That was why Lizzie had sought him out as a teacher, impressed with his painting technique and his reputation as an effective teacher. And, there was something else about him. She liked him for who he was.

She wrote to her friends in Boston:

"We have now been here four days and in that time have taken and moved into an apartment, hired a studio and engaged Duveneck as a teacher. I was so excited when this was accomplished that I wrote a card to Miss Ellis who will tell you long before this reaches you. We had a letter to a Mr. Dyer a painter of much merit living here. I asked him about teachers and he said there were many great ones but the best of all was Duveneck; that one of the old professors of the Academy had taken his son away from there and put him under Duveneck; that he had a real genius for imparting to others and had many scholars among young Americans. He did not know if he would take any more but I had better try. So try we did and he accepted at once and is to come tomorrow to my studio. Joy! Do you not all envy me?"

A little later Lizzie offered this description of her new teacher:

"He is very nice, genial, simple, and friendly and ready to talk by the hour and tell all he knows. He seems to me a born painter, perfect in technique, too realistic to be interested ever in sentiment, perhaps in fact making things invariably uglier than they are. Ugly always, but the bare startling fact he gives you with such force and truth that it is admirable."

The teaching experience with Duveneck was far different from her instruction in Paris during previous summers, which consisted of "the lecture on high art and *'la verite dans le beau'* from poor Couture." She was now in the hands of the young master, Frank Duveneck, her mind set on learning, her heart set on him.

Change was in the air for Munich, a large attraction for artists, and for the entire western art world. Munich was superseding Dusseldorf as an art center. Meanwhile, Paris was paralleling Munich, fast becoming the key focus of whatever was new in art.

Lizzie was anticipating a fresh experience and instruction in technique. In having Lizzie as a student Duveneck had just engaged his first female for private instruction. Soon the painter-teacher would form two classes along gender lines, the Duveneck Boys, comprising young artists who later would lead a transformation of art in America, and the class for women, making their initial inroads as practitioners. That summer proved fateful for the world of art, personally for Lizzie and for her artist-teacher who was to become the love of her life. Suddenly, bustling Munich, was exciting, and her new young instructor and her rented studio became fresh focal points of her life.

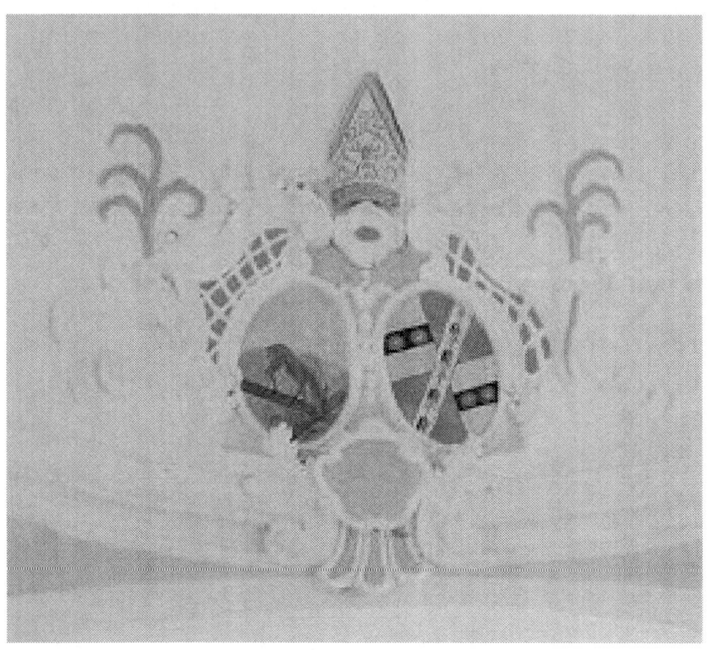

Coat of Arms in the Chapel of the Holy Cross in Polling

Much of the artistic action for Duveneck remained in Polling. The village is situated halfway between Munich and the Alpine resort area of Garmisch-Partenkirchen. The landscape is wreathed by villages and churches, a few onion-shape-domed and some restyled with rococo interiors in the fashion of the Eighteenth Century. Polling itself is known as the "monastery village" for its medieval monastic buildings and church dedicated to St. Augustine. Small ponds, flush and narrow waterways and broad lakes shimmer in the sunlight, and some of the area is marshy.

Artists took advantage of nature for *plein air* paintings of lovely pastoral scenes. Duveneck painted landscapes around Polling, one of the few places where he chose the outdoors. He also completed several studio projects, *Portrait Sketch of Georg von Hoesslin* and *Portrait of an Artist*, even while he had his hands full teaching. Hundreds of young artists had flocked to Polling in this period, and as many as eighty were Americans. Karl von Piloty, the head of the Munich academy, observed: "There is more talent in Polling than in the whole Academy put together," And he added presciently, "the time will come when European students will go to America to study painting."

Duveneck could make his way around Bavaria with few problems except for the shortage of money. He spoke German like a native, though Bavarians could detect a north German Oldenburg accent. In the American atmosphere at Polling, everyone spoke English if they were able. Duveneck instructed in both languages depending on his audience. His essential personality was unaffected by all of the recent attention and the mid-seventies' success of his paintings in Boston and his early achievement of quickly grasping instruction of lights and darks from Professor Diez of the Munich academy. As a student he had won wide recognition, prizes and even a studio of his own. Older now and adept at his craft after nearly a decade of steady work, he carried himself, albeit lightly, with a new authority, that of a teacher.

During those private sessions in Munich, Duveneck grew to know Lizzie and learned of her native capabilities. He loved to watch her paint, actually to do anything. In turn, she loved to see him work and, during a visit to Polling, adored him as he moved among his students through the old monastery, sat with her in evenings and bade her good night. She was a formidable and morally upright woman of the Victorian Age, not biding her time dabbling in art; rather, learning new techniques and building on her native talent and living life to the fullest. She found Frank to be a gifted teacher, easy to work with and pleasant to be around.

Lizzie's observation about him was affectionate and touching.

"I watched Duveneck paint and some of his boys. Every picturesque alley was filled with them and some of the sketches they made were excellent. The reverence and love which they bear to their master is delightful to behold. He is a man who endears him-

51

self to all who know him and apart from his artistic power the moral restraint which he exercises on these young men who are in Europe without friends or relatives is very great. One is struck by the contrast between this and some of the French schools where the master, if he does not encourage certainly does not discourage evil habits among the pupils. And this must convince us all the more that the standard of morals is higher among Americans than any other nation. It certainly would have been impossible in any other nation for ladies to associate with art students as we did with these [students] last winter. I think it surprises the foreigners in the class very much and pleases them at the same time. Last winter we organized a club which met once a week at the different houses for drawing in charcoal, modeling, etching, etc., combined with music and tea. We banished all parents quite in the American fashion and the meetings turned out to be very pleasant."

One can imagine Duveneck and Lizzie having their moments together during calm evenings after the clamor of departing students on a revel. They shared their endless interest in each other, their previous lives, their personal desires, and their hopes for the future. They took long walks in Munich and, on her visits, through the scenic Polling countryside. They stopped at inns, visited churches and joined gatherings of Bavarian music lovers in public and church recitals. They talked of art and artists, and about politics in Europe and America, the spread of revolution and republicanism in Europe, the rise of militarism in the new unified state of Germany and the Prussian Bismarck's Kulturkampf and its attempt at suppressing the Catholic Church.

Like many German Americans in Cincinnati, Duveneck was a faithful member of Lincoln's Republican Party. He could point out that Lincoln's top general, Ulysses Simpson Grant, was a native of the Cincinnati area who had become president of the United States of America. Grant's father, he liked to say, was the postmaster of Covington and lived in a fine house on Garrard Street.

"That's interesting," Lizzie would say, finding in his comments a lovable trace of provincial pride.

They talked of matters past and present.

Duveneck could not forget the horrors of the Civil War that had influenced his life as a young teenager. Cincinnati served as a supply center for Union Army and Duveneck's Northern Kentucky was an armed camp. He watched federal troops march across the Ohio River into Kentucky on makeshift bridges next to the massive piers of the incomplete John Roebling-designed Suspension Bridge. He saw the Benedictine sisters tend to the wounded and dying in their facilities near the Duveneck home. In the downtown area of Covington members of the Franciscan Sisters of the Poor, laboring at a recently founded hospital dedicated to St. Elizabeth, treated the wounded and set up facilities for orphans of soldiers and slaves.

The youngster heard the thump of artillery fire and picketers shooting at one another in the woods south of his father's home. He knew about the skirmishes at nearby Fort Mitchell and the city of Florence. Just before his fourteenth birthday, a massive Union Army, supported by "Squirrel hunters" mustered into the force from Ohio, stopped the vanguard of the Confederate army just south of Covington in September, 1862. No glorious victory by the Union, the military buildup caused the outnumbered Rebels to beat a humiliating retreat to Lexington. After the slim Union victory in Kentucky at Perryville, Confederate forces departed the state, never to return in large force. Most of all Duveneck remembered the war's aftermath. He and other members of his family fed ragged and hungry freed slaves who begged for food on their way north.

As an American expatriate in Europe Lizzie had avoided the reach of the Civil War, though some of her New England relatives were involved both militarily and politically. It was different for her. America was thousands of miles away in a place where she lived only eighteen months and so young in age that she was hardly conscious of it. Frank said he had seen the horrors of war and found it an exercise of insanity. He would rather paint as he was destined to do. Putting his talent to work at Polling he completed a *plein air* study that utilized his grasp of lights and darks of a brook and he captured the odd mystique of one of the flora-rich marshlands.

And, of course, each day he was occupied with his students at Polling, and then he enjoyed his routine of visiting Munich and meeting with his favorite, Lizzie.

An Unforgettable Summer

The relationship was growing more personal that summer of 1879. The father, Francis Boott, in Lizzie's words, had come with her on the Munich trip "to further the cause of my painting." He had torn himself away from his beloved Villa Castellani to satisfy her artistic interest, and disliked missing his usual summer allurements of Venice. He returned to Italy while Lizzie was taking instruction from June through September.

On August 12th, Lizzie wrote of Duveneck:

"Yesterday I had my last lesson for the week and Annie Putnam who is in Munich for a day or two was present. He painted for me all day as he generally does and I rack my brains to understand how he does it. His power of wielding paint is something marvelous and one must learn a great deal from watching him, only it is so excellent that one gets into a sort of despair over one's own trials."

In early September, trouble began to brew. Duveneck was out of town and had "forgotten to come in to give his lessons," Lizzie wrote to friends, in a matter-of-fact way but with an unmistakable note of a letdown. By the end of the month, the atmosphere between them had changed for the better. One can only imagine the scene of their meeting when the artist returned. He had some explaining to do and must have asked that his absence be excused.

This is surmise but it's possible that Duveneck wanted to party as the summer session with the boys had come to an end. It called for a night of celebration and fun. Perhaps he intended to leave the party early that evening because the journey to Munich was long and he, physically tired. Instead the beer revived him and he had a lot to talk about with his students, for one, another possible venue for his art school. The idea had come from Lizzie. She had spoken of the beauties of Florence and the Tuscan countryside even during winter, and suggested that he move lock, stock and barrel to Florence. More than this, the Uffizi Gallery and other sites of artistic interest were close at hand. Readily accessible paintings and sculpture of the Italian Renaissance were wonderful tools for the teacher. And so it could be that Duveneck talked and talked and had stein after stein of delicious beer; the night could have easily vanished in front of him and he retired very late having more than his fill. The next day, when he should have departed for Munich, he felt low.

His only hope was that Lizzie would understand when he did not appear for their weekly session.

Lizzie must have taken his absence in stride as many a good woman has done in similar circumstances, disappointed in a man's action but pleased when he adopted the right tone in asking for understanding and forgiveness. And she was cheered at his other news. He had taken her advice and planned to move his school to Florence and had won the boys over to relocation, and, furthermore, he would set up the class for ladies.

She told her friends in Boston:

"Duveneck is to migrate to Florence with ten of his pupils next month," she wrote at the end of September. "He is tired of Munich. Florence for a time will be a better place for him, though he ought finally to go to Paris. He is better known and appreciated here[,] and there (he) will probably make a revolution in art and make a name for himself."

Lizzie invited her Boston friends to join her in the class and promoted it as reasonably priced:

"He asks 250 francs a month for the class divided among as many as come and can be accommodated. To this would be added the rent of a studio about forty francs a month, and the models. So now is your chance. It seems to me after the experience of this summer to be the most admirable school to study color in, the use of the material, a hundred different ways of overcoming difficulties, or at least, trying to do so."

About this time Duveneck painted two studies for her. The first, a head of a Munich beer drinker done in his early style, similar to Frans Hals's broad brush technique, "full of life and superbly painted in three hours," wrote Lizzie, and a life-size reclining figure of a woman veiled in black, painted in two days. In contrast to the beer-drinking chap from Munich, the subject is a refined and idealized woman "perfectly true" in a style new to Duveneck.

In Lizzie's reckoning:

"It is really beautiful; full of repose and dignity and the best thing of his that I ever saw. You may imagine that I demurred at taking them, but he said he painted them for me and he is just one of those open-handed men that give away right and left and never make their fortunes or are, sufficiently appreciated."

Lizzie was fast becoming his primary audience. He was painting for her and had heeded her advice to relocate his school and all of his students. Clearly, an objective of this move was to be near her in Florence. They could continue their romance in new surroundings of near mythic proportions in the art world. She would continue as one of his female students, his favorite, *the* one and only, and still be close to her venerable father, Francis. As the father was in his early seventies, she fully realized, she strongly felt the noble and daughterly obligation to take care of him.

Enthusiasm in Florence

In reality the move to Florence was anything but easy in spite of boundless enthusiasm among Duveneck students.

One exclaimed:

"Three cheers for Italy. When do we start?"

Then the arguments commenced among the students over the best modes of transportation and routes southward across the Alps. What could they expect when they arrived? Where would they stay? What kind of paint would they be able to purchase? What about brushes, models? Does anyone speak Italian?

Duveneck realized that some ground work was in order before the school and its students made the move. He decided to lead an advance party in October on a train through the Brenner Pass. It had dawned on him that no one could speak Italian beyond "Si," posing an insurmountable obstacle to any commerce. Lizzie, preceding them in Florence, came to the rescue along with the assistance of a kindly multilingual official of the German consulate who spoke his native tongue, Italian and English. In a few weeks, the efficient pair found living space and arranged for studios for both the teacher and students.

In November, the second group of students got underway, taking a train junket southward. They were conspicuous for their mixture of clothing and sartorial styles. Some students wore frayed and faded corduroy clothing. Some stood out wearing the latest men's fashions. One wore a tam-o-'shanter, another a formal frock coat and tails. A few of the young gentlemen comically donned old-fashioned knee breeches.

They blended in with traveling peasants, often debarking at railway station stops for snacks, beer and pretzels. Once at the Florence railway station they gathered their bags and bundles, easels and canvases and paint boxes and moved off in a group. They only knew the name of the hotel where they were staying, not the address, and no manner of communication could inform puzzled officials to where that could possibly be.

Finally, a successful method was found, and the boys trudged off as church bells rang for Mass.

Duveneck was late to meet them, or the train was early, but he located the boys.

"I knew all that clatter could only be the boys," he said.

Duveneck led them to the hotel where they dropped their belongings and followed him immediately to the Uffizi and other highlights of the city in an exhausting first day.

As the young men, followers of the new Realism, stood before the work of masters in Uffizi galleries they scorned the works and proclaimed their opinions to any who would hear.

"No, No, you are wrong," the teacher said. "You'll change your minds later."

Duveneck was so right!

They did change as they matured in their art and in their lives. They were to become famous across America as the Duveneck Boys. Their time in Florence was captured in William Dean Howells' *Indian Summer*, a fitional novel, which depicts their youthful and outrageous charm that represented the promise of America to Europeans.

In the narrative a female character says:

"'They were here all last winter, and they've just got back. It's rather interesting for Florence.' She gave them a rapid sketch of that interesting exodus of a score of young painters from the art school at Munich under the lead of the singular and fascinating genius by whose name they had become known. 'They had their own school for a while in Munich, and then they all came down into Italy in a body. They had their studio things with them, and they traveled third class, and they made the great excitement everywhere, and had the greatest fun. They were a great sensation in Florence. They went everywhere, and were such fanatics. I hope they are going to stay.'"

The character Inglehart was drawn carefully after Duveneck. Howells described his Inglehart this way:

"He was so good-natured that he used to drink all the tea people offered him, and then the young ladies made tea for him in his studio when they went to look at his pictures. It almost killed him. By the time spring came he trembled so that the brush slipped out of his hands when he took it up. He had to hurry off to Venice to save his life. It's just as bad at the Italian houses; they've had to like tea."

In reality the Duveneck Boys were widely known for being particularly expressive in museums. They gathered around paintings, finding fault, praising, and talking shop that caught the interest of other spectators. On the whole, people loved them for their youth and their vitality.

Duveneck joined in the fun as well. His theatrical performances recall a slice of America's past that seems innocently quaint.

More than once he donned a soft hat that resembled a student cap, drew a red streak across his cheek to look like a scar and substituted a cane for a saber in a comic attempt to portray a dueling German student. The artist also gave a hilarious rendition of a dialogue between a tipsy old peasant and his long-suffering whining wife. His voice shifted from a slurred baritone to a high falsetto achieved by holding his nose and using a handkerchief to cover his mouth. He also did a droll rendition of a lost calf. When the Boys performed in *tableaux vivant* during evening parties, Duveneck would be called to join in. Recalling his Kentucky boyhood, he would sing out, "I'se coming, I'se coming."

In this period of fun and frolic Duveneck's paintings were to change under the influences of Florence and of his new-found love, Lizzie. The painter drifted away from the dark colors of his Munich work. A new direction can be seen in the *Guard of the Harem, Portrait of Amy Folsom, The Music Master* and the *Girl in a Black Hood.* He and many of his students began a schedule of fall, winter and spring in Florence and summer in Venice, a schedule adopted earlier by the Bootts.

Emulating His Teachers

Duveneck's Florence students numbered fifteen. The class size could be increased only by unanimous vote of the student body or at the request of the "Old Man," according to Charles Mills, a student from Dedham, Massachusetts. In December, 1880, he wrote to his father:

"This is done for his sake as there are so many applications that he cannot take them and really that number is a great deal of a tax on his time." The school operated with two studios, one with five students and the second with ten. "We paint from models every day, the hours being from 8:30 to 12 and from 1 to 4. Then we draw in the evenings from 7 to 9."

The master visited them often, the student wrote, two-to-three times a week. He had periods of less exposure to the students, but on some days he would balance out his teaching by painting with the students either half or a full day.

"We have no rules; each one is interested enough in his studies and keeping the school in order to behave himself and keep at his work."

Mills was aware of a coming split between Duveneck and Lizzie Boott. He wrote that Duveneck had talked of moving the school to Rome. In late December of 1880 he accompanied the painter to Rome, ostensibly to find studio space; but they returned on January 1 after only a few days in the Holy City. Mills innocently observed: "I do not remember spending much time looking for studios."

In a message dated February 13, Mills wrote:

"I think I told you there was some talk of going to Rome, but D. has reconsidered and thinks that it is very probable the school won't keep up for many years longer…"

Mills expected to spend the next season in Paris.

On March 27, at a dinner with students, Duveneck informed them that he was returning to America and not going to Paris as he had intended. The young student assumed a connection between Duveneck's change of venue for the school and the breakup with Lizzie. For his part, Duveneck visited England in 1881 when it was likely that he visited with Gertrude Blood and her family and made the faux pas at the table of a ducal estate.

Siding with Father

For the first time in the father-daughter relationship, Francis Boott encountered some competition in Duveneck. Characteristically, the elder Boott had nothing to say for the written record about his daughter's new love. He did learn that the painter's father operated a beer garden in Covington, and was appalled. Others among American expatriates such as Henry James offered plenty of advice and solace for the man. In his wildest dreams Mr. Boott did not foresee himself as a third party at the Villa Castellani.

James's biographer Leon Edel described the trio based on James's thoughts, first with Duveneck:

"'Aside from his painting, he seemed the strangest person in the world to be in the constant company of Lizzie Boott.' Lizzie, in her thirties, was a product of a careful education and a sheltered life.

61

Duveneck had what Henry termed an 'almost slovenly modesty and want of pretention.'"

Edel continued: "He was uncouth, vigorous and good-natured. Lizzie seemed to Henry to stand to him in 'a sort of double relation of pupil and adoptive mother—or at least adoptive sister. I hope,' he [James] wrote to his Aunt Kate, 'she won't ever become his adoptive anything else, as, though an excellent fellow, he is terribly earthly and (sic) unlicked.' They were a strange group, the father, the daughter and the painter, and Henry was to watch the evolution of Lizzie's love affair with her bohemian teacher with the interested eyes of a friend—who was also a novelist.'" [3]

In his days as an art critic in the 1870s James had discovered Duveneck, finding in some of his portraits qualities of Velazquez. He commented on the "extreme naturalness, their unmixed, unredeemed reality," and he found "they contain the material of an excellent foundation." James said he looked forward to Duveneck doing something first rate. On a visit to Florence in 1880, the first year of the relocated art school, James wrote to his father that Duveneck was "the most highly developed phenomenon in the way of a painter that the U.S.A. had given birth to," and he commended the "completeness" that was new to his work since the exhibitions in Boston and New York. He closely watched Duveneck's evolution, not always satisfied with the pace of his progress.

As to Lizzie it was during this period that James's attitude toward her broke away from a friendly base of admiration and praise, dating to their first contact in the 1860s. As an example of this dispositional change, James offered this scene in one of his letters. Lizzie, he wrote, had been ill over the winter, and when he first saw her he felt she looked elderly and plain. The Bootts were again living in a rented portion of the Villa Castellani, the fifty-room estate overlooking the Valley of the Arno River. Lizzie was working in her own studio focused intensely on her painting. In the letter to his father James bristled with criticism and sniffed: "She seems to spend her life in learning, or rather in studying without learning, and in commencing afresh, to paint in someone's manner."

James had begun *The Portrait of a Lady* and was taking it slow—diverted, he said, by the wonders of Italy. *Washington Square* was about to be released in the United States and in England, giving him valuable time to adopt a leisurely approach to his writing as he spent time in Florence. He had friends in Florence other than the Bootts. In particular there was Constance Fenimore Woolson, Constance Fenimore grandniece of the American writer, James Fenimore Cooper. The sometime poet was called Fenimore by James. An expatriate, devoted to James and his writing, she admired the author and became an inspiration for characters in several novels. With Lizzie, unavailable as she devoted most of her time to Duveneck, James turned on his charm to Fenimore who accepted it easily and well. Older than James, she became "a private resource," and a party to what James' biographer called a secretive relationship among the strangest in American literature.[4]

Finally, as to father Francis Boott, the musician and composer whose religious works had been performed in the Vatican, James reserved high respect. He was a frequent correspondent and always visited with him and Lizzie in Florence, and, they met in other European locales if their travel plans coincided as they frequently did.

In any case it was obvious to all concerned that Francis Boott regarded Duveneck as an intruder, beneath his daughter, at least socially, a disposition common among fathers towards many a prospective son-in-law. This attitude of distrust and rejection caused a lengthy extension of the courtship between Frank Duveneck and Lizzie Boott. Lizzie had sought him out and loved him. The artist loved her deeply in return, and they were now separated. In this round father Francis had won.

The next few years proved to be difficult, even painful. Lizzie wouldn't leave her father out of loyalty and tender regard for his exceptional and loving care, and therefore, she couldn't be with her artist, for whom she had an unquenchable fire. Concern for the impact of marriage on her own career in art may have furnished another barrier to her consent and another likely cause for her equivocation. It is clear, however, that they resisted the natural magnetism that brought them together, not an impossible task for mature people but one that makes demands on each unfulfilled person.

They were to marry eventually. And, for a wonderful period they were able to live in wedlock, though at times awkwardly with the father at the Villa Castellani, but that was still several years away. For most people the adage, two's company, three's a crowd, applies.

After the breakup in the early 1880s and the closing of the art school, Duveneck traveled, often with friends. Lizzie traveled as well, to Spain with friends, and it is thought they met without the father's knowledge over the several years. Meanwhile, Duveneck had experienced over the previous decade something new and charming in his life, and Lizzie had played a strong role. The society he knew differed drastically from his early life in a Midwestern world just emerged from the American frontier, from his years as a church decorator and his Bohemian student years in Munich. That Lizzie and Frank loved at all is a testament to each and to the enduring quality of their love. In many respects, their social and family histories stood in stark contrast, the lone notable exception was their co-dedication to art. Lizzie's devotion to art, whetted by her European upbringing, was nurtured by a fresh wellspring of artistic activity in Boston that had societal implications. Frank Duveneck's interest came about in a much different way growing up in Covington, Kentucky, a town across the Ohio River from Cincinnati.

---

[1]*The picture season at Villiers-le-Bel, 1876-78, Elizabeth Boott, Thomas Couture, and Henry James,* by Carol M. Osborne, *Apollo* 149, no. 447 (May 1999):40-51

[2]*Frank Duveneck, Painter-Teacher*, Josephine W. Duveneck, John Howell—Books, San Frankcisco, CA, 1970, quotation from Elizabeth Robins Pennell, p. 95

[3]*Henry James, The Conquest of London: 1870-1881*, Leon Edel, Avon Books, New York copyright, 1962, pp. 403-404

[4]*Henry James, The Middle Years: 1882-1895*, by Leon Edel, J.B. Lippincott Company, New York, 1962, p. 356-62

Chapter Three

Pioneer Roots to European Fanfare

Covington, Kentucky, October 1848

The river town of Covington occupies the northeast corner of land shaped by the westward current of the Ohio River and a narrow northward-flowing stream known as the Licking. A painting of the mid-nineteenth century, titled *View of Cincinnati from Covington* by Robert Seldon Duncanson portrays a small town growing back from the two rivers and, in the foreground, a large expanse of tilled land. The artist assumed a view from the southern hills that overlook the Ohio Valley and it encompasses both tiny Covington and sprawling Cincinnati. A daguerreotype of Cincinnati in the mid-century year crisply delineates a multitude of church steeples and a haphazard row of shops lining Front Street, many serving the steamboats, sternwheelers and side-wheelers, anchoring along the shore. A teeming boomtown of breweries, taverns, machine shops and slaughter houses, Cincinnati was feeding on steady immigration from Europe and on growing business and industry.

Frank Duveneck was born in Covington, on October 9, 1848, to Bernard Decker and his wife, Katharine Siemers Decker. The Deckers were among a group of immigrants from Duchy of Oldenburg in the north of what later became Germany. In her childhood Katharine's blood father had died and her mother, a widow with two toddler girls, Katharine and Margarethe, married Dietrich Harmsen, a farmer and an immigrant from the area around the town of Damme, not far from the North and Baltic Seas. Farmers in that region wore wooden shoes, useful especially to trudge through mud-slick farms, much as the Dutch and Danes did who lived comparatively short distances away. Unlike many other northern Europeans, most Oldenburgers tended toward Roman Catholicism, with Protestants in a small minority of the duchy's population. When they immigrated to America, the people of Oldenburg carried their religion with them as an extension of their culture, if not as a sign of their humility in recognizing who they were as people in God's world.

However admirable, the practice of the Oldenburger's religion and expressions of their Germanic culture, were not pleasing to rival immigrants, these largely from the Carolinas and Virginia who had moved to the Ohio Valley a few decades earlier. All newcomers sought the advantages of rich farmland available at comparatively low prices in what had become, by law, a unique new part of the United States, the Northwest Territory. Jobs were scarce for these European immigrants regarded as upstart rivals not quite American. An industrious band of people, they resented the prejudice; some hardy individuals looked to find a way out. In August, 1833, Katharine's mother and foster father journeyed on to the northern Ohio frontier where a former teacher from Damme, Franz Joseph Franz Joseph Stallo, had established a rural community of six hundred and eighty acres. From the entrepreneur Stallo, Harmsen acquired one of the 144 sections, a parcel of farm land for $8.50. He had to hack his way through his wilderness plot to build a log cabin and clear the area for crops. The family ate bear and deer meat. They made bread from corn meal and baked loaves in a clay oven. There were no cobblers in this remote region, shoes an unattainable luxury. Despite hardships and austerity, the Harmsens thrived as a family. The couple had two other children and the farm expanded as Harmsen cleared more land year after year.

Frontier Hardships

Then in 1840 tragedy struck as it often did in the untamed region. After a hard winter, the mother, Frank Duveneck's grandmother, died of an unknown illness. Death struck again only a few months later. On a trip in the company of the family dog to nearby Piqua, Ohio, the widower father fell from his horse-drawn wagon and died. Having no identification on him, local people buried him. The bedraggled and stressed-out dog dutifully returned to the farm, which gladdened the children's hearts; but it also represented for them a ghastly and alarming sign of the father's fate. Several tense weeks passed with no word of the father. Then a stranger on horseback confirmed the children's worst fears, relaying the tale of a man who had fallen from his wagon, died and was buried near a Piqua Road.

The orphaned girls faced a dilemma. Running the farm was an impossible task for the youngsters. Margarethe Siemers was just eleven years old, Katharine, ten. They decided to leave their even younger siblings with a local family and to return to Cincinnati. Barefoot, they walked on trails southward for a month in the summer of 1840 in search of relatives and friends from the Old Country, and they found them in Covington.

Katharine earned her first pair of shoes while working as a domestic for the nineteenth century artist, James Henry Beard, a specialist in portrait painting, and his wife, then living in the Cincinnati area. In this domicile, a citadel of culture to an unschooled, illiterate young girl, Katharine learned the value of art to an individual and to society. Fortunate for the future world of art, Katharine's new-found interest provided a seedbed that enabled her to encourage her son's knack for artistic expression and guide him in a time when most people, in contrast, focused exclusively on making a living. It's also possible that she considered her son to be uniquely qualified and a strong candidate to provide in future for himself.

The Siemers girls got on with their lives. Margarethe married Frank Decker, a local merchant, and Katharine joined them in their Scott Street household. When Katharine was about seventeen years old early in 1848, she married Frank Decker's brother, Bernard, in Muttergottes Kirche [Mother of God Church] in Covington.

Later that year, on October 9, Frank Duveneck, who was to become the famed artist and teacher, came into the world as Frank Decker. For Katharine, personal calamity was to strike again. The cholera epidemic of 1849 took the lives of one-seventh of the members of Mother of God's parish, among them, Bernard Decker, widowing Katharine and leaving her nearly one-year-old child without a father. The Decker family was devastated over an eight-day period that summer. Mary and Elizabeth Decker died within an hour of one another. Henry Decker was next, followed by Bernard, Katharine's husband and father of baby Frank.

For the 1850 United States census, Katharine recorded herself as a widow and mother of a year-old son. Not long afterward she married Joseph Duveneck, known as Squire, a justice of the peace who operated a tavern and beer garden on Greenup Street in a German-American Covington district known as Helentown. Young Frank, too young to know any different, adopted the name Duveneck. The family grew rapidly with its full share of triumphs, pleasures and pains. Some fifty years later, in the 1900 census, Katharine Duveneck, then known by Anglicized names of Catherine or Kate, testified that she had borne twelve children, five of whom were then alive.

Growing Up in Covington

Frank Duveneck grew up in a modest frame house at 1232 Greenup Street in a thriving new community. As the oldest he had responsibilities with the growing family, even baby-sitting. In one memorable story of his youth his mother assigned him to the task of watching a child in a cradle, and he was expected to rock the cradle slowly to induce sleep while she was away. Young friends were playing marbles outside and Frank wanted to join them. So he devised a technology to accomplish the rocking, by hitching a long rope to the cradle and tugging it once in a while to keep the cradle in movement while he joined with his friends. When Mother Duveneck returned to the house, she found the cradle overturned, the rope hanging limp and the baby playing on the floor. Frank didn't hear the end of that.

He also got into trouble when he looted a nearby orchard of some apples. He managed to stuff the fruit into his baggy pants, said to have been hand-me-downs, tightened at the ankles to contain the apples. He was ready to make his getaway when the orchard owner, who knew him, called him to stop, then inquired what he planned to do with the stolen apples. Frank replied—some for his mother, some for his sisters and some for himself. But don't you know that that is stealing, the man said. A model of tolerance and understanding, the farmer told young Duveneck that the next time if he wanted some apples he should come through the gate and ring the bell at the front door. The orchard owner allowed Frank some of his booty and advised him to be up front in his dealings with others and not to take the sneaky approach ever again.

Young Frank promised to do the right thing, then he started to climb over the fence to depart, and the man stopped him again. Use the front gate, he counseled, not only on this occasion but at any time he happened to come by. Many years later, the orchard owner and his wife visited the artist in his studio in Florence. He recalled the incident for Frank who then remembered it as one of the great lessons of his life. During the couple's stay in Florence they frequently dined with the artist. He painted the man's portrait and gave it to his wife as a gift. Its whereabouts is not known.

Covington, while eclipsed in growth by Cincinnati, still had its factories, a distillery, a tannery, and a pottery run by an English immigrant. Though growing, it offered the young person with some of nature's gifts. The Licking River, only a few squares away from the Duveneck home, served as a swimming hole, and the clear fresh water flowing straight from the Appalachian Mountains provided the opportunity for a young lad to fish and have fun. Frank Duveneck's first experience as a sculptor came when he modeled figures made of Licking River mud, dried them and gave them to his brothers and sisters as toys. He also made impressions of name plates on doors of neighbors' houses.

Much of the region's economic growth came about because of the intersecting rivers, busy with ferryboats carrying people, wagons and goods, and small commercial boaters plying their trade for individuals. As the 1850s decade drew to a close, giant stone piers of John Roebling's Suspension Bridge were sunk in the Ohio River. The opening of that famous landmark bridge would await the conclusion of the American Civil War, a conflict that was to levy a harsh toll on the Ohio valley and weigh heavily on the people including the Duvenecks.

Civil War and Slavery

The dispute over slavery that divided the nation split the people socially just as the river did geographically. Alexis de Tocqueville in his *Democracy in America* observed what this meant:

"So the traveler who lets the current carry him down the Ohio till it joins the Mississippi sails, so to say, between freedom and slavery; and he has only to glance around him to see instantly which is best for mankind. On the left bank of the river the population is sparse; from time to time one sees a troop of slaves loitering through half-deserted fields; the primeval forest is constantly reappearing; one might say that society has gone to sleep; it is nature that seems active and alive, whereas man is idle. But on the right bank a confused hum proclaims from afar that men are busily at work; fine crops cover the fields; elegant dwellings testify to the taste and industry of the workers; on all sides there is evidence of comfort; man appears rich and contented; he works."

When Frank was approaching eight years old in 1856, the divided Ohio Valley fell under the national spotlight for Kentucky's ugly commitment to slavery. Margaret Garner, a slave at the Gaines Farm in nearby Boone County, escaped with her family and friends on the intensely cold night of January 28. They made their way to Covington and later crossed the frozen Ohio River to Cincinnati, travelers on the Underground Railroad en route to Canada. Margaret and her family stopped at the Mill Creek Valley home of a former slave and cousin, Elijah Kite. But a posse from Boone County had tracked Margaret and her family to the Kite residence, and they were confronted in the Kite household.

As the slave hunters closed in, rather than witnessing the return to bondage of Mary, her two and a half-year-old daughter, the mother slew her with a butcher knife. She was attempting to end the lives of her remaining children when other people intervened. By such desperate acts Margaret Garner became a national symbol of the evils of slavery, a woman who would do the unthinkable to avoid the unbearable. She and other captured slaves stood trial in United States Court in Cincinnati under the federal Fugitive Slave law that required all states to comply with United States law that deemed the fugitives as a slave owner's personal property. Garner and others were convicted and were returned to Kentucky. She was never tried for murder under Ohio law. A requisition from abolitionist Governor Salmon Portland Chase to Kentucky Governor Charles Morehead for the return of the Garner woman to Ohio failed as she had been sent down river in the possession of other Gaines relatives and out of state jurisdiction. Novelist Toni Morrison captured the drama of Margaret Garner's life in her book, *Beloved*.

All during this period the 1852 novel, *Uncle Tom's Cabin*, by Harriet Beecher Stowe was bringing the horrors of slavery to the general public. The story was lived out in person in Northern Kentucky. A major route for the Underground Railroad lay just east of Covington near the town of Maysville, Kentucky, across the river from the town of Ripley, Ohio. An actual happening of runaway slaves inspired the tale. Surely, Frank Duveneck and his family, strongly Unionist, knew of the novel and probably read it. While Northern Kentucky had its share of Southern sympathizers, the region was divided, the majority favoring the Union. The border state's General Assembly had declared the state neutral and early in the conflict much of the commonwealth became an armed Union camp with points of military strength around Louisville and Cincinnati.

As a young teenager Frank Duveneck heard the drums of marching soldiers near his home. He was something of a "camp rat" for the Union soldiers. In September of 1862, a Confederate thrust northward from the central part of Kentucky stalled in front of the high hills south of Covington, where the Union Army had constructed a series of forts and artillery batteries in the defense of Cincinnati. Surely at night young Duveneck heard the crack of musketry and the booms of occasional shell fire as Confederate infantry probed fortifications.

His involvement grew intensely personal as the war wore on. On a horse-and- wagon trip to Squire Duveneck's small brewery to fetch a supply of beer, the elder Duveneck and young Frank heard the heavy pounding of men on horseback and encountered a band led by the Confederate raider John Hunt Morgan of Lexington, Kentucky. At a command from the soldiers, the Duvenecks raised their hands high and stood by as they were surrounded. Squire Duveneck pleaded, "Take the beer if you want it but leave me the horse and wagon. It's all I've got and there's a big family at home." The Confederates took some beer and left him and Frank with the horse and wagon. Frank remembered Morgan, known for his panache and gentlemanly ways. He said "a very decent man he was and riding a fine horse."

A series of small skirmishes in the Northern Kentucky theater and later in other parts of the state filled beds of the local hospital, St. Elizabeth, with wounded, and many soldiers were treated by Benedictine nuns who had settled in Covington in 1859 near the Duveneck's home in Helentown. He spoke of seeing sick, wounded and hungry soldiers, without shoes and poorly clad for the winter. Confederate prisoners were probably even more deprived, and black refugees "helpless, starving, not wanted, and sometimes very brutally treated by the people who tried to drive them away."[1]

Duveneck later said he abhorred war and its aftermath. His own personal experience helped him to sort out his feelings on the matter. His strong family connection with the Roman Catholic Church could have been another cause of his and his family's opinion. War making was regarded as an act of last resort, and there was no glory in it for Duveneck.

Benedictine Nurturing

A strongly positive influence on Frank Duveneck came from the Benedictines, both religious men and women, including Catholic lay people. The religious women came from Erie, Pennsylvania, in 1859 (originally from Eichstadt in Bavaria), chiefly to teach young girls. By 1862 the sisters lived in a convent on Twelfth Street, a short distance from the Duveneck home. In addition to the convent, they later staffed St. Joseph parish school. Young Frank perfected his reading and writing abilities under the tutelage of Catholic laymen whose names can be found in records at St. Walburg Convent in Villa Hills, Kentucky: Mohr, Auchs, Lemming, Folmerding, Wilmes, Rapp, Rebekamp, Volmeke, Teschner, Adams and Buhre. Under their guidance, the young artist secured a strong foundation for his logical written presentations and clearly stated narratives of his surviving letters.

The Duveneck family is listed as parishioners of the then new St. Joseph Church, according to parish records in the archives of the Benedictine St. Vincent Archabbey in Latrobe, Pennsylvania. Frank received his first Holy Communion and was confirmed at St. Joseph. He was an acolyte, or altar boy, and served the priest-celebrants at Masses. His time in cassock and surplice was not all religious and sincere, as this story, revealed more than a century later, suggests.

Come forward more than one hundred years to the 1970s. Helentown's demographics had already changed. Families of the original German-Americans had moved on, and St. Joseph Church was closed. Before the razing of the church, its historic organ, built in 1859 by Mathias Schwab, was removed piece-by-piece, pipe-by-pipe, by seminarians across two city blocks to the Cathedral Basilica of the Assumption. As the young men dismantled the open-topped pipes, wads of paper fell onto the ground. Many were autographed. One was signed, Frankie Duveneck. The seminarians took an interest in how that could happen and, through interviews, learned that altar boys, to bide their time, made paper wads and tried for three-pointers into the open pipes.

The Mathias Schwab pipe organ has another story to tell. What was to become a famous signature on his paintings, *FD* was carved on an inside wooden housing for the hand-and- lever-driven wind pump. No longer needed after a renovation, the housing has been removed and the monogram lost. The organ occupies a west loft beneath the east-facing rose window of the cathedral.

A study of parish records by Brother Nathan Cochran, O.S.B., of the Latrobe archabbey lists Frank Duveneck as a student at the St. Joseph parish school starting in 1856 through to 1861-62. He was taught by laymen. Upon leaving the school he made his first foray in the art world, working for the Benedictines.

In his spare time and encouraged by his parents, young Frank took up sign painting and created a wooden placard for his stepfather's beer garden and another for a local butcher. He was either twelve years old or fourteen when he painted his first picture on an easel. The first depicted the barefoot little *Match Girl* from the Hans Christian Andersen's tale. The girl saw visions as she lighted matches in the freezing cold and was assumed into Heaven in the company of her loving grandmother. The other painting offers a tender scene of a young boy holding yarn for his mother or grand-mother and bearing a woeful expression as young friends beckoned from a nearby doorway.

Mother Duveneck kept the two early works in the Duveneck house until the day she died. All through her life she encouraged the artist. Even as a child she took him to see prints in Cincinnati shop windows and statuary going up in public parks. She was re-membered for saying, "Frank, if you can ever make things like that, I shall be very proud of you."

Medieval Apprentice

In the year 1862, when Frank Duveneck turned fourteen years old that October, a profound change came into his life. A Benedictine religious brother, Cosmas Wolf, O.S.B., had been assigned to Covington from the Latrobe abbey. Born June 20, 1821, in Grosskissendorf, a small Swabian village in Bavaria and on the same day christened Johan Baptist, Wolf practiced and appreciated art. He had studied in Germany before entering the Benedictine order at St. Vincent's, and his love of art must have been strongly felt. Without permission from Abbot Boniface Wimmer, he returned to Germany in 1857 to pursue studies on his own under Johann Nepomuk Petz, a sculptor and church designer. But once there in Munich, Wolf defaulted on his individual quest. A letter from an acquaintance, Rev. Joseph F. Muller, court chaplain for King Ludwig I, recently found in the Latrobe archives, gives testament to the intensity of Brother Cosmas's vocation and his regret over his personal choice to depart the abbey without permission.

Father Muller wrote:

I reproached Br. Cosmas for being released from the monastery. The good man began to weep and fell at my feet and implored me without ceasing that I beg the abbot [Wimmer] to receive him again, for he certainly did not leave the monastery due to dissatisfaction but purely because of art. There was a craving in him that he could not withstand anymore. I promised to intercede. As anxious as he is here, I cannot say the least thing disparagingly about him. He is working industriously and is making great progress with the sculptor Petz. He has never uttered a word of dissatisfaction but always expressed his attachment and love for the monastery. He says the others made it hard on him because he is pious. According to what he says, he never conceded to the suggestions of the agitators. I saw and heard only good things in his regard. A letter is included in which he presents his case. Therefore be merciful and compassionate.[2]

A tolerant and understanding leader, Wimmer showed mercy and compassion. He agreed that Brother Cosmas continue as a monastic with ties to Latrobe while he studied sculpture. The young, talented monk stayed in Munich a total of five years. Clearly, Wimmer, the founder of the Benedictine order in the United States and Canada, foresaw the advantage of having a monk trained in art.

In the meantime, German immigrants were coming to America in waves, many settling in what became known as the German Triangle, the region within the three sides formed by Cincinnati, St. Louis and Milwaukee. In the decade of the 1850s the urban population of Cincinnati increased by more than a third, by some fifty-thousand people, mostly Deutsche speakers. Ethnic parishes sprang up including St. Joseph Church in Covington's Helentown. The pastor of St. Joseph's church, Rev. Odilo Vandergrun, O.S.B., a monk from St. Vincent's, petitioned Abbot Wimmer to send sculptors and craftsmen to Covington to build and decorate churches. Brother Cosmas, fresh from his Munich studies, got the assignment.

By the end of 1862, an eventful year for the war-battered region, a company had been formed, the Catholic Altar Building Stock Company, founded at St. Joseph Church. A studio was flourishing in a wood-framed building on nearby Bush Street. Brother Cosmas had plenty of help. He was assisted by another sculptor, Brother Claude. Paul Gestrein was a wood carver, Louis Steiner, a general painter. There were others in the studio, known largely by their last names: Grawe, Gehring, Roese, Geisler, Schroeder, Wehrle, Schroepfer, Meyer, Dressman, Wessel, Lohr, Liebler, Ewald and Becker. The formation of the company, also called the Institute of Catholic Art, was announced in a Munich newspaper.[3]

Duveneck "must have been a favorite in the studios because he quickly became an apprentice, much like in the medieval tradition."[4]

The story goes that young Frank wandered into a studio barefooted and eager to learn. Another story has his mother, knowing of his talents, bringing him to a painter in the company, Johann Schmitt, who had been recruited by Wolf. However he made contact, Duveneck was soon employed as apprentice much in the same fashion as a person of talent during Europe's medieval age. From Brother Cosmas and Schmitt he learned the use of tools, to carve wood, design friezes, paint frescoes and to focus on the eyes of his subject, the windows of the soul.

Church altars created by the artists, many extant in the Midwestern region, are invariably made of wood in the gothic style and painted white. Many paintings associated with the altars are given a gold leaf background following a white and gold scheme of baroque churches in Germany.

Another painter, Wilhelm Lamprecht, who learned his trade at the Royal Academy of Fine Arts in Munich, became a later influence on Duveneck. The Schroeder Brothers was another team of German-American specialists in sculpture and altar structures. In 1869 these artists launched the Society of Christian Art in Cincinnati, with Lamprecht the leading light. "Br. Cosmas, Johann Schmitt, and Wilhelm Lamprecht all had important roles nurturing, teaching, and mentoring Frank, and they eventually encouraged him to study at the Royal Academy of Art in Munich—a move that changed his life and artistic outlook."[5]

Just about the time he started working with the altar company, young Frank gave thought to becoming a priest.

"He was attracted by the ceremony and dignity of the mass, he loved the colorful vestments, the sonorous chanting and the light and shadow of the altar candles," wrote his daughter-in-law, Josephine Whitney Duveneck. His dedication to art prevailed, however, and Frank joined Schmitt and Lamprecht on assignments in Indiana, Pennsylvania, New York, and in Quebec in the church-decoration business.

In 1864 at fifteen years of age, Frank Duveneck painted *Our Lady of the Immaculate Conception*, oil on canvas, 38 x 24 inches. The painting is a product of one who has matured in his personal faith, done in the Neo-gothic Nazarene style, popular in Bavaria and known in Great Britain as the Pre-Raphaelite movement. Mary is depicted as an innocent young woman, modest and humble, her right hand over her heart and her left holding a spray of lilies. A sun glow of grace surrounds her.

Duveneck's painting was the first item in an exhibit dedicated to Brother Cosmas at the St. Vincent Gallery at the abbey, November 1, 2013—February 28, 2014. Among paintings were portraits by Wilhelm Lamprecht, of Cure Pierre-Telephore Sax of the Church of Saint-Romuald near Quebec City and of Abbot Wimmer. Sketches of altars, reredoes, baptismal fonts and of Christ at the Last Supper join with sculptures of St. Benedict and other figures created by Cosmas.

In 1868 Duveneck painted a Madonna and Child for the Benedictine Sisters in Covington. It is remarkable for the glowing almond-shaped eyes of the mother and the image of a knowing child. The painting hangs in the Benedictine St. Walburg's Convent in Villa Hills, Kentucky. Nearby, on a refectory wall, there hangs a portrait of St. Walburga, the seventh century English nun who joined Boniface in their successful mission to convert the Germans. The painter was Duveneck's teacher, Johann Schmitt.

Embarking for Europe

Duveneck's mentors encouraged the young man in his art work and naturally favored him as a candidate to pursue the same education they had experienced in Germany. Duveneck's family liked the idea of European studies. His father, Squire, had his concerns. He wanted young Frank to further his studies, having confidence in the young man's abilities and in the German system of education. Cautiously he placed a restriction that Frank wait until he was a more mature twenty-one years of age before pursuing his studies in

Europe. Meanwhile, Wolf negotiated an arrangement that young Frank would study at the Munich academy and that the Duveneck family would contribute $150 a year for two years to defray the cost of his room and board. To this arrangement by 1869, all were agreed.

Wolf expressed some concern that young Duveneck might stray. He recommended that he accept "absolute obedience" to his *in loco parentis,* a Herr Sharer. Lamprecht recommended his former teacher, Johann von Schraudolph, a professor at the Royal Academy who had founded and directed the Verein Fuer Christliche Kunst, the Society of Christian Art, which had attracted so many adherents in Cincinnati. From a distance these precautions for Frank's welfare looked to be more than adequate.

Frank Duveneck departed Cincinnati in the fall of 1869 in a new suit made of such sturdy material he thought even years later that it would never wear out. Suitable for the Midwest, the cut was out of fashion for Europe. So as an innocent abroad, a pilgrim in reverse, he sailed for Europe in steerage from New York, trading in his second-class ticket to fatten his billfold. He bought what he found later to be a creature-inhabited mattress that offered little comfort as he crossed the Atlantic Ocean. The ocean liner landed in a North German port and young Frank located his large trunk in a customs house where customs officials stood over it holding their noses. Mother Duveneck had packed cooked chicken, cheese and other of Frank's favorites and placed them in the trunk, mistakenly thinking he could have access to them during the trip.

Frank cleansed the luggage of the offending materials as best he could and promptly dispatched the trunk directly to Munich.

Arriving in Europe must have been a heady experience for Duveneck. In any era, travelers say that the first experience in a new land and a new culture can always be most vividly recalled. Surely, this was the case for Duveneck.

At this time picturesque Munich still possessed buildings from the time of its medieval founding and contained people who shared Duveneck's love and respect for art. In 1870, Munich had as many churches, mostly Roman Catholic, as Rome, and the city fathers educated the populace with sculpture and picture galleries, a state gallery and one for contemporary art. The Alte Pinakothek gallery exhibited paintings from the Dutch and Flemish schools that clearly caught young Duveneck's eye.

Munich offered everything for the six thousand artists who lived there, a lusty, beer-drinking town that loved life. Young Duveneck began classes in 1870, and he had his own plans for studies to the dismay of the *in loco parentis* Herr Sharer. Immediately, he fell in with Wilhelm Leibl, a painter and professor at the Munich Academy only four years older than Duveneck. The young painter and fellow American William Merritt Chase became members of the Leibl Circle, which included other German students and artists. Munich as a center of art was pulsing with change.

French painter Jean Desire Gustave Courbet had introduced to Paris a style that became known as the French version of Realism. An early advocate was Edouard Manet who later became a Master of Impressionism. In Munich, the artist Wilhelm Leibl was setting the stage for the rise of a Munich version called *Realismus*. Munich painters were throwing off the shackles of the academy, becoming more interested in light and color. Chief influences came from an 1869 international exhibit in the Glaspalast and a public showing of works by masters of the brush such as Rubens, Rembrandt, Velazquez and Hals. In keeping with this tradition of change based on a review of the past, Duveneck signed up not for classes with religious brothers or monks but for the Antique Class to learn from masters.

"All of these painters were in various ways affected by the art of Courbet; in order to give a firm basis to their own Realist aspirations, they embraced Leibl's principle of rendering essential nature under the impact of light in a unified totality."[6]

For example, the teacher Leibl spent much of his time in Bavarian villages painting his own family and peasants. "I paint men as they are; the soul will be there anyway," he said.

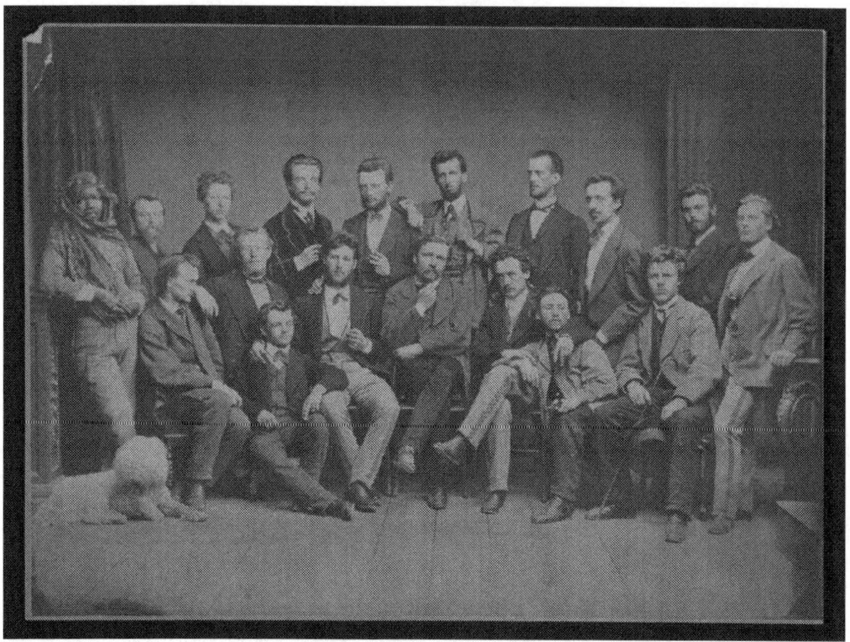

Duveneck is seated at the far right in this class at the Munich school.

-Diez class in Munich, 1871/J. Landy, photographer. Frank and Elizabeth Boott Duveneck papers, 1851-1972, bulk 1851-1919. Archives of American Art, Smithsonian Institution

Youthful Duveneck was a handsome roughneck in these years. His large head was topped with thick light-colored hair, his face was full and well-balanced in features, his pair of ambitious and discerning eyes brimmed with self-confidence.

Family stories from the Decker clan say that Duveneck was "a wild one" in these early years abroad. He loved to drink beer and carouse with his friends, a habit he kept for a lifetime, part of the

German tradition. He was young then, learning much and expressing himself in art, and by all accounts, he was enjoying life.

These years were also some of his most creative and productive. Growing in self-confidence he would carry his portraits to Munich's galleries and stand his work next to an acknowledged master's "to test them" he said, "because I wasn't going to have anyone get ahead of me."

Accolades came quickly. He won a silver medal from the academy, a top award that allowed him to set up his own studio within the school. Even so, his shirts fell into rags. In a letter to his parents he teased that his Midwestern suit of iron-like cloth "as thick as a board" was thankfully showing signs of wear. By this time he had completed more than two years in Munich studying with a professor he liked, Wilhelm von Diez, [sometimes referred to as Dietz] when he received a letter from home asking him when he planned to return to America.

He responded with a burst of loyalty for his comrades and teachers that also contained, presciently or by happenstance, about dates of his actual marriage:

"I can assure you that I have never before felt so happy in my life—first because I had the good fortune to fall in with such an able professor as Diez, who tries to do everything he can for his pupils.[2]

"Really coming home until December can't be considered! I think that nothing would be so hard for me now as to say goodbye to Munich and to all my colleagues here who all like me very much. Diez has advised me to stay in Germany, but of course that can't be considered. One day he asked me not to paint any more holy pictures but to make my studies exclusively from nature…

"You ask about marriage over here. But that does not go! Slowly and cautiously! Otherwise you grind off your own nose. I think I'll postpone it twenty years, and maybe I won't do it at all in the end.

Anyhow there's nothing to be done in Germany for there aren't any pretty girls!"

The parents must have been concerned that he was excessively loyal to his friends and professors, feeling perhaps left out or secondary to his friends in Munich. Duveneck replied:

"I received your letter in which you say that I seem to think more of my colleagues than of my father and mother. Surely, you don't think that!"

He wrote that their letter brought him to tears.

"I can assure you the first year I hardly knew where to turn for homesickness and longing to see you. But I was fortunate to find men to turn to here such as you rarely find in America, for they are not only companions who are good fun to bat around with, but they are also people with whom you can have real sympathy and understanding."

He also found himself defending his work schedule.

"If I had wasted my time and not worked day and night, as Mr. Tiemann and Father Gerard [likely visitors to Munich who had seen Duveneck] can tell you, I certainly should not have won the silver medal, which is very rarely won without first getting the bronze one."

Formal Studies End

Defensive about his work habits and elusive on a date for a departure from Munich, Duveneck still understood that he had to return to America. He was having difficulty subsisting on money from home, and he knew that he wasn't the only one who needed financial support in the Duveneck family. Yet, he wanted to make the most of what time was left. Luckily, he had sold a painting of a man and his dog to a Munich art dealer for 800 gulden that would help sustain him, for a while. But generous to a fault, if not plainly reckless with his money, Duveneck showed the packet to his young artist friends and allowed them to pinch some to meet their needs. Instead of saving up for a trip home, he used what was left over to buy a train ticket to Italy. He visited Venice and went off sightseeing, dazzled by that country's splendors, only to return exhausted to Munich, and to learn some interesting news.

The German painter, Franz von Lenbach, had seen Duveneck's work and asked him through the painter's teacher, Diez, to become Lenbach's assistant.

He wrote right away:

"I was quite dumbfounded and hurried immediately to my professor who welcomed me most warmly and said: 'Duveneck, you are the glory of my school. My colleague, the master Lenbach, offers you a place in his studio.'"

But it was not to be.

Lenbach had other plans. On a visit to Austria, Lenbach found a rich market for portraiture in the Hapsburg court. He painted Emporer Franz Joseph and others in the family, and dropped the idea of expanding his studio with an appointment of the young American painter.

Meanwhile, Duveneck sold a group of small paintings for 1,200 gulden in the summer of 1873 and invested it in some kind of business venture. But, it failed. He was stony broke and had to skip an exhibit in Vienna due to a shortage of funds and a lack of appropriate entries. Impecunious, he wrote home fatefully:

"There will be plenty of Expositions. To want everything all at once doesn't do."

The financial stresses Duveneck was experiencing provided an opening for father Duveneck. He referred to the church decorators Schmitt and Lamprecht as "rascals," who "are getting as rich as

Rothschilds. Lamprecht has made money enough to live on the rest of his life and doesn't need to work anymore. His assistant too is getting along splendidly. All the artists say that you ought to come home."

A dreaded outbreak of cholera, which had killed his natural father in 1849 and other members of the Decker family, likely hastened Duveneck's return to America. Cholera took the life of Wilhelm von Kaulbach, the head of the Munich academy. Duveneck's painting, *The Unfinished Portrait Study of a Girl's Head*, from that period, narrates a shocking story of its own. Duveneck completed the sketch in several hours, and the girl model was to return the following day. She didn't show up for the sitting; she had passed from the disease during the night. Still, Duveneck hated to leave, but he tried to make the best of it. His daughter-in-law Josephine Duveneck described his emotions and expectations at the time.

"With half-amused but none the less genuine elation, he anticipated the figure he should cut when he returned to Covington and met his old associates who had been plugging along in the same old ruts, while he had been rising to importance out in the great world! He imagined, as he watched the ocean from the deck of the westbound steamer, how everyone would be waiting to see him, and want to shake him by the hand, not only his family and his boyhood friends, but the neighbors, and his father's business associates. Above all, the artists would take him in as one of themselves (sic) and ask him all kinds of questions about what he had seen and done. Perhaps he would receive notices in the newspapers! Dreams of glory filled his mind and when he reached Cincinnati, he was in a state of high excitement."[7]

Church Work Pales

Sculptor Clement Barnhorn, a lifelong friend, offered a graphic picture of his friend upon his return. He remembered Duveneck in a *Kentucky Post* interview article, dated March 28, 1934: "He was a real swell, swinging a cane and tossing a Munich cape back from his shoulders."

Due to his stepfather's intervention, Duveneck got a job with a man named Tien, a church decorator, and painted a fifteen-foot-high fresco of St. Peter, surrounded by a flock of sheep, and receiving from Jesus Christ the keys of the kingdom. The fresco in Trinity Church in Cincinnati was lost in a remodeling, and the church building itself was destroyed in a later fire.

Hard-pressed for cash in Cincinnati, Duveneck tried to refuel his passion for religious painting, but it was not working.

"He was one who always wanted to satisfy those [people] whom he loved, but he was hopelessly bored by saints and madonnas and scenes form Bible history," his daughter-in-law wrote. He was trying to rid himself of a "fearful mannerism" in his painting that his Munich teacher Diez had observed and attributed to his works on holy pictures. In what must have been a process of his mind over a period of years he drew a distinction between church decoration and what he called real art. His study of the old masters in Munich art galleries offered him a new outlet for his artistic urgings that relegated his art on religious subjects to the dust bin.

Always attentive to his mother, Duveneck asked her opinion on a switch to secular subjects and inquired how distressed she might be if he stopped going to Mass. He must have felt hypocritical, his life having taken a new and different direction. If he had been attending Mass with the family, he probably would not have taken Holy Communion, a sign that he was not living in accord with Church teachings on proper preparation for reception of the Eucharist.

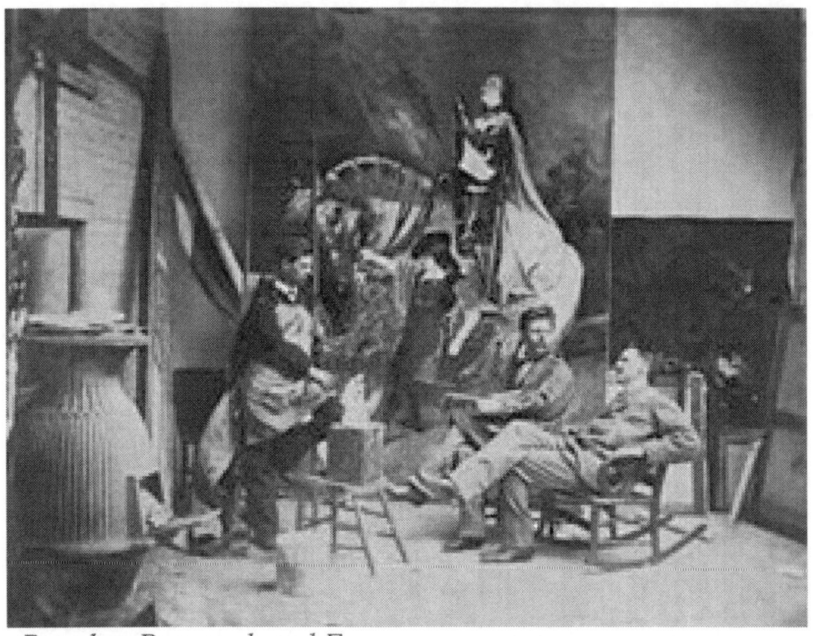

Dengler, Duveneck and Farny
-Frank Duveneck, in a studio, with Frank Dengler and H.F. Farny, 1874/unidentified photographer. Frank and Elizabeth Boott Duveneck papers, 1851-1972, bulk 1851-1919. Archives of American Art, Smithsonian Institution.

"I should like to have you do both those things of course," she responded, according to the family biographer, daughter-in-law Josephine Whitney Duveneck. "But now that you are a man you have to decide such things for yourself. It's all right with me whatever you decide." With that, Duveneck left the Church that had nurtured him and put aside his religious obligations, and he halted the practice of church decoration and religious paintings, at least for a time. As Shakespeare would say, he minded not his fair creed. One can bet that the tolerant mother, a religious woman, never stopped praying that her son would one day return to the Church.

A photograph taken in the winter of 1874-75 shows Duveneck in a studio he shared with sculptor Frank Dengler, which became an oasis for the art crowd in Cincinnati. He is with Dengler and Henry F. Farny, another Cincinnati area artist who made a name for himself as a painter of Indians in southwest deserts of the United

88

States. Behind them is a large painting of Joan of Arc, executed by Duveneck and exhibited at the Germanic Festival that year at Cincinnati's Music Hall.

In this period Duveneck, out of his generosity to fledgling artists, taught a no-tuition evening class at the Mechanics Institute. Fellow Cincinnatian John Twachtman took that class and later studied in Munich. Fortunately for his career, Twachtman pursued Impressionism and is known today for his rich landscapes. On commission in this period Duveneck painted a portrait of Mrs. Anthony H. Hinkle and he executed one, *William Adams*, the latter a work that attracted the eye of Elizabeth Boott.

In spring of 1875 there came an event that would propel Duveneck into the limelight in America's art world. He was asked by directors of the Boston Art Club to exhibit several of his paintings. An artist and teacher there, William Morris Hunt, had been instrumental in exciting interest in art, holding classes and lectures and extolling the trend of realism that had swept Europe. Duveneck sent five pictures, mostly portraits. The *Adams* portrait was purchased by Lizzie Boott who happened to be in Boston at that time and was studying art with Hunt. Lizzie may have met Frank Duveneck at the Boston exhibit but there is no evidence she did.

The Duveneck works attracted the eye of critic Henry James who wrote in the July issue of *The Galaxy* in 1875:

"The good people of Boston have recently been flattering themselves that they have discovered an American Velasquez. In the rooms of the Boston Art club hang some five remarkable portraits by Mr. Frank Duveneck of Cincinnati. This young man, who is not yet, we believe, in his twenty-fifth year, took, his first steps in painting in the Bavarian capital, and it is hardly hyperbolical to say that these steps were, for a mere lad, giant strides. He came back a while since, if we are not mistaken, to his native city, where his genius was not highly appreciated, and where depressing obscurity was his portion, until aesthetic Boston held out a friendly hand. It is of course of supreme importance that Mr. Duveneck should not be talked about intemperately, though we shall be surprised if his head is not too firmly set upon his shoulders to be easily turned. We speak in reason when we say that the half dozen portraits in question have an extraordinary interest. They are all portraits of men—and of very ugly men; they have little grace, little finish, little elegance, none of the relatively superfluous qualities. But they have a most remarkable reality and directness, and Velasquez is in fact the name that rises to your lips as you look at them. It is very evident that in so far as there is any question of Velasquez in the matter, the analogy of Mr. Duveneck's talent with that of the great Spaniard is a natural, instinctive one."

James praised the paintings for their "extreme naturalness, their unmixed unredeemed reality. They contain the material of an excellent foundation."[8] He added that he would find it disturbing if Duveneck failed to produce a work of primary importance. And, he watched the artist's career over the next decade, frequently at eyeball range as a close friend of the expatriates Francis Boott and daughter Elizabeth.

---

[1]*Duveneck, a Teacher of Artists*, L.H. Meakin, *Arts and Decoration*, July, 1911
[2]*Cosmas Wolf, monk architect sculptor designer*, The Saint Vincent Gallery, Br. Nathan Cochran, O.S.B., St. Vincent College, Latrobe, Pennsylvania, 2013, p. 4
[3]*Munchner Sonntagsblat,* November 23, 1862, p. 372.
[4]*Ibid,* St. Vincent catalogue, p. 14
[5]*Ibid*, St. Vincent catalogue, p.14
[6]*German Masters of the Nineteenth Century*: paintings and drawings from the Federal Republic of Germany, The Metropolitan Museum of New York, Harry Abrams, Inc., publisher, New York, 1981, p. 32
[7]*Frank Duveneck, Painter-Teacher* by Josephine W. Duveneck, John Howell—Books, San Francisco, CA, 1970, pp.35-48

[8]*Henry James, The Conquest of London: 1870-1881*, Leon Edel, Avon Books, New York 1962 p.187

Chapter Four

A Rebellious Brahmin and His Daughter

Boston, 13 April 1846

The Bootts of Boston were Brahmin, occupying the top level of the social scale.

They became better known in Beantown circles after members of the family founded textile mills on the Merrimac River in Lowell, Massachusetts, at least two generations before Frank met Lizzie in Venice. Societal acceptance of the industrialist Bootts was strengthened when Lizzie's father, Francis, married Elizabeth Otis Lyman, of a leading family of Boston, in the same social stratosphere with the Lowells and the Cabots.

Boston is a social center of its own unique design. Unlike England where heredity often counted more than money, commerce mingled more heavily with inheritance to provide feeding stock to gracious acceptance. Sheer wealth made the difference between the privileged rank of Brahmin and ordinary citizenry, though to be a Brahmin one had to follow an unwritten code and in later years be named in the Boston Social Register. The way to the top in most generations came through success in shipping, railroads, mining, banking, cod fishing, seafaring, or via such industries as fur and textiles.[1]

Mayflower descendants in the Boston aristocracy have been few and far between, and by the nineteenth century even fewer among the Brahmins could trace their families to the Pilgrims' landing at Plymouth Rock in 1620 A.D.

The Bootts came to America from England in the late eighteenth and early nineteenth centuries from the area around Derby. The family, originally named Boot [the Dutch and German word for boat] came from the Netherlands during the reign of Charles II and worked as surgeons in Lincoln. The additional "t" was added to the name by Kirk Boott, the most successful of the early immigrants in his founding of a mill in Lowell, Massachusetts. One of the Merrimac River dams is called the Boott Dam.

Kirk Boott joined in business with a Mr. Farrow in Boston. Francis Boott's father, also Francis, a nephew of Kirk's, started as a clerk in the counting room of Boott & Farrow, and later earned a considerable amount of money from furs on a business trip to the northwest of the United States. Having fathered a son and made a packet, the elder Francis Boott had plans to return himself and family to England. He departed Boston with $80,000 on a transatlantic vessel that put in at the Azores in an unseaworthy condition, according to reports. It was later lost. Boott was never heard from again.

Family antecedents of Frank Duveneck's wife-to-be, Elizabeth Otis Lyman Boott, won fame and fortune both in and beyond New England. Harrison Gray Otis, a spendthrift and nephew of revolutionary leader James Otis, built three houses in Boston. One residence on Beacon Hill was so large that it accommodated each of his three married children with private sitting rooms, guest rooms and, for each, a complete floor dedicated to their ballroom entertaining. Harrison Gray Otis was known for gold-laced hats and for wearing other expensive attire. A lawyer, merchant and successful investor in real estate, Otis (1765-1848) served one term each in the U.S. House of Representatives and in the Senate.

The Bootts not Apleys

A member of the Lyman family, doubtless a blood relative of Lizzie's from a later generation, was pilloried in Cleveland Amory's *The Proper Bostonians*, a post-World War II study of local society.

Amory wrote:

"No Boston Lyman, for example, has ever established a high reputation for humor, particularly in matters concerning Boston or a

93

Lyman. Emerging from the Boston opening of the play *The Late George Apley*, a Cunningham approached a Lyman and said hesitatingly, 'Very amusing, wasn't it?' 'No,' said Lyman severely, 'very exaggerated,' and passed on."

The Apleys of the fictional works are not the Bootts, nor the Lymans, though the Apleys of the stories and the real, historical families derived sustaining incomes from the Merrimac textile mills. The Boott mill was one of nine in the City of Lowell, and the one most frequently mentioned in the writings of Lowell native Jack Kerouac whose father counted among the many French Canadian immigrants to that city. The Lymans owned at least two mills.

The Apley play, the Hollywood movie version and a Pulitzer prize-winning book by John P. Marquand, offer a satirical view of the mill-owning Apleys as they transited from the Gilded Age to the Great Depression and endured, all the time under pressures of cultural and economic upheavals. The fictional George Apley was richly portrayed as a representative of the clan. Perhaps however, as the humorless Lyman suggested in his response to a Cunningham query, the character of George serves as an extreme version of the family type. In the novel, while forming at Harvard University in the 1880s, young George was advised by his father by letter that "nothing is more important than social consideration…Friends must be drawn from your own sort of people, or difficulty and embarrassment are very apt to be the result." The father, in his letters and actions, assumed the role of stiff-necked malefactor in the Marquand book; George is the malleable literary gentleman of a son, keeper of the flame, cut off from his Irish lass, Mary Monahan.

George Apley regards New York as "not an American city. We have our Irish and you have your Jews, and both of them are crosses to bear," he wrote to son John after visiting him in Gotham.

It would be unjust to apply this kind of attitude to the Bootts. It is a fact, however, that the Bootts owned mills in Lowell that are part of American history as the first-ever planned factory town. Working conditions in Lowell in the early days were exacting and hard when compared to contemporary standards. While laborers in America may have been better off than those in English mills, for example, still, not everyone approved of the workers' lot even in those days.

A primary example of the mixed opinion towards mill employment comes in the real life experience of entrepreneur Nathaniel Appleton, whose name is close to Apley either by chance or design. He helped establish New England as a world textile center and ushered the United States into the industrial revolution. A Whig in political circles, Appleton married Harriett Coffin Sumner, cousin of Charles Sumner, the abolitionist who served in President Lincoln's Cabinet. The abolitionist Sumner was critical of mill owner practices and had no use for southern slavers and plantation owners. In a public speech, for example, Sumner compared the "lords of the lash and the lords of the loom," grouping the slavers in the same stew with northern mill owners. Sumner made no bones about his feelings toward mill owners. In his mind they were hypocrites if they opposed slavery in the South yet tolerated abuse of employees in the North.

For their part, the real-life Messrs. Appleton and his partner, Francis Cabot Lowell rose to become kingpins of the American textile industry, known in business as the Boston Associates. They were responsible for setting up employment standards. They had taken the trouble of visiting England and witnessing first-hand the often brutish lives of workers there. Work policies shaped by the Boston Associates for American employees set precedent. They rejected child labor, a practice common to English mills, and hired young women, many from northern New England farm families. These "mill girls" lived in company boarding houses under supervision of older women proctors who enforced a moral code. Employees were required to attend church but it was a ceremony of their own choosing in keeping with their rights under the Constitution's first amendment.

Rigorous But Fair

The so-called Waltham System required girls to rise at 4:40 a.m. and to report to the mill by 5 a.m. Breakfast was served at 7 a.m.; lunch time was 45 minutes long. The mill girls worked until 7 p.m. each night, six days a week. Many labored only a few months, typically a fling to raise cash before they married.

"They were able to have educational opportunities they could get nowhere else and also were offered religious freedoms. They were paid in cash that went into their own pockets, not to a parent, spouse or company store, and the houses in which they lived were clean and of a high quality," claims a recent history of Boston.[2]

Charles Dickens, the vaunted chronicler of the impoverished, the supremely lucky and dreadfully unfortunate in nineteenth century England, visited the Lowell mills in 1842. He took pains in an alert to his readers of *American Notes* to insist that he was not a witness to a put-up show as he viewed the mill girls at the looms. The millworkers, he wrote, "were all well-dressed; and that phrase necessarily includes extreme cleanliness. They had serviceable bonnets, good warm cloaks, and shawls. Moreover, there were places in the mill in which they could deposit these things without injury; and there were conveniences for washing. They were healthy in appearance, many of them remarkably so, and had the manners and deportment of young women; not of degraded brutes of burden."[3]

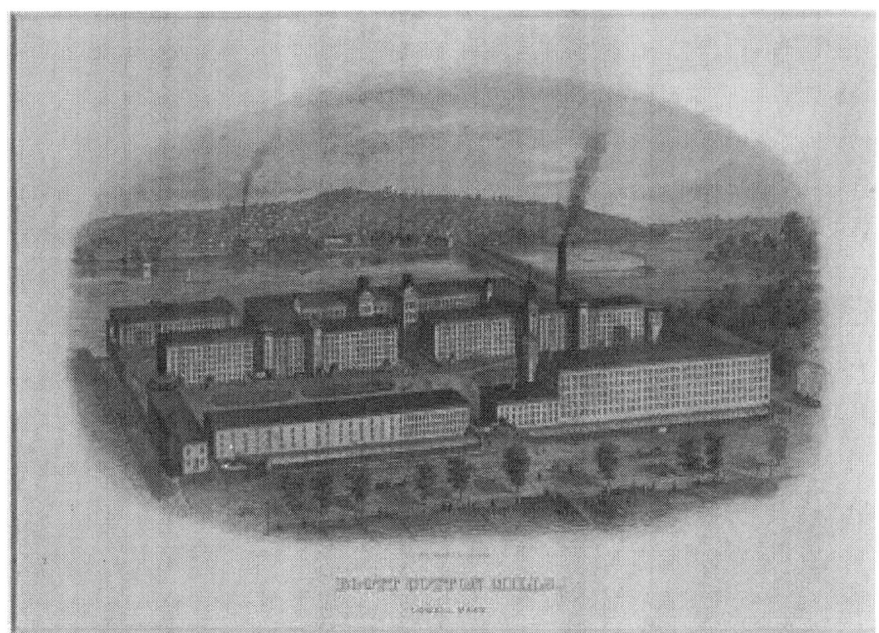

The Boott Mills in Lowell, Massachusetts
-Courtesy of the National Park Service

Dickens visited boarding houses and found that the women's rooms were clean, the residence halls even freshened by green plants. A great many houses were equipped with a piano. The girls subscribed to circulating libraries and produced a literary periodical, "The Lowell Offering," which he said had merit.

Duveneck biographer Josephine Whitney Duveneck, herself of an accomplished and distinguished New York family, was critical of working conditions at some mills but acknowledged that conditions improved with time. She wrote candidly:

"In the old days, the workers lived in houses within a brick quadrangle which included the mill itself, the company church and a school. The whole life of the employees was centered there. They labored fourteen hours a day, six days a week. On Sundays they had to go to church and were expected to support the minister out of their meager salaries. Children worked in the mill also, nine or ten hours at a stretch. Much of the blue cotton cloth worn by coolies in China in the nineteenth century was woven in the Massachusetts mills of Lowell and Lawrence."

Benefactors of this nineteenth century industrial environment, Elizabeth Otis Lyman Boott and her father issued no known public objections to working conditions, or to the industry that allowed them to live on a fairly high scale. They chose to base their residence in Europe as expatriates, a move that could be interpreted as a form of dissenting from the standard but more likely to pursue fashionable lives of art and leisure at the cultural base of western civilization. There is no evidence that either the father or the daughter found the sources of their money as reprehensible. In most ways they seemed to be members of the upper class whose families had fractured, in the first case by the death of Francis's father and in the next generation, by the death of his wife, Lizzie's mother.

Hardships in a Good Life

Young Francis Boott started his New England education in a private school that was located over a bakery in Boston's Temple Street. Then he began a Dickensian existence at a school called Ripley's in Waltham, Massachusetts. He compared the master, Mr. Ripley, to Squeers of the infamous and aptly named Dotheboys Hall in Dickens's *Nicholas Nickleby*. In his memoirs, Francis was more severe on Ripley's wife, "a very superior woman, who did not temper the wind to us poor shorn lambs. She had children of her own, too, but they seemed to occupy all the space offered by the *locus parentis*, to the exclusion of those of another's fold."[4] The schoolmaster enforced a regulation that all boys' letters had to undergo screening by him personally, a rule that inhibited discussion of any dissension in the ranks. But one missive from Francis Boott to his mother eluded Ripley's ophidian eye. Young Francis wrote from his confinement, a penalty for some infraction, and relayed the tale of a boy who in fun had shinnied up a swing rope and who received a like incarceration. The next day his mother, accompanied by others of the Boott family, arrived by coach at the school and summarily withdrew her son. Francis did better at the next private school. He qualified for Harvard and was selected to join the famous Porcellian Club, "and altogether that was the happiest year of my life." He completed his studies in three years and entered Yale law school, then switched to Harvard Law School.

"I found law no more to my taste, but went through the motions so to speak," he wrote in his *Recollections*. Upon leaving that pursuit he began a sojourn to Cuba and across the United States, and embarked in April, 1836, on a trip to Europe. He warmed to England and was enthusiastic about Germany, "then thought *the* land of poetry and romance, and her language and literature much studied." He resumed his interest in music and started lessons in singing, a peripatetic student of art, philosophy and music on a grand tour in Europe, until his return to Boston in April, 1840. Francis's personal life took an upswing at that point. He boarded with his mother in the Boott homestead on Mount Vernon Street, the same street on which the Lymans also maintained a residence. In three years he was engaged to Elizabeth Lyman, and they were married in her father's house in March, 1844. The first child, Frank Boott, born in spring, 1845, died in August of that year. Lizzie's birthing happened April 13, 1846, in the Mount Vernon Street residence.

The next year began a period of hardship for Francis Boott's young family. His wife suffered from lung problems, a common ailment among many women who lived a stultified existence in this Victorian era. Medical advice called for treatment in a more salubrious climate. The couple embarked for South Carolina. "But to no purpose," Francis later wrote. The cause of her death was a stomach ailment that interfered with digestion. She was buried in Boston at the Boott family tomb in Mount Auburn. Elizabeth Lyman Boott's death caused a radical change in the lives of Francis Boott and his young daughter.

As a full-time expatriate Francis Boott was something of a rebel. His particular form of rebellion was not wayward in any immoral sense. He abjured the common pathway to Brahmin success, the law, medicine, business, or the clergy. During his life he was not known for abusing alcohol or drugs, nor was he disposed to take risks on gambling or unreasonable stakes. As a public figure he appeared to be a patrician gentleman, fastidious, with elevated tastes. His course in life was unconventional only in the use of his ample funds to travel and live with little evident responsibility to anyone but to himself and to his daughter. In his memoirs Francis Boott wrote, "I spent many very agreeable winters in Rome, and came to the conclusion there was no more agreeable residence." He could trace Italian ancestry through his mother, Mary Turnaley, also from Derby, whose predecessor, either father or grandfather, named Tunalli, had immigrated to England.

A Brahmin and Daughter Abroad

After the fateful marriage, the birth of Lizzie and the death of his wife, Francis Boott and Lizzie, then a year and five months old, embarked for Europe with Lizzie's nurse, Mary Ann Shenstone, later known simply as Ann to avoid confusion with a friend's maid of the same name. Biographer Josephine Whitney Duveneck described tersely Francis Boott's unusual response to the death of his wife: "Francis Boott, who was something of a misfit in Boston society, gathered up his small daughter and her nurse and departed for Europe." He also inherited a considerable sum of money from his Lyman wife, an odd precursor to what was to happen in the next generation.

At first, Lizzie lived with her aunt, Fanny, Francis's sister, and her children in Genoa, while he took an apartment in the city.

He wrote:

"The winter was not a bad one; but this combination of families did not seem to work well, and it was decided to separate."

They moved about in Italy where they enjoyed friendships with other expatriates, largely American and including famous Europeans.

Francis Boott wrote home:

"(Franz) Liszt was then living in Rome , or rather on the top of Monte Mario. I met him at [the Sculptor William Wetmore] Story's and Madame Schwartz's. He gave a concert in the Capitol [sic] to raise money for the Pope [Pius IX] (Peter's Pence) and as he charged $3 a ticket he had the cream of Roman and Papal society. He did all himself, and it was a most remarkable exhibition, not only for the ears, but the eyes, as he acted out his emotions and illustrated the music by the expression of his face."

Francis gained some fame with a composition, a hymn for eight voices, *Momento Rerum Conditor*, which was part of a musical program in St. Peter's Basilica in Rome in spring, 1852. A slow movement of this work was published for four voices titled *Maria Mater*. He was self-deprecatory about this honor, saying that it was included in the church organist's annual program largely to attract support from Americans in Rome, which it did.

His memoirs say little about his personal finances except for a reference to loss due to the failure of a rolling mill in which a business partner had supported with $200,000. The loss does not appear to have severely dented his life of leisure and social swing. The reduced income may, however, have been responsible for the move from Rome to Florence where he rented rooms in the Villa Castellani at the budget expense of $55 a year in the currency value of that period.

Boott spent the autumn, 1854, in Paris and saw the author William Makepeace Thackeray of *Vanity Fair* fame at a friend's home.

He described him as a:

"large, awkward sort of man, intent and doubtless keeping his own counsel for his books." He also "saw the [Robert and Elizabeth Barrett] Brownings in Florence, then living in the Casa Guidi, the windows of which, looking on the Piazza Pitti, furnished Mrs. Browning a subject for one of her poems. She was a delightful woman—very modest, in spite of her great reputation. I did not fancy *him*."

His musical career received a lift when the Board of Examiners in a triennial competition at the Academy of Fine Arts in Florence accorded second place honors to his hymn, *Il Cantico di Zaccari*. The award found notice in the *New York Times* and, "I got a little notoriety among friends at home," he wrote. In 1858 he moved to the apartment in the sprawling fifty-room Villa Castellani on Bellosguardo overlooking Florence. It was there that Lizzie took her first art lessons and began studying piano, the violin, voice and French and Latin, among several languages. She learned to swim and ride to round out her Victorian lady credentials rendered with a European flavor. The villa became an important stop for Americans and English visitors. Little Lizzie's sketchbooks are filled with carefully drawn profiles of visiting literary and artistic figures.

Boott family and other Boston connections were maintained by letter-writing and by hosting the many and frequent visitors. Mr. Boott was a gentleman on an extended fling; she, a young lady of name and talent living in extraordinary circumstances under her father's cultural umbrella. They were Americans abroad, and were known for that circumstance; but these rare living conditions could not change who they were as persons with family attachments and New England culture. The Brahmin influence was in their blood. It was who they were.

Lizzie Boott was a cultivated young woman. She likely was familiar with *The Young Lady's Friend*, a manual written by the wife of a Harvard professor, regarded in mid-Victorian America as the Bible of social graces. The ideal gentlewoman was defined simply and indiscriminately as "the daughter of a rich man." Manners were pre-determined and fixed as if the Bostonians were members of Louis XIV's court at Versailles, each step defined from the opening of the hostesses' door to its close. There was to be no playing with cutlery, nor any touching of hair or blowing of noses. At table, suitable topics for conversation were a child, a picture, an animal, a worked ottoman or a bunch of flowers.

Even as late as 1865 women of the house were advised to place apart on shelves books by male and female authors following to some degree the same logic of far separate placement in George Apley's bookshelves of works by the father of modern psychiatry, Sigmund Freud and the beloved founder of the American Transcendentalism movement, Bostonian Ralph Waldo Emerson.

Little Evidence of Faith

Francis Boott's memoirs do not detail any clinging to any faith or religious feelings. Scholar Carol Osborne says that Lizzie was baptized a Unitarian in Boston's North Church. Having grown up in Italy she "was more sympathetic to Roman Catholicism than were her friends at home." She informed them that she felt religious while spending time in Santa Maria Maggiore, her favorite church in Rome, "which is more than I can say for myself in a Yankee meeting house." In her letter she assured friends in the art class under William Morris Hunt in Boston that she was not converting, however. Her "poor little faith" had been wilted under "the bare walls & white glare of a Protestant church." She found it agreeable that churches in Italy were open all the time "& not on Sunday morning when one has one's new blouse on," she wrote to her Hunt class friends in December, 1876

Still, it is difficult to assess how Francis and his daughter, or even the artist Duveneck, a fallen away Catholic in this period, may have been affected by the larger profound issues of life, death and afterlife. Personal letters also fail in this regard; but the movements and trends in high gear during their lives involved people they knew well and could have had influence.

A reading of Lizzie's correspondence and her interests and painting subjects show a tendency toward naturalism, which was coming into its own in nineteenth century Europe and America. Because of that tendency she may have found Duveneck attractive for his natural talents and honest and down-to-earth direct approach to life. When she reached adulthood, Emerson's Transcendentalism was still operative but it was beginning to fade in New England where religion, philosophy and pursuit of the spirit had always played a major civilizing role. "What linked them together," the transcendentalists believed, "was the conviction that all spiritual truths were known intuitively by the innate laws of the mind." A significant heritage of this movement was "the general creative expansion of the human mind as the instrument of knowledge and power."

Emerson regarded himself as an "endless thinker with no past at his back." Affiliated with English Romanticism and High German Idealism, American Transcendentalism encouraged individual seekers. Counted among them today are poets Walt Whitman, Emily Dickinson and, in the twentieth century, Robert Frost, author of *The Road Not Taken*. The movement is generally credited with engendering nature writing in America, sprouting with Emerson's friend, Henry David Thoreau, and including later writers, John Muir and Loren Eiseley. Mind-over-matter movements such as Christian Science can find a source in Transcendentalism. [5]

The nineteenth century Transcendentalism movement reflected philosophical idealism—sublime and wonderful in thought—which was affronted by such raw abominations as American slavery. To their credit, Emerson and other transcendentalists took up the anti-slavery cause. But the carnage of the Civil War served as the turning point for the movement. Philosophical focus shifted from the loftiness of Transcendentalism to a new kind of pragmatism, with Bostonian William James, brother of Henry James and friend of the Bootts, author of *The Varieties of Religious Experience*; Charles Peirce and John Dewey serving as standard bearers. Teaming with the pragmatism trend was the new emphasis on matter-of-fact science, arising from Charles Darwin's *Origin of the Species*.

Though perhaps not avid followers, the Bootts knew personally the thinker Emerson and Bostonian John A. Lowell, leaders of the nineteenth century evolution of the Unitarian religion. Unitarianism became established at Harvard Divinity School before that school's switch to non-sectarianism. After the Calvinist Pilgrims, Congregationalism had become the established denomination of New England. Later, a form of low-church Episcopalian faith began to spread. As Boston swelled with Irish immigrants, the Roman Catholic Church grew rapidly following the Irish Famine (1845-1850), a period prior to the Civil War when Lizzie and her father were abroad. The faith or life philosophy of Francis Boott and Lizzie remains, however, elusive and obscure.

What is known is that the Boott father and daughter based their residence in Florence and frequently visited other major European cities and resorts. Their closest friends tended to be either English or American artists, musicians or other expatriates. Father Francis and daughter Lizzie grew closely together in this nearly closed environment. It may be apt to compare them to Americans who today live in consulates abroad, or with military families on assignment overseas who are corralled and tend to stay together. As a consequence of this untypical rearing, though abroad, Lizzie appears to have thrived under the father's tender care and with her tutors. She had no problems quickly adapting to Boston society when she arrived there for the first time in her late teenage years. She even became a favorite of local society as she was so thoroughly imbued with Old World culture, noted "for her charm, wit and well-informed conversation" as she moved from house to house on Beacon Hill.[6]

105

The elder Boott may have depended on tutors to teach Lizzie languages and riding, but it was he who had a strong hand in her music, voice and art lessons. An Italian family with two daughters also lived in Villa Castellani, and young Lizzie spoke Italian, enhanced doubtless by frequent contact with them. Her father compared her Italian to her command of English, which seems to have been strong even at a young age. There is something fresh, precocious and lovely in her written expressions. She wrote from her home in Florence a touching thank you letter to her uncle, Arthur Lyman, in a scroll-like hand that carried the sweet message of a ten-year-old girl, dated April 27, 1856:

"I am much obliged to you for the beautiful dogs you sent me. Papa thinks them beautiful and says that nothing else would have pleased him more. The little French girl thanks you for having remembered her. She has been sick but is very well now. I am copying a picture of St. Catherine. We are going to Leghorn in the middle of May and I hope to see you there. You can live at the edge of the sea and take a bath every day. Ann is well and says she hopes to see you before you go."[7]

Apparently, Lizzie is "the little French girl," for that was another language in which she excelled. Ann is her nurse and companion.

The close, if not unusual, father-daughter relationship received fictional treatment from Henry James in at least two novels, *The Portrait of a Lady* (1881), and *The Golden Bowl* (1904). In *Portrait*, the father and daughter are Gilbert and Pansy Osmond, he something of a scoundrel who dreaded vulgarity, she a curious, obedient and lovely teenager. At a villa very much like Villa Castellani, her character is introduced while being delivered to her residence in the company of two nuns, religious women who had cared for her. A maternal orphan, Pansy refers to the elder nun not as, *"ma soeur,"* my sister, but as *"ma mere,"* my mother. The elder religious also observes about Pansy that as "good as she is, she's made for the world."

The close relationship depicted in *The Golden Bowl* lies at the heart of the novel's struggle. Maggie Verver, daughter of a wealthy American, Adam, marries an impoverished Italian nobleman, Prince Amerigo. In doing so, she realizes that her marriage has caused loneliness in her father and she persuades Charlotte Stant, a beautiful woman and friend, to marry her father. The plot thickens as Charlotte and Amerigo have a past as lovers. But the resourceful Maggie restores her damaged marriage with her Italian prince.

Lizzie, in reality, needed outlets for her drives. She took up writing including many poems and later a hand-written novel, *The Legend of Monteripido.* Though active in writing, art seemed her forte. She drew well, neatly. Among her early sketches is a profile bust of her first art teacher, Giorgio Mignaty, who had won commissions from the literary Brownings. Lizzie's sketch of Mignaty was presented to her father, and other of her sketches became her birthday gifts to him. The father preserved them all with loving care, and many have remained in the Duveneck family archive.

An arts commentator, writing an essay for an exhibit of her works many years later, summed up the relationship:

"The years abroad saw Francis and Lizzie, becoming exceptionally close as father and daughter. Without her mother's presence and influence, Lizzie gave her father twice the love and devotion a child could give. They were practically inseparable throughout Lizzie's life…"[8]

As one would expect for a lovely and talented young girl, Lizzie in her adolescence was attracted to the opposite sex. She experienced her first flirtation at sixteen. The love interest was with someone she met "at the palace, at the marques's dance," according to a line of poetry she wrote. One commentator claimed that father Francis disapproved and ended the youthful romance by removing her to Boston. Perhaps this was the case eventually, but if the unacceptable romance were the prompter, the flight to America came about in unusually slow fashion. Lizzie's return to America was not for several years, two if not three years afterward.[9]

Lizzie's American Debut

The return to Boston came after the Civil War ended in 1865 when Lizzie approached her nineteenth year. She must have been a formidable young woman whose manner would be perceived by Bostonians as authentic, perhaps superior, to the products of the best American finishing schools. She wrote poetry, played the piano, sang, sketched and painted, all very capably and in some cases, excellently, and doubtless in social gatherings she could offer stories that held high interest.

Summer, 1869, was a fateful time for Lizzie. , At a resort boarding house in Pomfret, Connecticut, she and her father met the vacationing James family, Henry Sr., his wife and sons, William, Henry and Wilkie, and daughter, Alice, a fortunate encounter for all concerned. Young William, who was to become the Harvard philosopher and examiner of religion in peoples' lives, wrote to a friend that Lizzie had rather dazzled him:

"Miss Boott though not overpoweringly beautiful, is one of the very best members of her sex I ever met...and I never realized before how much a good education (I mean in the sense of wide information) added to the charms of a woman. She has a great talent for drawing and was very busy painting here which, as she is in just about the same helpless state in which I was when I abandoned the art, made her particularly interesting to me. You had better come home soon and make her acquaintance for you know these first class young spinsters do not always keep forever, although on the whole they tend to in Boston.[10]

However, it was not William but Henry who befriended Lizzie and who played a large role in her life.

For someone with Lizzie's background and studies, it would not be long before she became connected with art education. In 1868, a few years after her return to Boston, the painter William Morris Hunt, opened an art school for ladies, a first for the United States. Hunt had studied under the French painter, Thomas Couture, and remained devoted to his style. In large part because of Hunt's influence, Boston in this period was becoming an arts cultural center of its own, assuming its place along with long standing New England traditions of literary and philosophical pursuits. Lizzie enrolled in Hunt's classes even as she was swept up in the social whirl, enjoying visits with family and friends and participating in all that America could provide.

Her father's tender care extended to this new venture in her life. It had to be interesting for her to experience, first hand, what she had heard about New England and family from him and from other relatives who visited them in Europe. She wrote to Henry James,

"America still pleases me on the strength of her own merits only."

Lizzie took up with Hunt and by 1873 enjoyed small successes in selling her paintings, not enough to "throw a glamor over anything," she wrote. Her pen-and-ink drawing of cupids and flowers was photographed by a dealer in Boston who charged four dollars each for the photo copy. Her share was a measly twenty cents for each sold.

Lizzie and the Hunt class painted in the village of Annisquam near the Cape Ann port of Gloucester in Massachusetts.

She wrote to Henry James:

"...we spent ten days there delightfully, sketching morning & afternoon, and the interval filled by many talks about this world & the next after the fashion of Boston women. We all think each other charming, & being thus encouraged by the good opinion of the others, each shows her best side, & all are sorry when the time comes to leave. This is one of the attractions of Boston for me. The

109

place is intensified New England, but there is something in the scenery which always pleases me. Green field studded with gray rocks, or rather rocks with a little grass growing between, wide spreading apple trees covered with a profusion of pink & white blossoms & the sun playing through the branches on the grass, gray houses & an occasional red chimney & beyond a long stretch of level beach, all this touches a certain Puritan sentiment which lives hidden in some out of the way corner of my heart & and has not been killed by a lifetime in Italy."[11]

Much time was spent on Coffin's Beach, and she was charmed by the people who lived on Annisquam. Boatloads of students were rowed across a creek by an old mariner named Uncle George. He charged $1 for the task. The next day Lizzie was astonished when the conscience-stricken boatman returned 25 cents, saying he had asked too much. Such experiences provided insight into the common man of her native place. Lizzie found America different, even exciting at times. But her early experiences in Europe had laid a different ground work for her life, one that she could never forget or outlive. In a June, 1874 letter, she chided Henry James for writing so effectively about his visit to Siena, its plaza and cathedral, places she knew well and cherished.

She wrote:

This, and your article on a return to Italy after Switzerland & Germany, made me desperately homesick, & I never confess to any Italian homesickness here, nor do I generally feel any, so will you please for the future, caro Enrico, be kind enough not to write any more such descriptions as they disturb my equanimity badly."[12]

Around this same period, the artist Hunt, Lizzie's painter-teacher in Boston, had come across a work by Frank Duveneck, then in Cincinnati after his first sojourn to Europe. It was a discovery leading to a personal connection having a profound impact on their lives. Hunt collected information on Duveneck and invited him to exhibit works in Boston. Five Duveneck paintings were part of an

1875 exhibit at the Boston Art Club. Lizzie saw them and immediately esteemed the painter's skill, taking note particularly of his brushstrokes and style critics likened to Rembrandt, Hals and Velazquez. She persuaded her father to buy one of the Duveneck pictures, a portrait, *William Adams.*

Within a year, the Bootts left the security of family and American friends and embarked for Europe. True to her calling Lizzie was taking her practice of art seriously. She and her father stopped in Paris where at Villiers-le-Bel she became a student of Couture, the inspiration for William Hunt three decades previously. The father and daughter took an apartment in the village where Couture allowed students to observe him while he painted and commented on the structure of his work. She studied with Couture for two summers. But she did not forget the works of Duveneck, nor the man, who had impressed her with his talent and his very being.

---

[1] *The Proper Bostonians*, Parnassus Imprints, Orleans, Massachusetts, by Cleveland Amory, 1984, p. 390

[2] *Beacon Hill, Back Bay and the Building of Boston's Golden Age,* Ted Clarke, the History Press, 2010, p.35

[3] *American Notes*, cited in *Beacon Hill,* p.35

[4] *Recollections of Francis Boott*, The Southgate Press—T.W. Ripley Co., 1912, Boston, p.7
Letter by Elizabeth Boott to the Hunt Class, Dec. 12, 1876, Archives of American Art, Smithsonian Museum, Washington, D.C.,

[5] *The Essential Transcendentalists, p. 231-235.*

[6] *Elizabeth Boott Duveneck: Her Life and Times*, exhibition catalogue essay by Michael P. Vargas, Triton Museum of Art, Santa Clara, California, p. 4

[7] *Letter from Elizabeth Boott,* Archives of American Art, Smithsonian Museum, Washington, D.C.,

[8] *Elizabeth Boott Duveneck: Her life and Times*, exhibition catalogue an essay by Michael P. Vargas, Triton Museum of Art, Santa Clara, California, p.4

[9]*The picture season at Villiers le-Bel, 1876-78, Elizabeth Boott, Thomas Couture, and Henry James*, Carol Osborne, *Apollo* 149, No. 447, May, 1999, p.42.
[10]*Frank Duveneck, Painter-Teacher*, by Josephine Whitney Duveneck, John Howell—Books, San Francisco, 1970, p.112
[11]*Letter to Henry James*, 13 June 1874. MSAm 1094 (32) James Family Papers. Houghton Library. Harvard University, Cambridge, Mass. Dear Henry James.org Ed. Pierre A.Walker et al 2005. Salem State College.
[12]Ibid

Chapter Five

Love At Last Leads to Marriage

Florence, 1880

From the distance of a century and a third, the off-and-on romance of Lizzie Boott and Frank Duveneck appears radically unconventional. At the start of the affair, there was normalcy. They fell in love and became engaged to be married. Then, their solemn commitments to one another were broken off, due to the father's objections and quite possibly some reservations on Lizzie's part. A full four years passed, their love supported solely by vivid memories and bolstered occasionally by clandestine meetings. Finally, they agreed to proceed with the original plan. For Lizzie's part, it sounds like a surrender of sorts. For Frank, it was a case of determination succeeding.

It's as if their mutual attraction and true feelings for one another finally overwhelmed any obstacle and societal influence.

During this time of personal upheaval and promise, Frank and Lizzie were not world renowned celebrities under society's magnifying glass. They were expatriates among hundreds of Americans living in the artistic mecca of Florence. Frank Duveneck was behaving like many other artists, enjoying favors of a life with few responsibilities. The Bootts, Lizzie and father Francis, were known and respected for their self-development in the arts that their wealth and cultural backgrounds made available.

The romance shared a common trait with the earlier and prominent love affair, also in Florence at mid-century, of poets Robert and Elizabeth Barrett Browning. After Elizabeth Barrett wed Robert, she was disinherited by her father, owner of a plantation in Jamaica. Members of her family joined him in opposition to the marriage, persuaded that Robert was a mere gold-digger.

Frank Duveneck and Lizzie encountered the same kind of resistance. Some of her friends and family suspected that Frank's chief interest lay in Lizzie's money. Duveneck's own students made a joke of his striving for his *prediletta.* They quipped that Duveneck's sole objective was the recovery of his painting of *William Adams*, which Lizzie owned.[1]

Against prevailing Victorian manners Lizzie appears to have exerted herself in pursuit of Frank, though the attraction was likely mutual from the start. She found him fascinating for his naturalistic ways, his bearing and his exceptional talent with the brush. Later in their relationship, Lizzie said she was captivated by his personal qualities of kindliness and generosity. These virtues served as final motivations that he was to be her man.

'*Love at First Sight*'

Biographer and daughter-in-law Josephine Whitney Duveneck wrote that Lizzie was drawn to Duveneck because "he was so different… The stories of his childhood and the tales of the midwestern community from which he had emerged were completely new to her."[2] Why this difference in him was important and attractive to her is not clear. Perhaps Lizzie's background as an artist and expatriate, which cleansed her of New England bias, enabled her to see through externalities to the real person who dwelled beneath the skin. It's likely that the feeling was simply an expression of love itself.

"When he fell in love," the biographer continued, "his direct and spontaneous courtship took her by surprise, accustomed as she was to being treated in the trained Victorian mode as a *lady* by a *gentleman.* [Italics, the author's] To be approached as a *woman* by a *man* broke through her wellbred (sic) restraints."[3]

What may be forgotten in any examination of their relationship is Lizzie's dedication to her own lively and successful career. Julie Aronson, curator of painting, sculpture and drawings, at the Cincinnati Art Museum, stressed that point in a lecture, "Duveneck Abroad," given at the Taft Museum in Cincinnati March 20, 2014. Successful women artists of the day did not marry, concerned over restrictions the married state would weigh against their freedom.

Frank Duveneck's intentions were obvious. Lizzie awakened his sexual interest. She was a lady of style and grace. He was attracted to her, and characteristically, he did something about it. Duveneck responded as one would expect, indifferent to the dictates of courtship established by a set of persnickety old women. Ties between them had progressed and strengthened from teacher and student, friend and friend to the bond of perfection, the exalted state of a loving couple.

Lizzie loved Frank Duveneck, there's no doubt about that. She persuaded him to re-establish his school from Munich to near her home in Florence, no small change. The move to another country affected him personally—he couldn't speak Italian—and his students had to follow him southward. Lizzie helped him relocate, found lodgings and studios, one in Palazzo Russo that entailed an apartment with two bedrooms and a salon, for Duveneck a lavish luxury. Then she continued her own studies under his special care. After the move to Florence, there followed a period of rare joy as their love bloomed.

Duveneck in this period was learning and adapting. He shifted into an Italian period in his painting, which replaced brown, dark colors and sometimes earthy subjects of Teutonic *Realism,* with bright colors of a new pallet, influenced by Lizzie and sunny, golden Tuscany. In 1880, he painted *Venetian Girl,* a large-eyed and full-mouthed exotic so unlike Lizzie. He gave the painting to Lizzie, and it was kept in the family for many years. During this time Duveneck shed the Germanic artist's attire and acquired a formal overcoat and kid gloves, the start of a conscious change in personal style. He was mirroring the habits and attitudes of the instructors he knew in Germany. He became Herr Professor to his students and to the outside world.

115

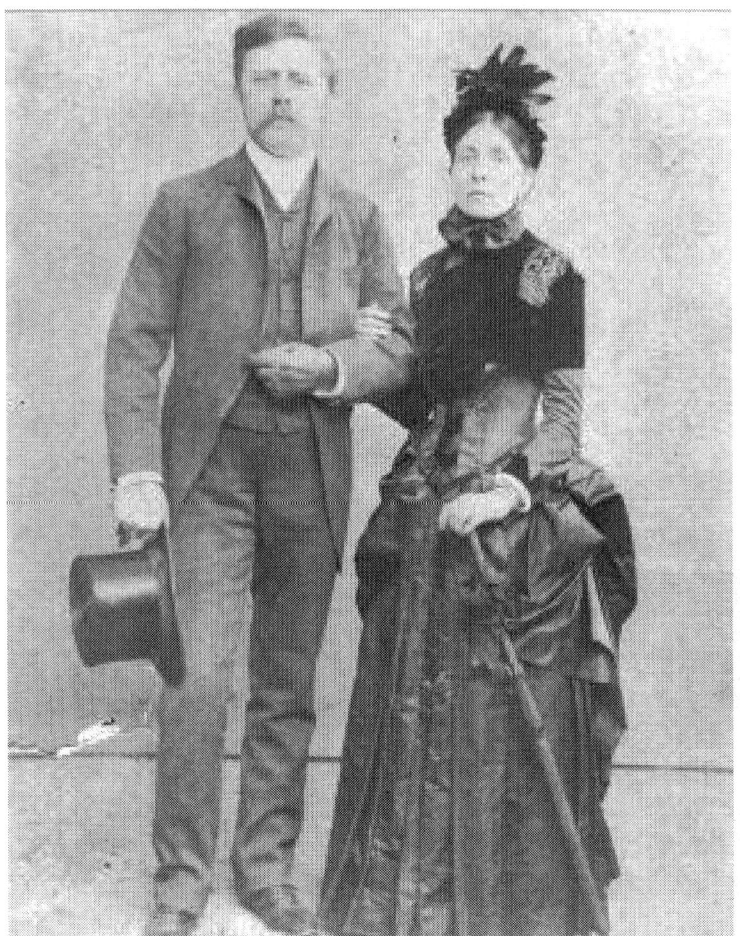

Frank and Elizabeth Duveneck
-Courtesy of the Kenton County Public Library, Covington, Ky.

The great obstacle to their union was the father. Francis Boott had strong reservations about Duveneck as a *sposo* for his daughter. While he recognized the painter's talent, he did not completely trust him. The father was wealthy, educated and from New England's upper class. His daughter meant everything to him. He nursed her in Europe's culture and created "a hothouse flower," as

James's biographer Leon Edel aptly put it.[4] About this same time, 1881, Henry James's novel, *Washington Square*, was published, later made into a play *The Heiress* and a Hollywood film. The plot revolves around a wealthy father's forced breakup of a romance between his backward daughter, his heiress, and a suitor who the father judged to be a fraud, only questing for his daughter's wealth.

By no means was Lizzie the backward daughter of *Washington Square*. She had responded to her father's meticulous care and evolved into a good, intelligent, talented and loving daughter. One can deduce that the elderly father may have preferred the scion of an American or English family, or even a European aristocrat to take an interest in his daughter. Perhaps no one would have made the high mark he set for his daughter; but there is little to go on. Francis Boott was always fussy about her. She experienced infatuations as any girl, and one teen-aged crush has been cited as cause of the return of the father and daughter to America. It is unknown whether she had affairs as an adult or any kind of romantic liaisons, except for Duveneck.

What is certain is this development: In the glow of a budding relationship, Lizzie agreed to marry Frank Duveneck. The engagement sent the father reeling. Lizzie was facing the arduous question of what would happen to her father if she and Frank were married. She felt keenly the sense of obligation to her father and would never abandon him nor neglect him in any way. She owed him too much, and while she may have anticipated that he would not be a pushover and easily endorse the marriage, she probably did not anticipate the stubborn and intractable position he adopted.

It's unlikely that she kept this dilemma to herself. She had many friends among American and British expatriates and close friends in Boston.

James's Opposition

Henry James was one of Lizzie's friends, dating from 1869. The author may have been a love interest. He was the *caro Enrico* of her letters, she the *cara Lisa,* of the return letters as they exchanged views on art, gossip and personal matters for years. While there may have been affection and mutual interest, perhaps both of them understood any sexual relationship would have been stunted, given the ambiguity of James's sexual life and his deep commitment to his special art.

James was close to Lizzie's father as well. He was among those who openly sided with the father, unable to comprehend why Lizzie had consented to be Frank's wife. He respected Mr. Boott and, after a fashion, may have loved Lizzie. They came from his kind of people, civilized in his opinion, possessing a ranking American pedigree. In his mind they exhibited in their every move a singular kind of Yankee cultivation that harked back to the earliest days of the United States of America, the start of the Industrial Age and to achievements and directions in the lives of the mind and the soul.

Arriving in Florence as spring was turning northern Italy into a lovely garden— and in need of a vacation, he ensconced in the Hotel de l'Arno. Lizzie was concentrating her time with Duveneck, leaving James to take up with his other friend, Constance Fenimore Woolson, inhabitant of another villa on Bellosguardo. Surely, James visited Villa Castellani out of friendship and to observe the Boott's life first-hand. Perhaps coincidentally James began writing *The Portrait of a Lady,* his novel that explores the unique relationship between an American expatriate father and his daughter, Gilbert Osmond and Pansy. Critics have no doubts that the Bootts served as models for these characters.

The novels, *Washington Square* and *Portrait,* were published the next year, 1881.

On this visit to Florence James was to personally see Lizzie for the first time in many months. He had tried to sell some of her art works on his recent stay in London, and he had a lot to talk about.

She was recovering from an illness. When they met, accustomed as he was to her youth and spontaneity, he thought she appeared elderly and plain, "but happy in her indefatigable industry." Then he added, brutally, in a letter to his own father that she had stymied herself by "studying without learning" and focusing her art on styles and derivatives of others.

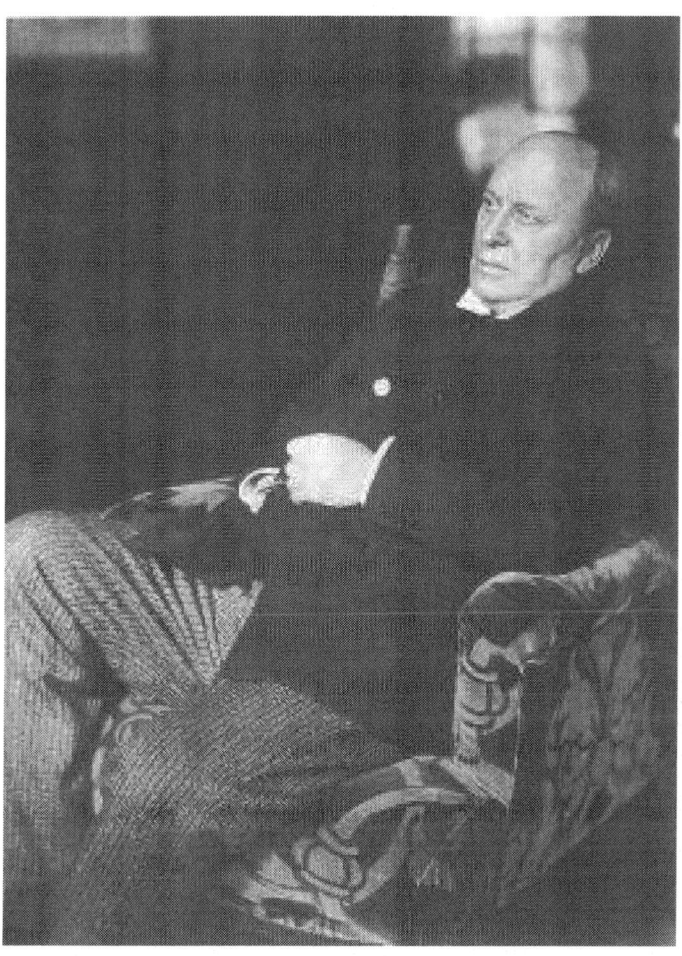

Henry James
-Wikipedia

119

James zeroed in his novelist's eye on Duveneck, calling him "her simple-hearted and simple-minded painting master," and found the image of the threesome including the father an oddity. [5] In this opinion Frank Duveneck and Lizzie Boott had been fashioned by widely divergent life experiences that should have made them incompatible. He wrote to his aunt Kate that Lizzie maintained a two-sided relationship with Frank, "pupil and adoptive mother, or at least adoptive sister. I hope she won't ever become his adoptive anything else, as, though an excellent fellow, he is terribly earthy and unlicked (sic)."[6]

The writer joined heartily in the opposition to the marriage, expressing his concerns in harsh and over-stated terms:

"…he is illiterate, ignorant and not a gentleman (though kindly and simple). His talent is great though without delicacy. But I fear his indolence is greater still. Lizzie however will urge him forward and be an immense help to him. For him it is all gain, for her it is very brave."

Under this withering criticism and the strong opposition of the father, the engagement did not take. Her historic filial devotion bested her new love for Frank Duveneck. The engagement was broken off, and for a time, the relationship lapsed into a state of limbo. On one hand, around this period, 1882, after the breakup, Lizzie's influence on the James family led to commissioning Duveneck to do the portrait of Henry's father, Henry James Sr. Duveneck dutifully carried it out. Still, the breakup left Frank desolate and Lizzie emotionally damaged. Travel and commitment to work intervened for both and perhaps these preoccupations softened for a while the blow of separation.

Frank spent much of his time in Venice. His companions included the etcher Joseph Pennell and his wife, journalist Elizabeth Robins Pennell who chronicled the lives of expatriates from their base in Florence. Their concerns for Frank's welfare grew. He squandered his talent and loafed, the Pennells said. In their opinion only marriage would save him from himself.

Clandestine Meetings

After the 1881 breakup, Lizzie spent time in Spain before joining her father in Boston. She worked hard to make use of her European training. Her works, thirty-one oils and thirteen watercolors, chiefly scenes of Spain and Italy, were exhibited at the J. Eastman Chase Gallery to some acclaim. In 1884, she had a successful exhibit of works at Doll & Richards gallery in Boston. She fell ill at one point. A nurse was engaged. Frank attributed the illness to the emotional damage from the breakup. He was likely correct in that assessment.

When he could come into close contact with Lizzie, Frank continued to pursue her despite the broken engagement and the relentlessly steely opposition. During a difficult period when they were forcibly estranged, stifled in their hope and desire for a union, a rare kind of durability emerged. The love between them was mutual and lasting. It was something special, yet their love remained unfulfilled for more than four years, 1881-1885.

One can only imagine how each person in this triumvirate felt about the turn of events. The written record reveals nothing of the emotions, yet it is easy to understand and feel the hurt. Lizzie and Frank kept the flame alive, meeting at times clandestinely, at sites in Europe and in the United States, probably at venues related to the art world. During this period Frank spent time in Boston, working on commissions including the portrait of the elder Henry James. He returned to Europe, putting an ocean between him and Lizzie and dividing his time between Florence and Venice.

Later, in 1885 just prior to their reunion, he moved to Paris, possibly in anticipation of a renewal of the courtship. Paris had become the center of the art world; he had to be there with or without Lizzie.

Lizzie's father probably was not aware of any of his daughter's and Frank's liaisons. He no doubt believed himself to be justified in his rejection of the painter. Something of a rebel himself in his youth, later living away from his own family, the elder Boott persisted as a steadfast opponent. Frank Duveneck had painted the father around the time of the break up in 1881, portraying him as a handsome, stern man standing erect as if he were blocking a doorway. Indeed, he was doing just that.

In this romance, time became a healer. The years allowed for a fresh and deeper examination, and a new understanding. The elder Boott was aging, and his daughter was reaching the end of her child-bearing years. One wonders whether the question of their future wasn't put into a realistic light that played a part in the occurrences that followed. In effect time was running out for all parties, and yet, the fire of the couple's love was still burning.

To Wed, Come What May

Early in the year, 1886, Frank and Lizzie were both in Boston and almost certainly had to know the whereabouts of each other. He learned that Lizzie was to depart for Europe on an ocean liner from the local port. He managed to meet her and wish her *bon voyage* and accompanied her to the ship. He asked to see her to her cabin. When they arrived there, he closed the door. Biographer Josephine Duveneck filled in what happened next.

"In her hand she held a pair of gloves. Gently he removed them and slipped them in his pocket. Then taking her small hands into his big ones, [he] said, 'Now we have to decide this once for all. I'm not going to ask you again. This ends it. In spite of your father, will you or will you not be my wife?"[7]

Lizzie accepted this final offer of marriage.

She wrote to a friend in February of that year about her surprise news:

"I am going to give up the life of single blessedness which I have led for so long and marry Frank Duveneck, the artist. I don't know whether you ever saw him, but if you do not know him now you will someday and like him I am sure. I am happy to say there is but one opinion of him and he and I have known each other so long and so intimately that we feel the most natural thing and in fact the only thing to do now is to take up life together for better or for worse. It has been a long affair for years. The thing was given up entirely at one time but on meeting again we find that the old feeling is not dead and we are going to take up life together as we did not like it very well apart.

"This is a very solemn and momentous step for me and it involved, I felt, so much that was dear to me in my past life. I could not have been separated from my father after all these long years together. As it fortunately happens [sic] this will not be. We shall all live together, most happily, I hope."

Introspectively, she added, "Send me your blessing, dear friend, and say you think I am right. I crave human interests in life. The abstract ones of art are not enough for me."

Lizzie Boott wanted more than art; she wanted the real thing, a man to love, and Frank was able to provide that relationship she needed. Duveneck's daughter-in-law explained that Lizzie, apparently realizing the potential for finality in the relationship, "dared not [to] refuse" the marriage offer from Frank. She insisted on the provision that "marriage would not mean permanent separation from her father."[8]

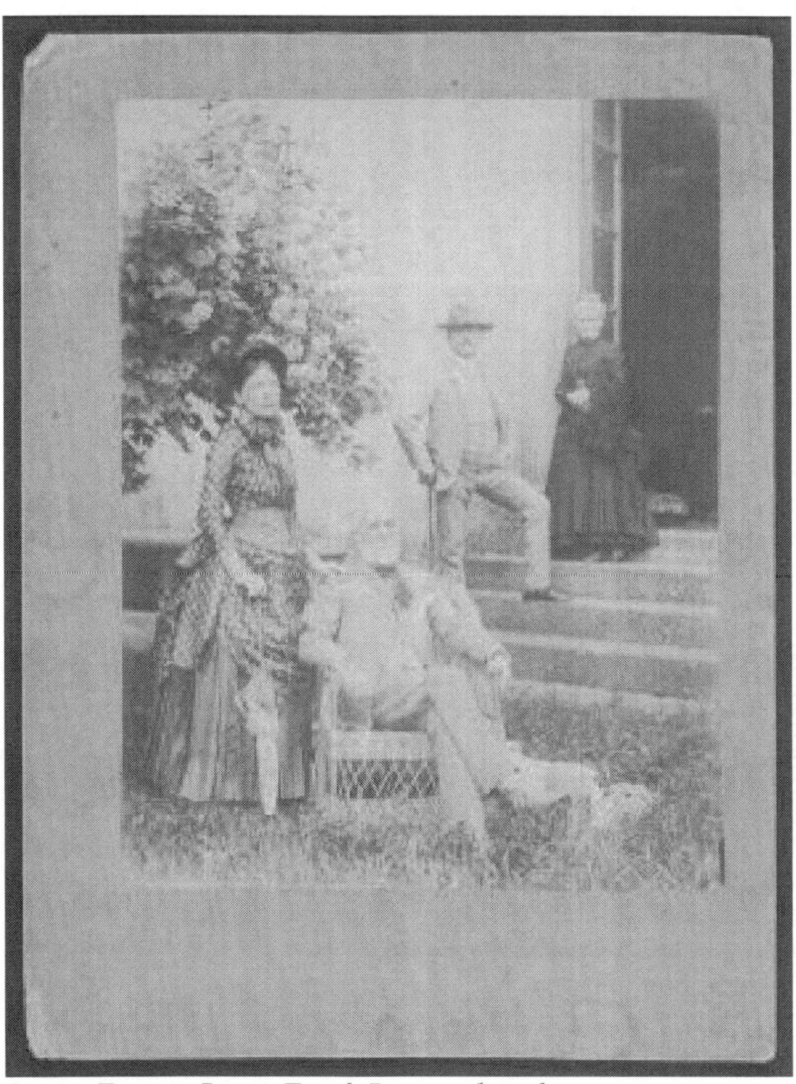

Lizzie, Francis Boott, Frank Duveneck and
Ann Shenstone at the Villa

-Frank and Elizabeth Boott Duveneck papers, 1851-1972, bulk 1851-1919, Archives of American Art,
Smithsonian Institution

Details of how the couple approached the problem of the father are
obscure. It's only known that the three lived together in the ram-

124

shackle villa on Bello-sguardo. That particular living arrangement for the trio was likely the only alternative. At least for the two men involved in this uncertain beginning, it must have been a trial. Frank Duveneck had to feel like an intruder. It's likely that the father had at times the same feeling. A photograph of the trio shows the father seated, Lizzie standing to his right with her left hand on his shoulder. Frank's position on the steps behind them is remarkable. He strikes an almost comical pose, his left leg cocked on a high step, the right on a lower one. He wears a broad-brimmed hat rather low on his head. Near the doorway is Lizzie's long-time nurse and companion, Ann Shenstone.

By this time Frank and Lizzie cannot be construed to be young lovers. At their marriage on March 25, 1886, she was a month away from her fortieth birthday. Frank was thirty-eight years old, to become thirty-nine in October. Mr. Boott was seventy-three years old, and deep feelings that he held toward his daughter and future son-in-law died hard in the old man. In testament to this begrudging attitude are copies of a legal marriage contract filed in the U.S. legation in Paris and in Kenton County Court in Covington, Kentucky, and dated the previous day. The contract specifies that Lizzie's fortune was to remain hers "for her sole and separate use forever." Frank relinquished all claims to Lizzie's properties, largely shares of stock in American companies. The elder Boott also signed the contract, which created a trust in Lizzie's name in his keeping.[8]

Frank Duveneck may have gotten his way with Lizzie, but the prenuptial agreement put him in his place in the new living arrangement. He signed the contract, perhaps he even suggested it as a way to prove that he was not after Lizzie's money as some in their circle believed. It is possible that the contract could have been his idea; he certainly endorsed it and willingly signed it, perhaps for the same reason, in effect, to clear his name and to satisfy the elder man's concerns. It's ironic, since Duveneck was never known as venal or power hungry, or even self-seeking. Signing such a document had to have been onerous for him no matter what positive results it may have had for him. It seems typical of Duveneck that he would be willing to go the extra mile if marriage to Lizzie was the outcome.

Virtually any way one looks at the pre-nuptial document, it represented an inauspicious start for the family relationship. It would take a few years for this uncomfortable situation to change for the better.

Inadvertently, the court document delivered a surprise for Frank Duveneck. The clerk in Kenton County referred to him in the contract as Frank Decker, also known as Frank Duveneck, the latter being the only name he ever knew. He learned through this document that his original name was Decker. His family in Covington, likely his mother, Catherine or Kate as she was known by then, had to have been the source of the astounding information that his blood father, Bernard Decker, had died in the cholera epidemic of 1849. Squire Duveneck, the man he thought was his father, was actually his step-father, Kate's second husband.

To all and to the generations that followed, he remained Frank Duveneck.

When the document was signed in March of 1886 Frank and Lizzie and her father were living in Paris temporarily. The painter lived at No. 72 rue Notre Dame des Champs. The Bootts had lodgings at No. 14 rue Tilsett. They each had knowledge of Paris, Lizzie as a student of Thomas Couture in the 1870s, her father as an art-loving expatriate who traveled widely. Duveneck was acquainted with the city from previous visits. It was, he said, the place to be in the art world.

Paris at Center Stage

All in the art world were aware of the turbulence aroused by the rise of Impressionism in painting that had its center in Paris and in annual exhibits, the famous salons. While still controversial in the

1880s, the works of Impressionism's practitioners had begun to turn a corner and attract financial investment. The year 1886 marked the eighth and last Paris show of works of Impressionism under the management of art investor and gallery owner Paul Durand-Ruel. The fame of the new style had spread to London where Durand-Ruel shows were held in 1882 and in 1883 and to New York City in 1886. Some seventeen canvases by Edouard Manet were exhibited in the New York show.

Henry James, writing as a critic for the *New York Tribune*, had dubbed Impressionists as the "Irreconcilables," a tribute to their persistence and steadfastness in delivering a new style to painting. While not an enthusiast, at least in the early years of controversy, he found paintings in an 1874 exhibition in Paris "decidedly interesting."[9] By temporarily moving to Paris in 1886 the Bootts and Frank Duveneck were perhaps mixing a bit of personal business, their marriage, with the attraction of possibly learning from the latest artistic trends. It's easy to see Lizzie's hand in this visit to Paris. She had more of a business head and had been encouraging the painter for years to go there.

The wedding was a civil affair before a magistrate in the Boott's apartment at the Tilsit address off the Champs Elysees. Lizzie wore street clothes, consisting of a bustled brown dress, bonnet, cape and gloves, in the fashion of the day. She and Frank each signed the certificate, *artiste, peintre*. Frank knew no French and had to be prodded by Lizzie to say at the appropriate time during the ceremony, *oui*. Typical of him Frank, short of cash, had to borrow the equivalent of one hundred dollars to pay marriage costs.[10]

It's not certain who attended the ceremony, though it is clear that a party had been held in their honor prior to the wedding. In attendance was a friend to both, Edward Darley Boit, an artist from Boston who is known today for a painting by John Singer Sargent commonly titled the *Four Daughters of Edward Darley Boit*, completed in Paris in 1882. Like Lizzie, Boit had been a student of Couture's in Paris. Henry James referred to the Boit daughters' painting as the "happy play-world…of charming children." Later interpretations have enlisted psychology to reflect on the attitudes of the two older girls. The painting hangs in the Boston Museum of Fine Arts.

Among other attendees at the pre-ceremony party were two of Duveneck's students, Ralph Curtis and Julian Story. Ralph Wormeley Curtis (1854-1922), a graduate of Harvard University, was a founder of the Harvard *Lampoon.* He was the heir of wealthy expatriate parents who lived at a palace on the Grand Canal of Venice. Portrait painter Julian Russell Story (1857-1919), an Oxford University graduate, was the son of sculptor William Wetmore Story. Also there was George Henry Clements (1854-1935) who had studied at the Union Art League in New York City prior to his academy training in Europe. He is known today for coastal scenes and marine and figure painting. Another attendee was a Lyman cousin who came representing the family for the wedding.

Frank and Lizzie's honeymoon trip lasted a month. They joined the father at Villa Castellani, and a studio for joint use was created in the villa. Lizzie, it was reported, began work on a painting of a barefoot mother seated with an infant and a child, a grouping "not unlike the modern Madonnas of William-Adolphe Bouguereau."[11] However, during a conservation of the painting at the Cincinnati Art Academy, the date on it is earlier than the marriage year. It is known that Frank began a life-size sketch of Columbus before the Council of Salamanca, which was never completed. He preferred *plein aire* paintings and the period of the next two years reflects the warmth of the people and Tuscan region. Life for him—and Lizzie—had taken on an ethereal glow.

Lizzie emphasized her new happiness in letters to Boston.

She wrote to a friend, Bessie Lee Shattuck:

"I don't think I was ever suited to a lonely existence any more than you were. I am sure we shall be infinitely happier than in single blessedness. It seems such a natural thing for people who love each other to belong together & it makes life so much more interesting to share all one's thoughts and feelings with someone close." [12]

Bessie's husband, Frederick C. Shattuck, was a professor of medicine at Harvard. Each had met Duveneck in Boston and liked him. In her letter Lizzie assured the Shattucks that Frank would write to them as well if he would break away from his new-found interest in politics. Duveneck had been spending evenings reading English newspaper accounts of the debates over Home Rule for Ireland.

Naturally, Frank had informed his family of his marriage. On a day that summer Lizzie, now Mrs. Elizabeth Duveneck, received a letter from Frank's mother, Katherine Duveneck, offering her best wishes to the new couple. Lizzie wrote a reply on August 15, addressing the letter to "My dear Mother."

In her casual, even loose handwriting style, Lizzie wrote:

"I was delighted to get your letter not long ago, and to hear that you were pleased that Frank was married.

"I assure you he seems to [have] taken to married life very [handily] and to understand how to make a woman happy. He makes me thoroughly so..."

During this time, Lizzie conceived of a child, and as winter approached in 1887, the family moved from the Bellosguardo hilltop to No. 9 via Garibaldi near the American Embassy in Florence. There, on December 18, a son was born, christened, Francis.

---

[1]Mahonri Sharp Young, "Duveneck and Henry James: A Study in Contrasts," Apollo, August, 1970, p. 214]

129

[2]*Frank Duveneck, Painter-Teacher*, Josephine W. Duveneck, John Howell—Books, San Francisco, California, 1970, p. 114

[3]Ibid, p.114

[4]*Henry James, The Conquest of London: 1870-1881*, Leon Edel, A Discus Book, Avon Books, 1962, p.404

[5]Ibid, p. 404

[6]*Henry James, The Middle Years: 1882-1895*, Leon Edel, *J.B. Lippincott Company, New York, p.197*

[7]*Frank Duveneck, Painter-Teacher*, Josephine W. Duveneck, John Howell—Books, San Francisco, California, 1970, p. 114

[8]Contract on file in Kenton County Clerk's Office, Covington, Kentucky

[9]*The Judgment of Paris, the Revolutionary Decade That Gave the World Impressionism*, by Ross King, Walker and Company, New York, 2006, p. 362

[10]*Frank Duveneck & Elizabeth Boott, an American Romance*, Owen Gallery exhibition essay by Carol M. Osborne, p.25.

[11]Ibid, p.26

[12]Letter to the Shattucks, Roll 1097, Duveneck Papers, Archives of American Art, Smithsonian Institution, Washington, D.C.

Chapter Six

The Judgments of Paris

Florence, summer, 1886

When they arrived in Florence after the March wedding in Paris, Frank and Lizzie Duveneck found Bellosguardo ripening with spring. Lizzie remarked on it in her letters. She, too, was blossoming, having already conceived with her first and only child. She appears to have borne the burdens of pregnancy very well. There is no record of morning sickness or any other difficult symptoms. Instead, she and Frank reported themselves busy combing the Tuscany region for fresh subjects. They were enjoying life during a glorious and peaceful summer at the Villa Castellani.[1]

They didn't go far to find a mutually selected subject, the villa itself. The structure takes its place prominently on the hilltop of Bellosguardo overlooking the Arno River valley. The front opens at a piazza and its fifty rooms spread throughout a long, flat structure. James Fenimore Cooper, author of *The Last of the Mohicans*, lived on Bellosguardo. Later, Horatio Greenough, famous for his ludicrous sculpture of George Washington in a toga, occupied rooms there. His wife was Mr. Boott's sister. When Boott first rented his ten rooms in the villa, he paid the equivalent of a modest expense of fifty-five dollars a year.

Villas are common in the hills surrounding Florence, some dating to late medieval pre-Renaissance period. Galileo Galilei occupied a house on Bellosguardo to be closer his beloved daughter, Sr. Maria Celeste, a member of the cloistered Poor Clares in the nearby convent of San Mateo. British and other European expatriates discovered Florence and its villas during the period of the Grand Tour in the eighteenth century. The city, its sensational history, extraordinary weather and lighting, became even more popular in the 1870s, after Florence became the capital of a united Italy.

Author Henry James regarded Florence as a treasure, and Villa Castellani provided for him a new, if not, premonitory experience. He wrote Lizzie after attending a party there. "It was an enchanting day, the views from the windows were lovely, the rooms were perfumed with a wealth of spring flowers—and the whole thing gave me a sense that it might yet be strangely pleasant to live in that grave, picturesque old house. I have a vague foreboding that I shall, someday."[2]

James visited the villa often but never used it as a residence. He took rooms in the nearby Villa Brichieri, occupied by Constance Fenimore Woolson, who had become a close friend of Mr. Boott and the Duvenecks and was a godmother to baby Francis. James, it seems never one to be outdone, boasted that Villa Brichieri had an even better view.

The author described a villa in *The Portrait of a Lady* that fits exactly with Villa Castellani:

"The villa was a long, rather blank-looking structure, with the far-projecting roof which Tuscany loves, and which, on the hills that encircle Florence, when looked at from a distance, makes so harmonious a rectangle with the straight, dark, definite cypresses that usually rise, in groups of three or four, beside it." He described the villa as standing on the summit of "an olive-muffled hill…"

Standing at the parapet of the broad terrace, upon which the villa sat, a person could lean on it and take in the view of the river valley below. From the terrace, the ground slipped away into the stand of olive trees, crops and vineyards. Above, on the villa grounds, a narrow garden produced tangles of wild roses, and mossy stone benches were conspicuous among a patchwork of colors. The Bootts employed a gardener who raised grapes, apricots and peaches, likely under the system of *mazzadria* through which the owner and the tenants shared in the yield and profits, much as one of the hill's famous men, Galileo.

In her water color of the villa completed in 1886, Lizzie adopted a side close-up view. The weight of a road falls on the right in her picture and is balanced by a tall green cypress tree on the left and the sloping hillside. The next year, Frank executed the same subject masterfully in oil-on-canvas, taking the view from farther below and on the right. The same cypress as in Lizzie's water color stands tall in the upper center of the painting, and the villa glistens in warm light, its white walls accented by green overgrowths.

Before and after the Duvenecks occupied these grounds, expatriates who chose Florence as a residence were as diverse as the Brownings, the sculptor Hiram Powers, Mary Cassatt, Gertrude Stein, the novelist Ouida, and artists John White Alexander, Cecilia Beaux, Giovanni Boldini, George deForest Brush, Lilla Cabot Perry, William Merritt Chase, Arthur Bowen Davies, Joseph Rodefer DeCamp and John Singer Sargent. Florence was always home for Sargent, born there in 1856 to American parents, his father an eye surgeon originally from Gloucester, Massachusetts.

Among Florentines today, there is a generous yet reasonable point of view that expatriates such as these contributed to its culture and were responsible for extending Italy's Florence into a cosmopolitan mecca of art and its appreciation.

"Florence was a city that had been turned into a myth, whose allure still attracts them today, once again entranced by the light and the civilized landscape." This observation comes from *Americans in Florence*, a commemorative book in connection with a 2012 exhibit of contributions by American artists and writers. Paintings by Frank and Lizzie Duveneck were displayed and figured strongly in the exhibit.

Further, the book makes the observation, "…for aspiring artists arriving in Venice, Florence and Rome the encounter with Italy was, without exception, an adventurous discovery, a sort of initiation, after which they went home transformed."[3]

The American *Vanguard*

Before this cadre of American artists set foot in Florence, trickles of Yankee adventurers had wended their way to Italy in the antebellum years of the mid-nineteenth century, notably the writer, Henry James, then youthful art student, and artists John LaFarge and William Morris Hunt. Hunt is a critical figure in the renaissance of art in New England. It was he who had studied under the master Thomas Couture in Paris and recommended Couture to Lizzie. LaFarge, talented and wealthy, was the person who advised Lizzie Boott to take instructions from Duveneck. As evidenced by these counsels, a significant collegiality was working among the Euro-enthusiasts who comprised the vanguard of Americans on the Continent.

Even earlier, in 1837, the Cincinnati sculptor, Hiram Powers, famous for *The Greek Slave*, arrived in Florence with his wife and two children, and never left Europe. His travels were funded by art connoisseurs Nicholas Longworth, also hailing from Cincinnati and a former Speaker of the United States House of Representatives, and John Preston, brother of Senator William C. Preston of South Carolina. Preston bankrolled Powers' visit to Florence with a three-thousand dollar stipend.

The leader of the vanguard to Europe, Hunt, the son a Vermont congressman, left Harvard College to study under Couture. Upon his return to America in the late 1850s, he started an art school in Newport, Rhode Island, later moving it to Boston. There, Lizzie Boott on her first trip back to her extended family's home in Boston, became a prize student, and she followed his advice to study in Paris before her fateful sojourn to Munich and Duveneck's school.

Unlike Frank Duveneck, most of these American expatriates came from Protestant households that historically had qualms about art and graven images. The Puritan's influence in New England continued strong. New Englanders grew into a bookish people who emphasized a taste of Calvinism in religion, naturalism and tran-

scendentalism in philosophy and were dedicated to worthy introspective literature from such luminaries as Nathaniel Hawthorne,
Ralph Waldo Emerson, Henry David Thoreau, Herman Melville
and Henry Wadsworth Longfellow. In many cases the New
Englanders ignored or stifled the natural urge to create in the artistic forms of painting, sculpture and sketching. Only after the Civil
War in the United States, the region's culture began to open up itself to other traditional forms, due in large part to William Morris
Hunt. The Bootts, then in Boston on a lengthy visit from Europe,
were among those who broke new ground for societal acceptance
of art and artists.

Around this time Henry James wrote to his brother, William, a letter that combines criticism with personal praise for Duveneck and
stipulates what he believes to be a mistake of judgment in Lizzie's
marriage.

James wrote:

"She is much in love with her husband—who will not do much, I
think, but who is all the same a fine, pleasant, polite (though perfectly illiterate) man, whom it is impossible not to like." James referred to the painter as a "good frank fellow without many small or
nasty qualities." But he said it was impossible to converse with
him for more than two minutes. James, of course, was Harvard-
educated and highly literate, a voluble know-it-all, and a representative of what most would regard as an advanced New England
culture. He wrote that he feared Lizzie, in accepting her talented,
though grade-school educated artist as a husband, was taking on a
burden:

"I mean socially, and in the world. He is only half civilized—
though he is very civil."[4]

Yet, it was at this villa that Lizzie joined with the painter-genius
from Cincinnati in forging a new and challenging bid in their personal lives that was to be productive for art and for life. Their hap-

piness was obvious and it was reflected in their writings and in their work. They were together and deeply in love. *Americans in Florence* makes this observation about Duveneck's painting of the villa: "And so this picture with its transparent tones seems to reflect the harmony of those summer days…"

Evidence of Mutual Love

Lizzie's letter to her uncle, Arthur Lyman, refers to this period and to nature's rebirth and relates the joy of those early months of marriage.

She wrote:

"I wish you could see our villa and garden now in all its spring beauty. When you were last in Florence the summer dust and heat had begun. Now it is perfect and delightful for all kinds of expeditions. We have not had much time for anything of that kind for since our return we have been very busy and are invited on all sides by our friends. It's pleasant to be made so much of and we are getting quite pampered and spoiled"[5]

And, she added forthrightly, "I should like you to know your new nephew whom I am sure you will like (though I say it). But other people say the same."

In July Lizzie wrote to a friend that "I wish you could see our villa now. Everything is in full bloom… Papa is here and well and my husband is hard at work." One of Frank's subjects was Christopher Columbus, she wrote, and he was working on a mural on a villa wall depicting Columbus laying out his arguments at the Council of Salamanca for a voyage of discovery. [6] In the letter she takes note that exhibiting his paintings at the Paris Salon was a personal goal.

Exuding the same happiness as Lizzie, Frank responded with much humor to Miss W, (Miss Adelaide Wadsworth, an adoring former student) three months after the wedding.

To his former pupil, he wrote:

"Your very kind letter of congratulation on my marriage reached me safely. I thank you very much. It seems a long time since the festive event took place in Paris. We move along with apparent ease and happiness. Maybe the time will come that Lizzie in one of her off tempers will secure a few of my beautiful curls when I shall remind her to save one for you. [The reference to curls, obviously his blond hair curls, must stem from Miss Wadsworth's request or is a private joke.] However, so far there seems little chance of her losing her temper with me—in fact she seems particularly well and is growing fatter every day and I don't doubt but what if she keeps on at this rate that we will make a good show in the way of size. So you see that I make a good husband and women after all are natural things.

"Your present (pepper and salt shakers) seems to be very appropriate and," he added, "so very useful to pepper up when the long monotonous days of married life set in!"[7]

Also in July, the father, Mr. Boott, observed to a friend, "Lizzie and her *sposo* are painting downstairs. We have a number of large rooms on the lower floor they use for studio purposes. Duveneck seems to be quite in the vein."[8] The painter was working on the Columbus scene in a room described as being as large as a church, using as a model sketches he had worked on earlier. It appears that the little family of three was getting along a little better than anticipated, living in joyous expectation of a fourth member.

Lizzie was sincere in writing:

"I am very happy in my hopes for maternity, and I already feel that this double life within me gives a new richness to life. I have been perfectly well and very active and this no doubt prevents any misgivings for the future. Frank is of a calm, equable placid temperament which is very soothing and my married life so far has been

137

most peaceful and full of happiness and rest. Papa is very well though I fear a little alarmed at his grand-paternal prospects."[9]

Perhaps to further ease any tensions from the ménage situation, each of the three traveled in that first year of Frank's and Lizzie's marriage. The couple was away from the villa on a honeymoon for at least a month after the vows. In August of that year, Mr. Boott spent a month in Switzerland. Around that time Lizzie wrote her father from Vallombrosa, the resort area near Florence where a Benedictine abbey stood. Ever the supporter of Frank, she seems to want to reassure her father of Frank's love and devotion.

She confided:

"Frank and I took a splendid walk yesterday. Two hours through the woods to the top of one of the high mountains behind the convent. We took our lunch and we spent two or three hours on the top eating, sleeping, and enjoying the magnificent view and reading Praetoria (sic),[10] (*Praeterita*), Ruskin's autobiography. On our return we went through the most beautiful beech woods. The fallen leaves under our feet were so thick that they were knee deep. It seems such a natural thing for people who love each other to belong together and it makes life so much more interesting to share all one's thoughts and feelings with someone else."

Lizzie was painting, though the pregnancy likely deprived her of her usual drive. She had submitted two paintings, a still life and another portrait of Mr. Boott, for the Paris Salon of 1886 and had intended to visit Paris in winter. Her condition naturally kept them in Florence. As the weather worsened and the date approached, they moved from their residence on the hilltop to No. 9 via Garibaldi in the city where baby Francis, later Frank Jr., was born. ,

Baby Changed Everything

The blessed event brought great happiness.

"It seems strange after so many years of spinsterhood to get so much domestic life in so short a time. I am so thankful for all this wonderful happiness," she wrote to a friend. To another on January 22, 1887, she penned: "You have probably heard by this time of the birth of my little son. It seems strange does it not? I cannot quite believe it yet myself though this small thing with a strong likeness to his father and to some old photos of me when I was a child is constantly present to remind me of the fact."[11]

Later, Lizzie, who had help from a nurse, wrote:

"I am beginning to work again, though not very steadily yet[,] for the baby is very absorbing. I find I am constantly thinking about him and wondering in my ignorance if everything is done that ought to be." In August, she added, "It is difficult to hold him now. He dances so in one's arms and is full of life and spirits. I laugh to think I should have a child like him. I was always so mousey and such a half-baked little woman…"[12]

One can assume how the atmosphere had changed at No. 9 Garibaldi. First, there had to be great joy, beyond the simple emotions, a joy that was to last and to change the lives and attitudes of those involved. Secondly, no doubt Lizzie was trying to minimize the impact of a new-born on her father, rushing to manage the child as he awakened crying for attention and milk, soothing him in his travails as only a mother can do, on watch duty constantly.

Perhaps as a break from the new routine of their lives, Mr. Boott traveled to America to summer in Boston in 1887, just to visit his old home for pleasure or business. Prior to his departure, he revoked the prenuptial agreement, "having to see his son-in-law for the good fellow that he was." The trust for Lizzie set up by the father and administered solely by him was terminated in an order issued May 9, 1887, by the clerk of courts in Kenton County, Kentucky. A copy of the original orders, dated in April and signed by the U.S. Counsel, Isaac R. Diller, was filed in the court. Lizzie was given "sole and separate use" of her fortune, including interest accruing from the trust created a year earlier.[13]

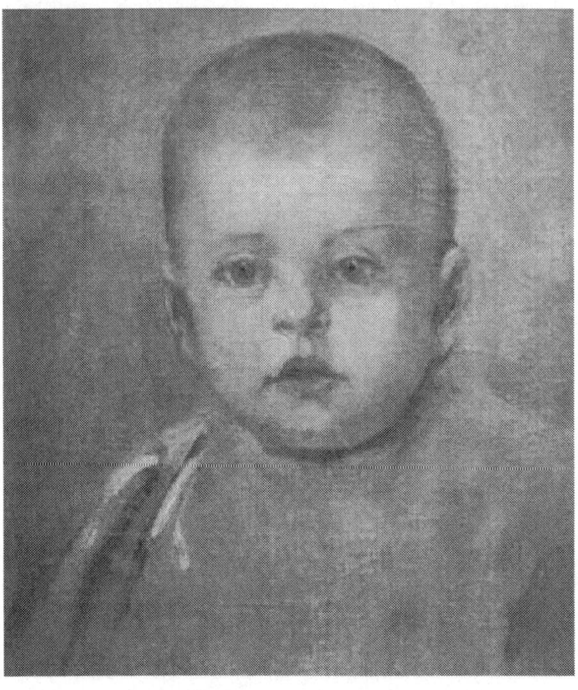

Frank Duveneck Jr.
Courtesy of the Kenton County Public Library, Covington, Ky.

Duveneck was not exempt from change. He was proud of his "strapping big fellow" of a son, whose presence it seems erased any animosity between the two men in Lizzie's life. The affront of the legal steps taken earlier by the father was eradicated by his father-in-law's own hand. They had something in common, the love of woman and daughter and the love of a son and a grandson.

With strong elements of joy and exuding sincerity, Frank wrote to his father-in-law in Boston:

"I think you will be surprised to see the great change in him. I think we have been very fortunate so far considering the heat he had to go through and never a moment's illness. He is a strapping big fellow for his age and seems generally happy and contented. Ten days ago his first tooth made its appearance and another is expected in a few days. His diet seems to differ a little from other babies. He does not favor the usual baby mixture but prefers good broth with something in it and a good sized piece of bread dipped in gravy! And wine without too much water. So you see he has made headway since you saw him last."[14]

The artist signed the letter, "Your affectionate son."

A New Duveneck Dimension

Henry James was correct about one aspect of the marriage of Frank and Lizzie. He predicted that Lizzie would serve as an asset to him, a manager of sorts who would further and direct his career. Otherwise, the author was dead wrong in his assumptions about Frank and the marriage. It appears that he could not comprehend Lizzie's honest motives and true feelings about Frank. He worried that she might "adopt" him as if he were a wayward child. In truth, she became a helpmate to the artist with whom she was deeply in love.

The main gain for Duveneck, other than having a loving partner, was that Lizzie recognized his talent and understood him. She possessed an inner drive to be a successful practitioner that transferred to his career. Lizzie had overcome prejudice in her quest to be, herself, an artist. For his sake, she knew that Munich may have been interesting to him, Florence fascinating, but she knew that Paris was the place to be for a practicing artist. She had encouraged him to work and exhibit his paintings in the City of Light as the cultural Babylon of the nineteenth century and the center of the new Impressionism. All the while she was a good wife and the mother of his only son.

Duveneck's paintings came under new influences in the decade of the 1880s as he matured, discovered other tricks of the trade, married Lizzie and moved to Florence. "Golden light saturates the atmosphere of Duveneck's genre paintings dating from the two halcyon seasons he spent at Bellosguardo, with his wife, *Italian Girl with a Rake, Siesta, On a Golden Wall,* among them."[15] Lizzie almost certainly engaged models for him. Daughter-in-law Josephine Whitney Duveneck observed that there is a marked similarity between the types we find in her sketches and his drawings around this time. His so-called Italian period began in this decade. He chose subjects like flower girl, water bearers and rosy-faced peasants. "The paintings are much lighter in tone, the planes less sharp, the brush strokes less emphatic and the subjects he chose less 'ugly.'"[16]

Plein Air paintings and sketches reflect a shift in approach, especially sunlit renderings of villas and courtyards. Portraits are lighter and warmer. Munich-style dark brown backgrounds are a mode of the past. The region and his new wife had their impact on Frank Duveneck. Landscapes in the period feature a fresh treatment of sunlight; landscapes show interest in naturalism.

"Boott had always disliked the dark realism of his Munich portraits and now, undoubtedly encouraged by her taste for Salon painting, Duveneck too, spun out sunny peasant women in the picturesque costume of the region. Occasionally, husband and wife painted from the same model."[17] Lizzie's influence is manifest in Duveneck's *Head of a Florentine Girl with Parted Lips, The Girl in White, The Little Italian Boy, The Boy Wearing Cloak,* each owned by the Cincinnati Art Museum.

The commemorative book, *Americans in Florence,* observes, "...for aspiring artists arriving in Venice, Florence and Rome the encounter with Italy was, without exception, an adventurous discovery, a sort of initiation, after which they went home transformed." The magic of Florence and its ancient villa rejuvenated the Duvenecks, and the birth of a son served as a unifying factor for the family. The future was looking brighter than ever.

---

[1]Author's note, for historic references to Bellosguardo and nearby villas, see *Galileo's Daughter,* Dava Sobel, Walker & Company, New York, 1999

[2]*Henry James, The Conquest of London: 1870-1881*, Leon Edel, Avon Books, p. 164

[3]*Americans in Florence, Sargent and the American Impressionists*, edited by Francesca Bardazzi and Carlo Sisi, Marsilio, Palazzo Strozzi, Florence, 2012, p.243

[4]Henry James, The Middle Years: 1882-1895, J.B. Lippincott Co., New York, 1962, p.208

[5]*Frank Duveneck, Painter—Teacher*, John Howell— Book, San Francisco, 1970, p. 115

[6]The mural was apparently lost in a redecoration of the facility, which became a boarding school, closed in 1966.

[7]*Frank Duveneck, Painter—Te*acher, John Howell—Books, San Francisco, 1970, p.115

[8]*Ibid*, p. 117-118

[9]*Ibid*, p. 118

[10]*Praeterita* is the title of Ruskin's autobiography. Josephine Whitney Duveneck's biography of Frank Duveneck refers to the Ruskin work as Praetoria, likely a mistake.

[11]*Frank Duveneck, Painter-Teacher*, John Howell—Books, San Francisco, 1970, pp. 118

[12]Ibid, pp.118-119

[13]Document copies on file in the clerk's office, Kenton County, Kentucky

[14]*Frank Duveneck, Painter-Teacher*, John Howell—Books, San Francisco, 1970, p.119

[15]*Frank Duveneck & Elizabeth Boott Duveneck: An American Romance*, essay by Carol M. Osborne for a Duveneck exhibition at Owen Gallery, New York, 1996

[16]Ibid

[17]*Americans in Florence, Sargent and the American Impressionists*, edited by Francesca Bardazzi and Carlo Sisi, Marsilio, Palazzo Strozzi, Florence, 2012, p.243

143

Chapter Seven

'An Unspeakable Shock'

Paris, 1887-1888

The new grandfather, Francis Boott, stayed in Boston for the summer of 1887. Lizzie missed him. His absence left an aching vacancy in her heart and she invited him to join her and Frank as they embarked together on a new venture in Paris. She made it clear in a letter that her love for him as a father would last forever, no matter what her circumstances. The letter shows cleverness, intelligence and sincerity.

Lizzie offered this to her father:

"I should so much like to see you. I do not think the great affections of one's life are not more or less but only different and do not interfere with each other. Certainly I never expected happiness as I have now. A healthy natural life was necessary to me and the joy of this dear baby is more than I can tell when joined to the perfect unity between Frank and me."[1]

This is a persuasive appeal, equal to the best of Cicero. An inherent quality of the letter is that he is not only loved, but needed. Lizzie says that she, *anyone*, is capable of loving more than one person. It may be a different category of love, she writes, and that the gift of heart, mind and will not be subdivided. Her marriage to Frank Duveneck contributes to a "healthy natural life," she asserts, and her son brings new joy. What else can a father do? He naturally responds positively.

Already by November of 1887 Francis Boott had made the transatlantic crossing and reconnected with the couple and child at the former Boott apartment on rue Tilsit where the marriage had taken place. Their residence became a social center. Living in Paris were Duveneck friends and former students Louis Ritter, Julius

Rolshoven and Theodore Wendel. The Bootts knew Paris well and had lived there when Lizzie studied under Couture.

In a letter Lizzie commented, "It is a great place for an artist to be here, and Frank has never had enough of the advantages offered in Paris. One also sees so much that is interesting and profitable."[2]

The Salon of 1888 provided an immense opportunity to see what was new and making money. Between twenty and thirty schools of painting were represented and as many as fifteen thousand works, largely paintings, were "sent back" by the jury. Historical paintings had fallen out of favor, a likely reason for the high number of rejections. They had enjoyed decades of acceptance and praise including the works of Salon organizer Jean-Louis-Ernest Meissonier, the famous painter of *The Campaign of France* and *Friedland.* Critics were active as usual, decrying the existence of an Old Boy Network that allowed acceptance of works, in some cases without examination.

In the decade of the 1880s, American painters became a new and fresh force at Salons. Participation increased annually starting in 1875 as the threat of insurrection diminished in the wake of the 1870 fall of the Second Empire of Napoleon III. American participation in 1875 was a mere twenty-three artists, increasing to one-hundred and seven in 1880, one hundred and seventy-seven in 1890, and two-hundred-and-thirty four in 1899. Moreover, the French government acquired thirty pieces by Americans in the period 1878-1900, which lent prestige to them and their works.[3]

Salons were always gala affairs. The opening each year on May 1 signaled the beginning of the spring season in Paris. The intense popularity among Parisians and artists during this period can be compared to the interest by audiences of the televised Hollywood Oscar awards each year.[4]

Among the more interesting sights in 1888—and dozens of years before, no doubt discussed by the Duvenecks—were works by

Edouard Manet, whose work has placed him as a bridge between Realism and Impressionism, and Jean Desire Gustave Courbet, a radical product of his independent study, the founder of the Realism movement. Manet had studied under Thomas Couture and was influenced, like Duveneck, by the Dutch painter Frans Hals and the Spaniard, Diego Velazquez.

More than two decades earlier, Manet's painting, *Luncheon in the Grass* (*Le Djeuner sur l'herbe*), delivered a shock, presenting a nude woman seated at a picnic in close proximity with two fully attired men. The work roiled the tempers of the academic judges of the Paris Salon and was rejected along with hundreds of others. The large number of rejections, many of quality paintings, some controversial, provoked an uproar among artists and resulted in the intervention of Napoleon III. Another Manet painting, *Olympia*, traumatized judges and critics alike as the subject was a woman unabashedly displaying her body. To calm the storm, Napoleon ordered the creation of Salon des Refuses in 1863, an alternative exhibition that existed off and on for decades.

When the Duvenecks arrived in Paris years after the controversies Manet and Courbet had already passed on, yet their works had augured a new era, and Impressionist painters Mary Cassatt, Claude Monet and Paul Cezanne were among the celebrated personages. Among newcomers was the neo-Impressionist George Pierre Seurat, painter of the masterpiece, *A Sunday Afternoon on the Island of La Grande Jatte.* That very spring of 1888, Vincent van Gogh, virtually unknown and disturbed by a heavy late winter snowfall in northern France, had chosen to head south to Arles where he painted apricot, peach and plum trees in his inimitable way. An entirely new generation of artists was coming into its own. For the Duveneck family, the time period was auspicious.

'To rest in that beautiful country'

Winter weather in north central France is typically cold and damp, and the season in 1887-1888 was no different. At the start of their stay in the fall Frank found so fascinating what was going on in schools that he reduced his time in studio. By March, however, he was busy doing a portrait of Lizzie, she attired in the brown dress, bonnet and cape that represented that day's fashion and which she had worn for her wedding. Frank was working steadily at the project, and she spent lengthy hours posing as they hoped the painting would be completed in time to apply to the Salon.

The painting ranks as one of Duveneck's best portraits. Lizzie is an idealized figure of serene beauty, standing alone wearing a slightly wistful expression. She wears a bonnet and her dark hair is parted in the middle and swept downwards. The line from her left eyebrow comes down gracefully to form the frontal line of what Duveneck later said was the most perfectly shaped nose on a human being. The face is an oval, of quattrocento beauty. Only two years earlier Duveneck completed a close-up portrait head of a more carefree Lizzie. She is a formidable woman, wearing a somewhat audacious expression, peering out with her head tilted backward.

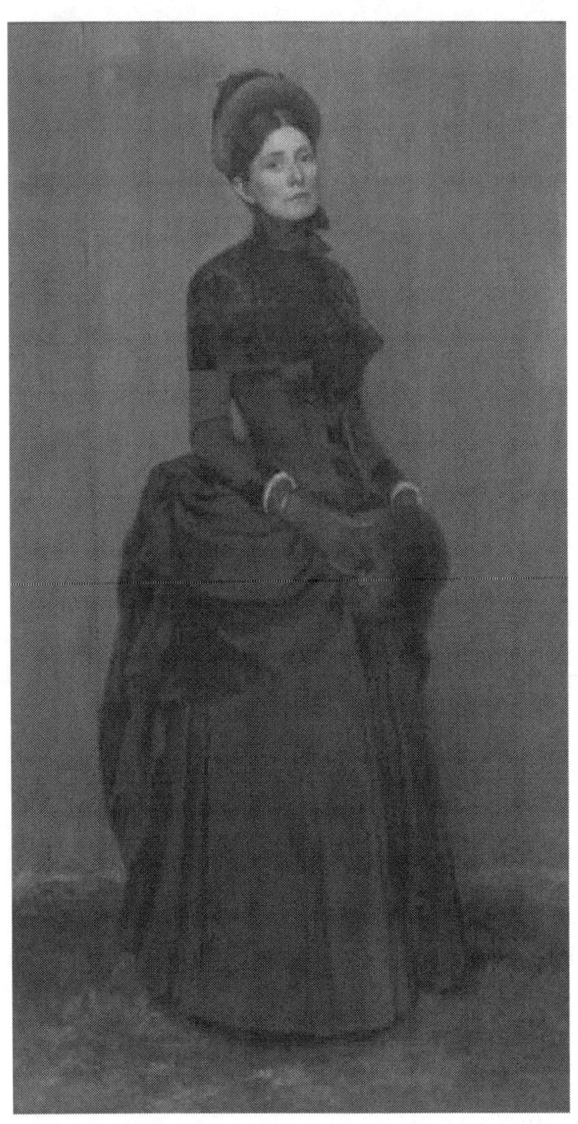

Lizzie Duveneck in her wedding dress

-Frank Duveneck (American, 1848-1919), Elizabeth Boott Duveneck, 1888,
Cincinnati Art Museum, Gift of the Artist

Busy in her new role, yet standing for the full-length portrait and working on a water color study of the Villa Castellani, Lizzie became more vulnerable to medical issues than ever. In late February she engaged an English nurse, Bessie Girling, to help with caring for the child. However, the accumulative effect of her expanded activities must have taken a toll on her never robust physical condition. Like her mother and many women of that time, she suffered from lung ailments. The winter's inclement weather affected her, and she paid a price for the demands on her as wife, counselor to her husband and attentive mother. She was also running the household and managing the consequent increase of social obligations for all concerned.

She revealed the difficulty of her new circumstances in a March 13 letter. Duveneck's portrait "has taken much of his time and of mine and I am always much occupied with the baby," she wrote.

A few days later, on May 18, after a shopping trip, Lizzie complained of a chill and took to her bed. She weakened as a bacterial or other type of infection irritated her lungs. Pneumonia had set in, a devastating development in those days, and she was unable to cope. After four days of suffering, with her helpless family beside her at half-past seven on the morning of March 22, she died.

The family biography says Duveneck left the apartment in a state of shock and grief and was nowhere to be found for a day and a half. Finally, a student, Theodore Wendel, combed the city and located him at a corner table in café that artists frequented. He was speechless in a drunken stupor. Before he went on a tear that dreadful morning Duveneck had summoned the will to model Lizzie's face in what is referred to as a death mask,[5] an act possibly incredible to some. Yet he was behaving in the only way he knew, as an artist. Perhaps he may have had already in mind a plan to memorialize the woman he loved so dearly. Another former student, Louis Ritter, aided the memorial project by providing a charcoal sketch of the recumbent Lizzie. Ritter's sketch is part of the Duveneck collection at the Cincinnati Art Museum.

When Duveneck regained his senses, he informed his family in a brief letter and then a second one a few days later to his brother, Charlie. His words evoke the depth of his sadness and misery.

"Yesterday I sent a few lines to say that my dear wife has departed from me forever. She died yesterday at half past seven after four days of suffering from pneumonia. I can hardly get used to understand this sad blow. I suppose I must understand it like many others must and in fact all of us must experience sooner or later.

"It was just two years yesterday when we were married and from this same house that we have lived in this winter. We were married two years ago this same day.

"I hoped [on] some day (sic) soon that we would come to America and we would have met together and she was anxious to meet you all. However, there is no use dreaming about many possible things in the future when anything might happen at any moment and the best I suppose is to be prepared for it. I shall try and make the best of it.

"My little boy is very well and well taken care of. My wife's father is with me and we are all very well.

"This morning my wife was taken to a temporary resting place and in the month of May we will take her to Florence her favorite home where she has lived most of her life, there to rest in that beautiful country of flowers she so dearly loved."[6]

James's Insensitivity

The grief was heavy in other homes that night. Henry James had lost a good friend, one with whom he had shared personal views as a regular correspondent of some eighty letters over more than twenty years. The author's hand was shaky as he informed others by letter of her death. Lizzie had told him, he wrote, that they all were stretched by the "tyranny of the baby" and that she decided to paint with water colors simply as a time saver since the colors were more easily composed compared to oils. He said she was overtaxed by the duties of motherhood, wife and artist. Mr. Boott, in a letter to Henry, must have said that Lizzie had taken on too much. In an unthinking, obtuse and inconsiderate response to Mr. Boott, James wrote:

"She staggered under it and was broken down by it."[7]

 Lizzie's death brought out the worst in James. To the grief-stricken father he wrote that he didn't believe Lizzie was as happy, that she donned a mask of sorts in her new roles. He said the happiness she displayed at a recent previous gathering had been all superficial. "The infirmity was visible beneath the optimism—the whole thing seemed to me without an issue. This particular issue [her death] is the most violent—but perhaps after all it is not the most cruel (sic)—the most painful to witness—for perpetual struggle and disappointment would have been her portion. I mean on account of the terrible specific gravity of the mass she had proposed to herself to float and carry.—It is not fault of his [Duveneck's]—but simply the stuff he is made of."[8]

James simply could not understand why Lizzie, the polished woman he called the most civilized he had known, had married Frank Duveneck, a great artist who in most other respects, at least in James's estimation, was an ordinary, if not ignorant man. He wrote of the "unspeakable shock" her death gave him. In a letter to Mr. Boott he recalled the time he had recently spent with her at the villa. Together they beheld the view from the parapet, and he said she stood in the tall grass on the terrace. He wrote that he would always remember her in those circumstances. In his way he loved her. A close friend had departed from his life. "She was a dear little quiet, gentle, intelligent laborious lady."

The author departed from this sentimentality and turned to philosophy in his grief. "What clumsy situations does fate bring about, and with what an absence of style does the world appear to be ruled!" Henry told a friend. He was constitutionally unable to

151

comprehend the presence of Duveneck in the new situation. The grieving husband Frank Duveneck and father Francis Boott were "strange companions, held together by that child."

Duveneck, the Bohemian, he concluded, was not the person to be in charge of the rearing young Frankie, adding this odd sentence: "My imagination can scarcely take in Duveneck's *afloat* condition again—after his having embraced the faith that he was, for life, safe from all winds and water. I kiss the child and shake hands with Duveneck. For you my dear Francis, I can only repeat that I bear you constantly in the participation of my thoughts."[9]

He inquired of a correspondent who had seen Duveneck's portrait of Lizzie, "Is it good or interesting?"

The author Somerset Maugham offered an insight to James's character in an essay, "Some Novelists I have Known," that explains in short order what Leon Edel and other James biographers have attempted in their writings. He observed of James:

"He did not know the English as an Englishman instinctively knows them and so his English characters never to my mind ring quite true. His American characters, at least to an Englishmen, on the whole do. He had certain remarkable gifts, but he lacked the quality of empathy which enables a novelist to feel himself into his characters, think their thoughts and suffer their emotions."

Further, Maugham wrote: "The great novelists, even in seclusion, have lived life passionately. Henry James was content to observe it from a window. But you cannot describe life convincingly unless you have partaken of it; nor, should your object be different, can you fantasticate (sic) upon it (as Balzac and Dickens did) unless you know it first. Something escapes you unless you have been an actor in the tragi-comedy."

Then he added significantly:

"Henry James regarded his relations and friends with deep affection, but this is no indication that he was capable of love. Indeed he showed a singular obtuseness in his stories and novels when he came to deal with the most deeply seated of human emotions; so that interested and amused as you are (often amused at him rather than with him), you are constantly jolted back to reality by your feeling that human beings simply do not behave as he makes them do."

James lived in an England where class-consciousness affected all who drew a breath. Maugham believed James accepted this way of life in his writings and applied this high-toned attitude toward characters of humble origin. To James, the unfortunate poor were required to earn a living, a circumstance that was slightly ridiculous to him.

"I think he took himself a good deal too seriously," Maugham wrote. "We look askance at a man who keeps on telling you he is a gentleman; I think it would have been more becoming in Henry James if he had not insisted so often on his being an artist. It is better to leave others to say that."

Ink had scarcely dried on James's insensitive letters when rumors circulated in Boston that, firstly, Frank Duveneck had murdered Lizzie for her inheritance, and secondly, that she had committed suicide. Neither insulting speculation had any basis in truth. Perhaps driving the speculation was the grim fact of a series of untimely deaths and suicides among Brahmin women that had shaken local society.

The author and critic Jean Strouse, author of the biography of Alice James, sister of Henry and William and a friend of Lizzie's, raised a question about the cause of Lizzie's death. She affirmed in her book that Alice James had considered the possibility of Lizzie's suicide. Her evidence was a remark that Alice James made to her brother, William, that Lizzie's "having so violently discontinued herself (sic) was a great shock."

In a collection of articles in *Italian Presence in American Art*, critic Carol Osborne questioned Jean Strouse on her interpretation of Alice's remark. In their exchange on the subject, Osborne says that Strouse agreed the remark was ambiguous. In the nineteenth century tuberculosis and pneumonia were frequent causes of death for both young and elderly. Lizzie's mother had died of a similar ailment. Osborne, in trying to clarify the situation, also learned that 'discontinued herself' is a euphemism for dying, not a reference to suicide. So, there is certainty that Lizzie died of pneumonia and was not a victim of anyone's hand. The death certificate reads that she suffered a mortal case of pneumonia.[10]

As the Duveneck family's personal tragedy was unfolding in Paris, the jury of the 1888 Salon accepted both Duveneck's portrait of Lizzie, and Lizzie's water color study of Villa Castellani. By coincidence, the jurying took place the day she fell ill. The two works were exhibited the following May. Frank Duveneck's painting of Lizzie won honorable mention. It is a feature of the Duveneck Room at the Cincinnati Art Museum.

In May the sad assembly of two heartbroken men escorted Lizzie's body to Florence, the baby and recently hired nurse, Bessie, with the artist Louis Ritter in tow. Lizzie's many friends in the city bade her farewell at her final resting place in Allori Cemetery. On that day flowers mounded high on the grave. Lizzie's friend, the writer and Bellosguardo, neighbor Constance Fenimore Woolson, attended the final ceremony. She described Mr. Boott as calm while Duveneck openly sobbed. She wrote to Henry James that Duveneck's "demeanour has won all hearts here."[11]

Duveneck had to have been asking the nagging unanswerable question, *Why did this happen?* Doubtless he was as confounded as anyone. The ache from her loss he carried to his own grave. The passing of time offered some healing, and doubtless, as a fellow Victorian, he would have shared the sentiment expressed in the poem of sorrow by the Victorian poet Alfred Lord Tennyson:

I hold it true, whate'er befall;
I feel it, when I sorrow most;
'Tis better to have loved and lost
Than never to have loved at all."

Fortunately, the English nurse, Bessie, solved a difficult problem for Duveneck. She felt an obligation to assume a greater role in caring for Frankie and agreed to remain on duty. She was with Mr. Boott and Frank Duveneck and son when they returned to Villa Castellani and, for each of them, an uncertain future.

Returning to America

The family biography says that Mr. Boott rallied first from the family catastrophe. It is perhaps an odd, if not eerie coincidence that he, too, had inherited a large sum of money after the death of his wife, Lizzie's mother. Perhaps his learned experience as a widower, left to raise a motherless child, prompted him to prepare to meet the obligations to his grandson. In any case Mr. Boott took the reins of the situation as Frank languished in his grief. "He was distraught and perplexed and at a loss which way to turn," wrote biographer Josephine Whitney Duveneck. She also pinpointed the problem for the two men: "How could an old man and an inexperienced artist father care for an infant barely old enough to walk?"

A friend in Florence offered to raise the child. Mr. Boott and Frank Duveneck were mulling over that prospect when an opportune cable arrived from Mr. and Mrs. Arthur Lyman, Lizzie's uncle and aunt, of Waltham, Massachusetts. It contained an invitation to young Frankie to join them as a member of their family. The offer was generous since the youngest of the Lyman children, Ronald, was already nine years old. And, it was also sensible since the aging father had wondered about the child growing up in Europe far apart from his mother's relatives and friends in Boston. [Apparently, the Duveneck family in Covington was not given any or much consideration as potential guardians.] Grandfather and father were

155

relieved and agreed to give custody of young Frankie to the Lymans to be raised in Waltham.

For the sad duty of packing household goods and paintings, the author Constance Fenimore Woolson, the baby's godmother, helped the two men. A trunk of Lizzie's personal items contained the wedding dress she wore for the portrait, "which no one had the heart to abandon."

In August the family set sail for Boston and new lives for all concerned. They arrived in Waltham on the Shore Line railroad to an enthusiastic welcome. Mrs. Lyman recorded in her journal, "We were in such a state of excitement that it was hard to settle to anything. I went over to the street to make my first purchase for the baby. The afternoon seemed very long. We expected them at four, but they did not come till 6:30."[12]

Mrs. Lyman found Duveneck "simple almost boyish very straight forward and affectionate. The baby is a winning little fellow with a sweet smile."

They settled in quickly in the Lyman's home. Mrs. Lyman records a tender scene before and after breakfast in her journal dated August 22. Duveneck brought out and displayed the Ritter deathbed sketch of Lizzie. "He spoke of their engagement ten years ago having been broken off and said it had a very bad effect on Lizzie's health." Then Duveneck said that he was deeply grateful for their taking responsibility and rearing his son, saying that Mr. Boott had considered remaining in Florence with the child. "…but I told him it would be a great deal better for him to take the baby home and he said the Lymans' [sic] was the only place he should be willing to have the baby go." When Mrs. Lyman said that she thought it unselfish of Duveneck to part with Frankie and added, "You must come to see him often. Mr. D. Where upon the poor fellow burst into tears and sobbed aloud."

156

Despite the heavy emotional pulls of placing young Frankie with Boston relatives, Duveneck developed a rationale. "Where he would not have had good care[,] then if anything happened to him I should have felt it could have been helped[;] but now I feel as if he were under his mother's care, for it is just what she would have wanted. If anything happens to him now, I shall feel it has been in the course of nature."

Duveneck told the nurse, Bessie, that he "wanted the baby to be as much as possible one of the family and that he felt for himself it was better to keep off and go to work and get interested in that and in his friends."

The grandfather "was not quite so willing to allow Mrs. Lyman to have a free hand with the boy. When he was only three[,] Mrs. Lyman comments[,] that his grandfather expected the boy to have 'the perfected manners and instant obedience of a colonel to a general." She also said "Uncle Frank," presumably the grandfather, continued anxious for little Frank's health, morals and even his clothes. The decision about hats for Baby Frank was so difficult that thirteen hats were sent up from the store and four of them bought."[13]

Lizzie's death also brought changes to other lives. Mr. Boott ended his long odyssey in Europe and moved in a residence in Cambridge with his sister, the former resident of Rome and widow of sculptor Horatio Greenough. He renewed his friendship with William James, then teaching philosophy at Harvard, who lived nearby. After Mr. Boott's death in 1904, James wrote a memorial that captured the unusual, if not unique, character of Lizzie's father.

Some of it was quoted in the family biography:

"A certain appearance comes in here of a self contradictory (sic) character, for Mr. Boott was primarily modest and sensitive, and all his interests and pre-occupations were with life's refinements and delicacies. Yet one's mind always pictured him as a rugged

157

sort of person, opposing successful resistence (sic) to all influences that might seek to change his habits of feeling or of action. His admirable health, his sober life, his regular walk twice a day whatever might be the weather, his invariable evenness of mood and opinion so that, when you once knew his range, he never disappointed you—all this was at variance, with popular notions of the artistic temperament. He was exact and accurate; affectionate, indeed, and sociable, but neither gregarious nor demonstrative; and such words as 'honest,' 'sturdy,' 'faithful' are adjectives first to rise when one thinks of him—our old friend Boott was identical in spiritual essence all his life, and the effect of his growing old was not to alter but only to make the same man mellower, more tolerant more loveable. Sadder he was, I think, for his life had grown pretty lonely; but he was a stoic and he never complained either of losses or of years and that contagious laugh of his at any and every pretext for laughter rang as free and true upon his deathbed as at any previous time of his existence."[14]

Deeply grieved by her friend Lizzie's death, Fenimore contributed a memorial of sorts in a short story, *Dorothy,* which was based largely on Lizzie. It appeared in *Harper's New Monthly Magazine* in March of 1892, a tale of a young woman who lived in Florence on Bellosguardo in Villa Dorio, a fifty-room villa capable of harboring five families. She begins as something of an ingénue described by the author in a perched position on a parapet to take in the view of the Arno River valley. "And Dorothy herself generally led them in the dangerous experiment. But one could never think of Dorothy as falling; her supple figure conveyed the idea that she could fly—almost—so lightly was it poised upon her little feet; in any case one felt sure that even if she should take the fancy to throw herself off, she would float to the lower slope as lightly as this-tie-down."

In writing style, the story is similar to any written by her close friend Henry James's works that devote many words to recreate scenes and deprecate action. Fenimore's story of a lost love is truly sentimental as is Dorothy's lingering death by an unknown cause.

More to the point, the novel, *Esther*, a story by Henry Adams, was likely inspired by circumstances similar to those faced by Lizzie. A Brahmin woman faced an irreconcilable conflict between choosing a career as a creative artist and devoting her life to good causes. The theme was repeated in writings of more recent feminist writers who find tragedy in a talented woman subordinating her career to a man's as was the case with Lizzie.

Frank Duveneck returned to Covington, and began work on an effigy of Lizzie for her tomb in Florence. He engaged the aid of a young sculptor, Clement Barnhorn (1857-1935) of Covington who became a close friend and later a colleague at the Cincinnati Art Academy. Their pairing in Barnhorn's studio in the Pike Building on Fourth Street in Cincinnati was to raise prospects for Barnhorn and to launch Duveneck into a new form that won honor and praise. As his former student, Aileen McCarthy, said of Duveneck, with conviction, "he could do anything."

---

[1] *Frank Duveneck, Painter-Teac*her, Josephine Whitney Duveneck, John Howell—Books, San Francisco, 1970, p. 119

[2]Ibid, p. 119

[3]Jugen von Jagow, The Salon of 1888, *The Connisseur*, Vol. 3, No. 1, September, 1888, pp. 24-27

[4] Lois Marie Fink, *American Art of the Nineteenth-Century Paris Salons*, Smithsonian Institution, Washington, D.C., and Cambridge University Press, Cambridge, 1990, pp. 113-142

[5]Interview with Aileen McCarthy, a student of Duveneck's at the Cincinnati Art Academy. The death mask, said to be a plaster cast, came into the Howell family when they acquired the Duveneck House. For a time it was exhibited at the Behringer-Crawford Museum in Covington's Devou Park. A Howell descendant, Frank Droege of Boone County, Kentucky, was a one-time owner of the mask. It has been sold twice and is now the property of an unnamed Cincinnati resident. The mask was studied recently at the Cincinnati Art Museum. Curator Julie Aronson is of the opinion

159

that the mask is actually a sculpture and not the work of Duveneck. A death mask may have been taken, she says, but the one studied by the museum specialists is not it.

[6] *Frank Duveneck, Painter-Teacher*, Josephine Whitney Duveneck, John Howell—Books, San Francisco, 1970, pp. 121-122

[7] *Henry James, The Middle Years: 1882-1895*, Leon Edel, J.B. Lippincott Company, New York, pp. 245-246

[8] Ibid, pp. 246-247

[9] Ibid, p. 247

[10] *Alice James: A Biography*, Jean Strouse, Boston, 1980, p. 70. See footnote to "Lizzie Boott at Bellosguardo" by Carol Osborne, Ibid, pp. 246-247

[11] *Henry James, The Middle Years: 1882-1895*, J.B. Lippincott Company, New York, p. 248.

[12] *Frank Duveneck, Parent—Teacher*, Josephine Whitney Duveneck, John Howell—Books, San Francisco, 1970, pp. 123-124

[13] Josephine Whitney Duveneck, notes, Duveneck Papers, Archives of American Art, Smithsonian Institution, Washington, D.C.

[14] *Frank Duveneck, Parent—Teacher*, Josephine Whitney Duveneck, John Howell—Books, San Francisco, 1970, pp. 123-124

Chapter Eight

Return of the Native

Cincinnati, Ohio, spring, 1890

Frank Duveneck returned to Cincinnati in 1890 somewhat unsure that he was doing the right thing. He was offered an opportunity to teach a class in a studio at the Art Museum in the early days of the Art Academy. The class had been formed by Maria Longworth Nichols Storer, a noted ceramicist and founder of Rookwood Pottery, the wife of U.S. congressman and later diplomat Bellamy Storer.[1] Duveneck, an experienced instructor and now famous for his art, was a natural and desirable fit for the class. He named his terms in a letter to Mrs. Storer written from 77 Boylston Street in Boston, dated May 8. The semester was to last six months, from November 1 to May 1, and he was to be paid $25 a week. He would teach for two days of the week. He noted drily that six months was quite sufficient in length for a painting school and he gave the name of his former student, Joseph DeCamp as an able assistant.

The decision to return was not easy. Compatriots in Europe had tried to dissuade him. He wrote from Florence in July of 1889, "My friends strongly disapprove of my going to Cincinnati and think I ought to settle either in New York or Boston and get used to it in course of time. Of course I have other reasons for going to Cincinnati," and added, "the beginning of a new school is not an easy task and my dislike of the place would probably not make it very pleasant in the long run. So I shall steer for Boston in the coming winter."[2]

Duveneck dithered in Boston that winter but he demonstrated that he had not lost the knack of portraiture. He associated with family and other artists and completed a painting, *Marie Danforth Page*. The portrait of Miss Page was rendered in the style of the period, as an elegant young lady, jauntily wearing a summer floppy hat.

As always Duveneck focused on the subject's charming face, her blue eyes, well-formed nose and luscious red lips. She herself was an art student of Helen Knowlton (1832-1918) and continued as a working artist for the rest of her life in Boston.

Still, Duveneck returned to Cincinnati for "those other reasons," perhaps having something to do with his mother and family living in the region. His return also could be motivated by the developing art scene in Cincinnati and the opportunity to be master of his own career. Again, there were his many old friends and former students. Economy, also known as stinginess, may have played a role. He delighted in telling a friend that "prices for studios are about 1/5 the price they are in Boston."

Cincinnati had matured since his last visit. New and taller structures lined downtown streets. Hotels and office buildings, some designed with style by the local architectural firm, Samuel Hannaford & Sons, were cropping up on the city's surrounding Seven Hills. Five funicular railways, known as the inclines, connected the downtown with suburban hilltops. Hannaford also designed Cincinnati's City Hall and its famous Music Hall. And the more famous name, Henry Hobson Richardson, had completed in 1889 the Greater Cincinnati Chamber of Commerce building in the downtown area.

Despite these advances Cincinnati retained some of its essential character of the old brawling town of frontier days. The many slaughter houses gave it the nickname, "Porkopolis." The Ohio River teemed with steamboats mooring at the city landings. In the decade of the Nineties, Vine Street, the major north-south thoroughfare, counted one hundred and thirteen saloons, dance halls and beer gardens between McMillan Street and the Ohio River, a distance of two miles. Saloons were concentrated between Twelfth and Thirteenth Street on Vine, twenty-three offered whisky and beer and food. A patron could get a free wienerwurst with a paid-for shot of Kentucky whisky. The city supported five opera houses that hosted such celebrated entertainers as Lillian Russell and Sara

Bernhardt. Vaudeville's Weber & Fields and Trixie Friganza delighted audiences. The famous boxer and world champion John L. Sullivan so frequented Vine Street bars, before and after prize fights, that people thought the Queen City of the West was Sullivan's second home.

Cincinnati was lively if nothing else. A half-mile area known as the Circle, containing the city's central business district, radiated northward from the Ohio River and mixed tenement life, labor and business twenty-four hours a day. Dozens of ghettos were patched onto this Circle—enclaves of Blacks, Jews, Italians, Greeks and Irish. Between them, often sustaining them, were open air markets, shops, factories, warehouses and saloons, with numerous cross-topped steeples of churches dominating the skyline. Some Germans lived in the Circle. Most had shifted to north of the city and called their home Over-the-Rhine, as it lay just north and east of the Erie Canal that crisscrossed the city.

In the busy Circle electric-powered street cars clattered and horse-drawn wagons rattled over cobblestone streets. Duveneck used a streetcar that traveled through Covington and across the John A. Roebling-designed Suspension Bridge and then changed cars at Fountain Square for the art school on top of Mount Adams. Cincinnati was not Florence, nor Paris, nor even Boston; but it was home and Duveneck had solid friends there. From today's vantage point one can easily say that the prospering and lively city should have provided a wonderful opportunity for Duveneck to capture the true soul of the town and its people. He had done just that two decades earlier in Germany and later in Italy especially in Rembrandt-like portraits of common people and street scenes in sunny Florence. Perhaps he thought the old realistic approach was passé, and that Impressionism had taken over. The future for him, perhaps, lay in portraiture, scenes of the sea and harbors of Gloucester, and in teaching.

Duveneck's native town of Covington had grown, too, at a slower pace and primarily as a residential suburb of the larger city across

163

the Ohio River. Helentown, the German residential area, absorbed wave after wave of hard-working European immigrants who enriched the town and strengthened the economy. "It was a place," a one-time congressman said, "where all the fine Germans lived."[3] In the Nineties, the Duveneck family house was no longer the beehive it had been. His stepfather, Joseph or Squire, had died in 1883. Many Duveneck siblings had moved on. Mother Catherine, known then in her *kaffee klatsch* as Kate, was proud of her son and his accomplishments which had given fame to the family.

In May 1890 Duveneck adopted a positive tone about the art school when he wrote from Cincinnati.

"The prospectus of my school in Cincinnati is very promising for next winter and I have agreed to take charge of it for one winter. The Art Museum Trustees have just decided to make the necessary alterations in the upper part of the Museum at considerable expense and give it to us free of all charges. My agreement is for six months beginning November 1 to May 1st and my days for teaching at my own convenience."[4]

At the conclusion of that first session he sounded a distinctly human note in his expression of fatigue in a May, 1891 letter. "I wish that I were through here and could get away. I am tired of studio and art in general. Next week begins the horse races which are always exciting and interesting here and with baseball and good whiskey in addition, we ought to manage to get along." Six months later, he changed his tune to the positive for teaching. "My school is already full and somewhat larger than last year and on the whole more promising."[5]

The Effigy's Story

Renaissance funerary monuments in Florence were one of the attractions for artistic-minded Americans and Europeans in the nineteenth century. A centerpiece and place of homage for women in the Florentine network was the white, marble sarcophagus dedicated to Elizabeth Barrett Browning, author of *Sonnets from the Portuguese* (How do I love thee, let me count the ways). In 1885, Julia Lyman, a relative of Lizzie's, was with Lizzie when they viewed the Browning memorial and they also saw an effigy designed by Donatello situated then in the Florence Baptistery, a part of the Il Duomo di Firenze complex, comprising the baptistery, the Basilica de Santa Maria de Flora, and Giotto's Campanile. Florence was observing the five-hundredth anniversary of Donatello's birth, and of particular interest was Donatello's gold-tinged bronze figure of St. Louis of Toulouse.

No doubt, Frank Duveneck was well aware of these works. Always a student of the arts, he learned from his studies and experience, typically placing his own stamp on his creations. The memorial effigy to Lizzie would be no different. He picked up some pointers from his Cincinnati friend and sculptor, Clement Barnhorn (1857-1935). Duveneck admirers today regard him as the author of Lizzie's face and hands, while Barnhorn is given credit for the palm branches and other aspects of the effigy.

Duveneck's point of view was to present Lizzie to the world as the lady he knew—a woman serene and beautiful. He chose as his model the recumbent figure for the Tomb of Ilaria del Carretto by Jacopo della Quercia. In 1406 Ilaria at twenty-six years of age had died in childbirth. The memorial, commissioned by her husband, a man of commerce, presents the young woman as a person of self-sacrifice. Her hands hold her swollen stomach. The Jacopo work was well known at the time. The original was installed in the cathedral at Lucca. Casts of it could be seen in Florence.

The artist was fortunate to have the support of Barnhorn who had begun his artistic work as a wood carver under Henry L. Fry, an Englishman who had done work in the House of Parliament in London and produced marvelously detailed furniture now in the Cincinnati museum. Barnhorn studied sculpture under Louis T. Rebisso, an instructor at the Cincinnati Art Academy, and assisted

165

him as he completed the Ulysses S. Grant memorial in Chicago's Grant Park.

Interestingly, Barnhorn's career took off after assisting Duveneck with the Lizzie effigy. His performance at the art academy brought him a scholarship, awarded by the directors, which enabled him to study in Europe for three years in the early 1890s. He spent most of his time in Paris studying under William-Adolphe Bouguereau, Mercie, Puech, and Fremiet. His idealized figure, *Magdalen*, won honorable mention at the 1895 Paris Salon. He took a silver medal at the 1900 Paris Salon for another *Magadalen* and a silver medal at the 1904 Louisiana Purchase Exhibit in St. Louis, which also honored a Duveneck portrait of his mother.

Works also received honorable mention from the 1901 Pan American Exposition. That same year he began instructing in sculpture at the Cincinnati Art Academy, around the same time that Duveneck signed on as a master teacher. Their academy studios adjoined for nearly two decades. Barnhorn assisted Duveneck in the sculpture memorial to Ralph Waldo Emerson, completed in 1905 and then installed in Emerson Hall at Harvard University.

Barnhorn and Duveneck first met in 1875 when Barnhorn was barely eighteen years old, a student of Xavier College, now Xavier University. At that time Duveneck was about to return to Europe, but the meeting was remembered by each. They had a lot in common. Each traced their family histories to the Duchy of Oldenburg in Germany so they were two Americanized sons of German parents who enjoyed life and sought to portray it truthfully. In their approaches to their art, they were opposites. Duveneck was actively busy while Barnhorn was calm and methodical. The deep and long-lasting friendship was solidified as they worked together on the Lizzie memorial and continued for three decades. Barnhorn's wonderfully sad-eyed Teutonic face was marked by a drooping mustache; and he grew bald in his later years. A twin, born in Cincinnati on January 9, 1857, he came from a large family headed by Clement Barnhorn, keeper of a public house and later a dealer in liquor, another piece of personal history that he shared with Duveneck.

Former Duveneck student Aileen McCarthy believed that Barnhorn, though younger and always the assistant in joint works, was a good and positive influence for Duveneck. He was devout as a Catholic who attended Mass daily. Much of his work had a strong religious bent. It was only natural and expected that the two Covington artists received commissions from Bishop Camillus Paul Maes, a Belgian who oversaw the design and construction of the city's French gothic-styled Cathedral Basilica of the Assumption. Duveneck spent five years working on a large-scale, three-panel mural, and a side panel, the latter work somewhat hidden from normal view in the basilica's Blessed Sacrament Chapel. Barnhorn sculpted a statue of the Blessed Virgin Mary which stands today in a frontal niche at the Cathedral Basilica and completed a tympanum depicting the Assumption of Mary above the main doors.

Ably assisted in this great memorial, Duveneck's mind was full of the plans for the effigy of Lizzie. He consulted Augustus Saint-Gaudens, the sculptor who in 1891 unveiled a striking memorial to Clover Adams, wife of the author and essayist Henry Adams. Situated in Rock Creek Cemetery in Washington, D.C., the memorial features a statue of a haunting, hooded figure the public called *"Grief."* At the same time, the sculptor and Duveneck friend Daniel Chester French (1850-1931) unveiled a memorial in Forest Hills Cemetery near Boston titled, *The Angel of Death and the Sculptor,* commemorating the life of a local sculptor and his brother. Saint-Gaudens encouraged Duveneck in his effigy project. Knowing that he lacked sculpturing experience and training, he promised to help with technical details. Later, his friend Daniel French praised Duveneck's careful rendering of Lizzie's face.

Duveneck worked on the clay model of the effigy in Barnhorn's studio in the Pike Building located in or near the famous Pike Opera House on Fourth Street between Vine and Walnut Streets.

Unfamiliar with the clay modeling process he relied on Barnhorn to instruct him. As for his own resources for the project he had his treasured memory of Lizzie's face, his talent and his own procedures and style. For example, he used to tell students that nature provided a flawed specimen and it was the artist's duty to improve on it. He applied that kind of thinking to an artist creating a portrait of an individual who had a blemish on his or her face. The flaw should be blotted out, he said, and the artist should focus on the character of the person in the portrait especially in the eyes. A blemish only served as a distraction, in his mind.

The effigy project, his schedule of teaching and, no doubt other, time-consuming art works busied the life of the painter-teacher, perhaps causing his general fatigue. He also experienced some eye problems and was forced to see a doctor who prescribed glasses with corrective lenses. After completing a second six-month term at the Art Academy, he told others that he needed time to complete casting work for the effigy, and he asked for and received a leave of absence from the Cincinnati academy. The clay model he and Barnhorn had fashioned was to be used to form a mold from which the bronze effigy designed for Allori Cemetery and plaster casts could be produced.

Meanwhile, Duveneck's concept for the sarcophagus had jelled. From a practical standpoint he perhaps had access to a death mask of Lizzie's face, and he had a deathbed sketch of Lizzie executed with skill in the sad Paris apartment by former student and artist Louis Ritter. The realistic sketch from the side view displaying the death-distorted face of Duveneck's beloved is in the collection of the Cincinnati Art Museum. In the final work it is obvious that his own romantic and idealized view of his wife prevailed.

By late June of 1891, the fashioning of the clay model reached completion. A reporter from the *Cincinnati Times-Star* came to the studio to interview Duveneck and see the model. The scribe wondered why Duveneck chose "somber and funereal bronze" rather than Carrara marble "from which angels take wings under skillful hands…"[6] Duveneck offered the explanation that a marble work in the outdoors would "too readily stain and mar from the weather" if used on a full-length reclining figure. He was concerned that a reclining figure in marble would sustain greater damage than bronze as it caught and held water.

"Of course I would prefer the marble, but I wanted something lasting as well as appropriate, and bronze fills that idea the best. Then marble is too apt to be marred, either by people or the weather. This memorial will not be more than three or four feet high, and could be earily (easily) got at. And relic hunters are not over-particular and it would not be long perhaps before there would be a finger gone or the nose broken off or other portions marked and hacked. So taking it all around, I found that bronze would suit the better of the two and would be best of all that I could select."

The reporter was then invited to view the model.

"There in the clay model lay (sic) the full-length figure of a woman. A face of exquisite sweetness in the clay, how sweet must have been that face in life. The likeness was of the dear being it was sought to memorialize. The delicate hands were folded over the breast and a robe sweep gracefully away, falling over the sides here and there like drapery. Over all is a long palm branch that completely takes away all that hardness and starkness of the reclining figure in effigy. There is relief, repose, rest. The work is the idea and possibly the ideal of a master artist to the most beloved of his wife."

Julie Aronson, the Cincinnati Art Museum curator, believes that Duveneck made a plaster of the clay model and shipped it to the Boston studio of artist Howard Walker where Duveneck completed the casting in bronze. "Shipping the clay would have been extremely risky," she noted.

Father-in-law Francis Boott, living in nearby Cambridge, a frequent companion of his grandson, young Frankie, expressed his pleasure with the memorial. He suggested that Duveneck make a copy that would be accessible to family and friends. His commission was to do one in marble that would be housed at the Boston Museum of Fine Arts. No doubt delighted with this plan, Duveneck asked the help of a former student, William Couper who had remained in Florence. Couper moved quickly and soon had an aide locate a large block of statuary marble from the site at Seravezza. A five-horse wagon bore the block to his studio on via Dante da Castiglione. There it was roughly blocked out for final treatment by Duveneck.[7]

Walker, the Boston artist, maintained close ties with Duveneck as he worked on the marble version. "He told me once of the almost reverent feeling he had in making the figure upon the sarcophagus of his wife, and that on a Sunday he entered his studio alone and worked with a great cmotion upon the face when suddenly he realized that he had cut too much of the stone away and had ruined the work in the intensity of his effort.

"He said, 'in all my life, I was never in such despair.'"

He sat and brooded over the ruin he had made, when the Italian workman came in and he told him that he had spoiled his statue. The Italian said nothing, took calipers and carefully measured the model and the stone, looked up and smiled, "No, Signor," he said, 'your heart is better than your eye or head. The face is right. It is only that the rest of the statue has not been brought to it."

"'You cannot imagine my relief,' said Duveneck."

The marble work was shipped to Paris. The Paris Salon of 1895 accepted it and a jury awarded Honorable Mention. The statuary was then shipped to the Boston museum where it is displayed today. There the elder Mr. Boott and his grandson visited the museum frequently "to look on the serene and quiet face. The old man would tell the child stories of his mother, who was known to him only through the words of older people. But because of the stories told him by his father and grandfather she became a living presence to him—an unseen but intimate reality."[8]

By this time the bronze version of the effigy had been installed in Allori Cemetery beyond the Roman Gate at Bellosguardo. Duveneck spent time in Florence visiting with his and Lizzie's many friends and acquaintances, including the philosopher and writer William James, Henry's brother. William praised Duveneck's work on the effigy:

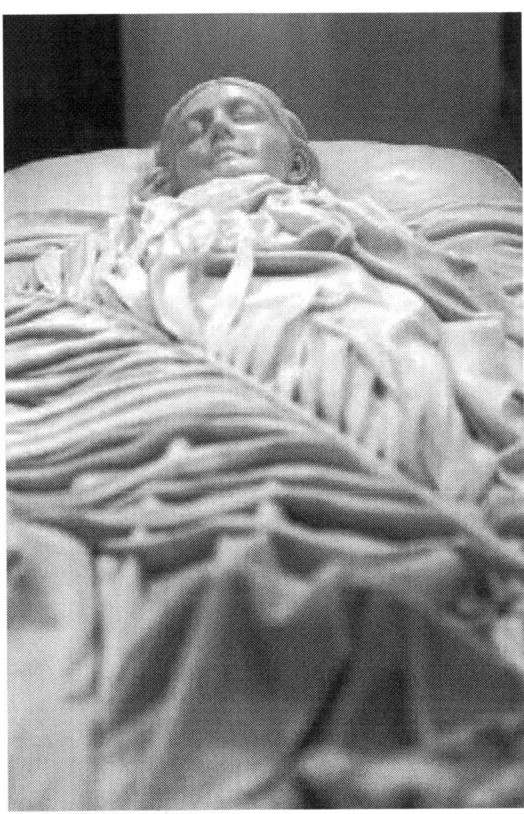

The effigy of Elizabeth in Boston.
-Photo by Lee Sandstead

"All I can say is that it is *beautiful, beautiful, beautiful*! The face with its solemn half-smile, the position of the head, the hands upon the somewhat flattened form as if sunk into the couch, the simple, delicate drapery, so modest and so real, the serenity and peace of the whole thing! It is a great work and a great monument, and I wish I could believe that our dear Lizzie herself took cognizance of it and knew that you had done it. It ought to make you very happy to have expressed in such a completed and permanent piece of work something of the feeling for her which has filled your heart. It will last after you too are gone, as one of the monuments of Florence which people go to see and it is better that, being a *painter*, you should have been able to do this thing than if you had done it being a sculptor. It is more particular and more exclusively for her."[9]

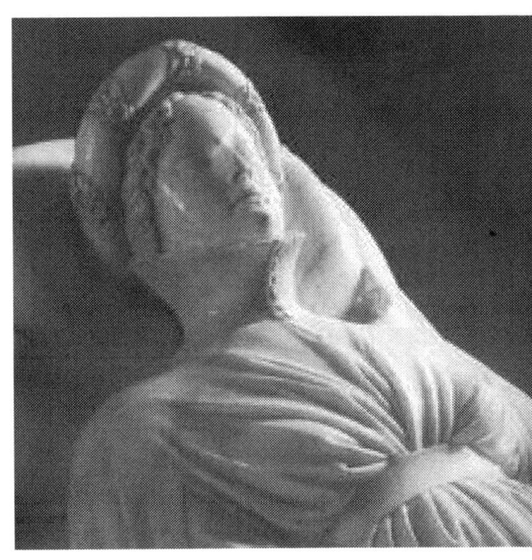

The effigy of Ilaria del Carretto
-Photo by Daniela Verzaro

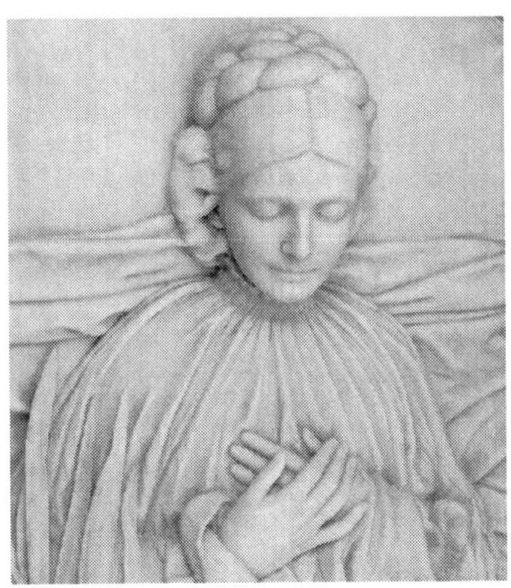

The effigy of Elizabeth
-Photo by Lee Sandstead

173

At first Henry James regarded the effigy as glaring and in bad taste. Later, after visiting the grave, James adopted a different view, according to his biographer, Edel, who summed up James's thoughts in this somewhat acidic manner, perhaps including his own: "He [Duveneck] envisioned her also as a knight's lady in death and so he posed her, recumbent with her hands folded on her breast amid flowing drapery...Today it is grey green and ghostly and Lizzie lies in her eternal sleep, her eyes closed to the Italian skies. Brown dry pine needles sift at certain seasons gently into the folds of the drapery."[10]

James assumed a philosophical and agreeable tone in his letter to Lizzie's father. "One sees in its place and its *ambiente,* what a meaning and eloquence the whole thing has—and one is touched to tears by this particular example which comes home to one so—of the jolly great truth that it is art alone that triumphs over fate."[11]

An Itinerant Traveler

Duveneck traveled considerably during the 1890s. He could afford it, having inherited Lizzie's, fortune which has been estimated variously at more than $600,000 and upwards of $1 million. She had owned shares of stock in Boott Mills and other American companies, which came to Duveneck as widower. The investments brought a steady income for the artist. He was never known as a spendthrift. His reputation had more to do with his generosity toward fellow students in his Munich days and later as a teacher when he quietly supported art students he regarded as capable.

The painter was in Venice in spring, 1894. He visited Florence and performed final work on the marble version of the effigy, returning to Venice where he spent much of the summer. Venice had been a preferred spot for Duveneck during his second stay in Europe in the late 1870s—it was where he first met Lizzie—and during his separation from Lizzie in the first half of the decade of the 'Eighties prior to their marriage. During Duveneck's lengthy 1894 stay Henry James reported that he had looked him up, presumably out of friendship, or curiosity, perhaps both. According to his daughter-in-law, Duveneck was painting fishermen and families in Chioggia and was planning a large canvas similar to one he had started several years previous at Villa Castellani. In any event James reverted to his critical view of the painter. He wrote to Francis Boott that Duveneck did not favor him "with the sight of a single stroke of his brush" and that he only displayed "the beauties of Chioggia and his robust and pleasant self." It may have escaped James that Duveneck had no desire to show him anything except perhaps cordial hospitality.

Later in 1894 Duveneck moved on to Paris. He reports in a February, 1895, letter that he enjoyed two pleasant experiences during his stay. He attended a dinner honoring Puvis de Chavannes on his 70th birthday, he, the French painter, muralist and founder of the Societe Nationale des Beaux Arts. The gala affair attracted five hundred artists and literary figures. Duveneck attended in the company of Julius Rolshoven. Secondly, he was privileged to see private art collections in the possession of two French patrons. These included works of Sir Joshua Reynolds, Thomas Gainsborough, Sir Thomas Lawrence, George Romney, John Constable and Richard Parkes Bonington. The number of J.M.W. Turner paintings in one collection exceeded that in the National Gallery of London, he wrote. Of Jean-Antoine Watteau paintings there were more than those owned by the Louvre.

From Paris, where he collected the Honorable Mention award from the Paris Salon, he traveled to Madrid with an early member of the Duveneck Boys, Charles Forbes, possibly Henry Sharp, the Cincinnati-based painter of American Indians, and Rolshoven. Over a two-month period they copied paintings of the Spanish school. Five large canvasses were completed by Duveneck; these were presented to the Cincinnati Art Academy. During this time he was given space to work in Arnold Bochlin's studio and Couper's in Florence, and Rolshoven's in Paris. All the while he continued to maintain studios in Boston, Cincinnati and in Gloucester. So accustomed to this near vagabond way of life, meeting with friends, staying a while here and there, when asked years later by a casual observer of Duveneck's works what kind of paint he used, his friend Barnhorn replied, "somebody else's."

Duveneck was not present in London in the early Nineties when John Singer Sargent uttered his famous praise, "After all's said, Frank Duveneck is the greatest talent of the brush of this generation." The well-known plaudit for Duveneck's skill came about in a discussion at a dinner party. Norbert Heermann, the former student recorded the words in his 1918 book. He wrote that guests were speaking of the merits of eminent men including the very artist who had instructed Sargent, Carolus-Duran, the portraitist of the Third Republic in France. Sargent's tribute would not be challenged by either artists or competent lay people of the day who understood technical expertise required of artists, according to Heermann. Those in the general public may have been surprised by it, coming from such a renowned artist, Heermann wrote. Duveneck's art was not widely accessible, though surely known within the confines of the art-loving community. Further, Heermann noted, students of painting best understand Duveneck's outstanding achievements with the brush.

Duveneck continued to travel later in the decade though his destinations tended to be in the United States. In 1895 he spent time in Boston and in Gloucester as well as in Cincinnati and Covington. "Duveneck's family in Covington was gratified by his return," biographer Josephine Duveneck wrote. "His half brothers and sisters were small town,* unenterprising (sic) people, apparently always sliding from one crisis to another. Poverty, ill health, improvidence, and irresponsibility seemed to follow them and their families, and they continually looked to the successful elder brother to extricate them from embarrassing situations." (A case in point is the plight of half-sister, Mary Catherine Duveneck, whom Duveneck nicknamed Mollie, the subject of the next chapter.) The painter used Mollie and several other family members, including the mother, as models for portraits. A room at the rear of the family home on Greenup Street, used as a laundry, was converted into a studio, complete with a northern-facing skylight.

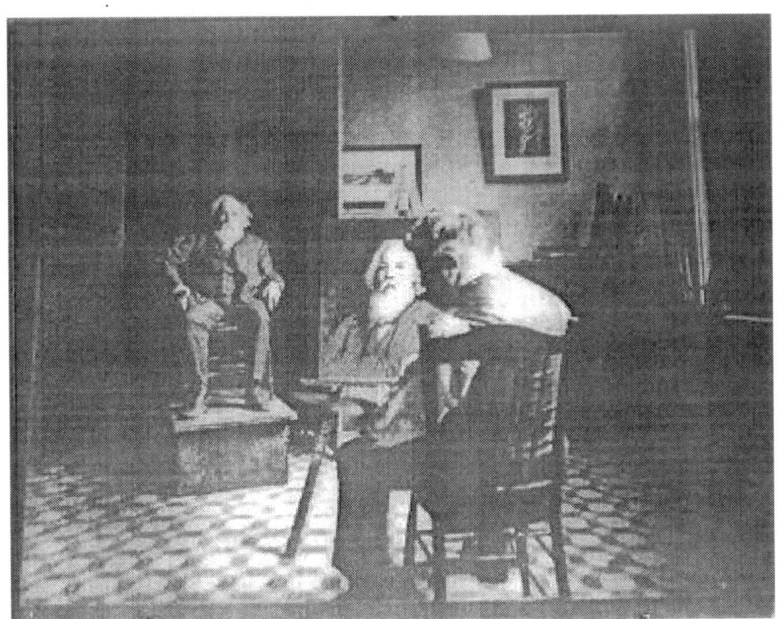

Duveneck at work in his Covington home.
-Courtesy of the Kenton County Public Library, Covington, Ky.

In 1896 the Society of Western Artists was formed in Chicago. By acclamation Duveneck was elected the first president. He felt uncomfortable in his role as presiding officer, writing to his father-in-law that "I had to face the music and do the best I could."[13] When Chicago artists invited the newly formed society to a banquet the next evening at the Art Institute, Duveneck squirmed in discomfort at the prospect of giving a talk. "I have never felt so sorry for myself that I could not make fine speeches, especially when I received such an unexpected ovation as I did that evening. I think that my whole history from early dawn was unveiled as a painter and my influence over young American artists, and in another speech I was held forth as a sculptor who has no equal in America. I was perfectly staggered and did not know what to say and then someone

177

got up and proposed to drink to the health of the American Phidias and the first President of the Society of Western Artists!"

Duveneck described speakers from other cities as good performers, but the Cincinnati artists attending, himself, Barnhorn and Louis H. Meakin could not match that output. Luckily, he wrote his father-in-law, that an easy speaker, Henry Farny, famous as a painter of American Indians, another Cincinnatian and sometime Covingtonian, showed up and gave a good representation for his hometown.

The family biographer wrote that Duveneck was incapable of exploiting the recognition given by his peers that night. "While he could tell a good story to a small intimate group, a larger audience seemed to freeze him. He shunned publicity, indeed he became extremely adept in outwitting newspaper reporters and ladies who desired to lionize him at their evening soirees." This attitude prevailed through the years. In a 1915 letter to Barnhorn, written around the time of the Panama-Pacific International Exhibition, where Duveneck received special honors, he wrote:

"I do not want to come in touch with any newspapermen. I have managed to keep out of their way so far but I was caught one day coming out of my hotel in S.F. I found a noisy picture machine pointing at me. I should like to pay a nickle to see it."[14]

Duveneck paid a penalty for this disdain for social networking, according to his daughter-in-law. "His diffidence in regard to the elite society in which Chase, and Sargent and other lesser men flourished and became known, cost him many desirable commissions and contacts which could have stimulated artistic creativeness." Mr. Boott, his father-in-law, was impatient with him on that account and expressed his opinion in a letter to him.

The painter responded:

"I do not mind in the least your criticism. Quite the contrary I am grateful for your kind interest in me and I think you have the right to express yourself as you like. It has always been the greatest puzzle to me why I should have to be contented with reputation only in America and nothing else and then have to see how mediocre men have every success they want. Only lately there was a man sent to me from West Virginia who was instructed to see me about having seven portraits painted of governors of that state for their State House and I was told that the retiring governor would soon come to Cincinnati and give me settings. I suppose that that will be much the same as other promises. However the present condition of the artist here or elsewhere has been hopeless for sometime (sic) and everyone is hoping for better times."

In his letter Mr. Boott must have brought up the sculptor, Daniel Chester French, and Duveneck responded. "You must not compare me with Mr. French. No sculptor outside of St. Gaudens and French need apply in Boston for any work unless it is by some extraordinary influence and that I do not have in Boston. All work that goes out from Boston for public monuments is done by invitation and to these two men only and if they cannot do the work they recommend their pupils. Some time ago you sent me a Boston Herald growing description of Mr. French's monument to Boyle O'Reilly of which I saw the original model in Chicago. All due credit to Mr. French's good work which he has done as well as any American of today could do, but his Boyle O'Reilly monument would not pass muster in the third class."[15]

Lizzie's death had sheared away for him her contacts with Boston society. Duveneck was "alone, and a westerner with relatively little education, among Boston blue-bloods, his only claim for acceptance was the somewhat tenuous relationship with the Lymans through the small boy growing up in their household." In the biographer's view, Duveneck's son, whom he visited multiple times each year, prevented the artist from returning to Europe and perhaps rediscovering his talent and pursuing new directions. Instead, he focused on his son and spoke frequently of his mother. "It was important for him to be able to share the dear reminiscences with his own flesh and blood and hers."

In this later period of the nineties he also began a series of studies of nude models, sketches and full-scale canvasses. Duveneck traveled to New York and to Chicago, responding to invitations to teach, and he conducted classes in each city. During a stay in New York in 1898 a cast of the effigy was exhibited by the National Sculpture Society and created much interest in Duveneck and his work. Afterward, officials of the New York Art Students' League and the Art Institute of Chicago asked him to take permanent assignments. The writers of the proposed Chicago contract even left blank a space where he could have filled in his own salary. But Duveneck declined the offers. He said there were plenty of capable artists in each city and officials there should choose from among them, as Cincinnati's arts community did with him.

Duveneck introduced to the Cincinnati arts scene the use of nude models. His own sketches served as examples for his students for learning. He completed fifteen to twenty sketches of models in standing, sitting or reclining poses. He also used pastels to create a near life-size rendering of a sleeping nude woman. He called it "Siesta." A Cincinnati tavern and restaurant owner, Theodore Foucar, bought the work for $250 and put it up in the bar room where only male patrons could see it. In time word spread about the enticing picture of a beautiful woman, leading women to look upon it as improper and agitated for its removal.

Foucar was offered $25,000 for the pastel work, a hundred-fold multiple in price. He declined the offer. "When the good women of a town get on the warpath, a wise man heads for the tall timber," he was quoted as saying. "So I decided to play a little joke on them and give the picture to the Art Museum. That girl was too naked for my saloon, but she was not too naked for high society."[16]

---

[1]Mrs. Storer was an aunt of Nicholas Longworth IV, Speaker of the U.S. House of Representatives (1923-1931) and the husband of Alice Roosevelt.

[2]*Frank Duveneck, Painter-Teacher*, Josephine Whitney Duveneck, John Howell Books—San Francisco, p. 130

[3]Interview with Orie Ware, former U.S. congressman, deceased

[4]*Frank Duveneck, Painter-Teacher*, Josephine Whitney Duveneck, John Howell Books—San Francisco, p.130

[5]Ibid, p. 140

[6]Report in the *Cincinnati Times-Star*, July 7, 1891

[7]Letter from Couper, a Duveneck student who remained in Florence, Archives of American Art, Duveneck Collection.)

[8]*Frank Duveneck, Painter-Teacher,* Josephine Whitney Duveneck, John Howell—Books, San Francisco, p. 127

[9]From Private Grief to Public Monument, the Funerary Effigy of Elizabeth Boott Duveneck, *Italian Influence in American Art*, p. 205.

[10]Henry James, The Middle Years: 1882-1895, Leon Edel, J.B. Lippincott Company, New York, 1962, p. 248

[11]"Frank Duveneck & Elizabeth Boott Duveneck: an American Romance," Carol M. Osborne, 1995-1996, p. 30, an essay for the catalogue of Duveneck exhibition, February12-March 24, 1996, Owen Gallery, New York.

[12]Ibid, p.13

[13]*Frank Duveneck, Painter—Teacher,* Josephine W.Duveneck, John Howell—Books, San Francisco, p. 133

[14]Letter is maintained by the Archives of American Art, Smithsonian Institution, Washington, D.C.

[15]Frank Duveneck, Painter-Teacher, Josephine W. Duveneck, John Howell—Books, San Francisco, p.134

[16]Ibid, p. 136

Chapter Nine

A Family Affair

Cincinnati, late spring, 1895

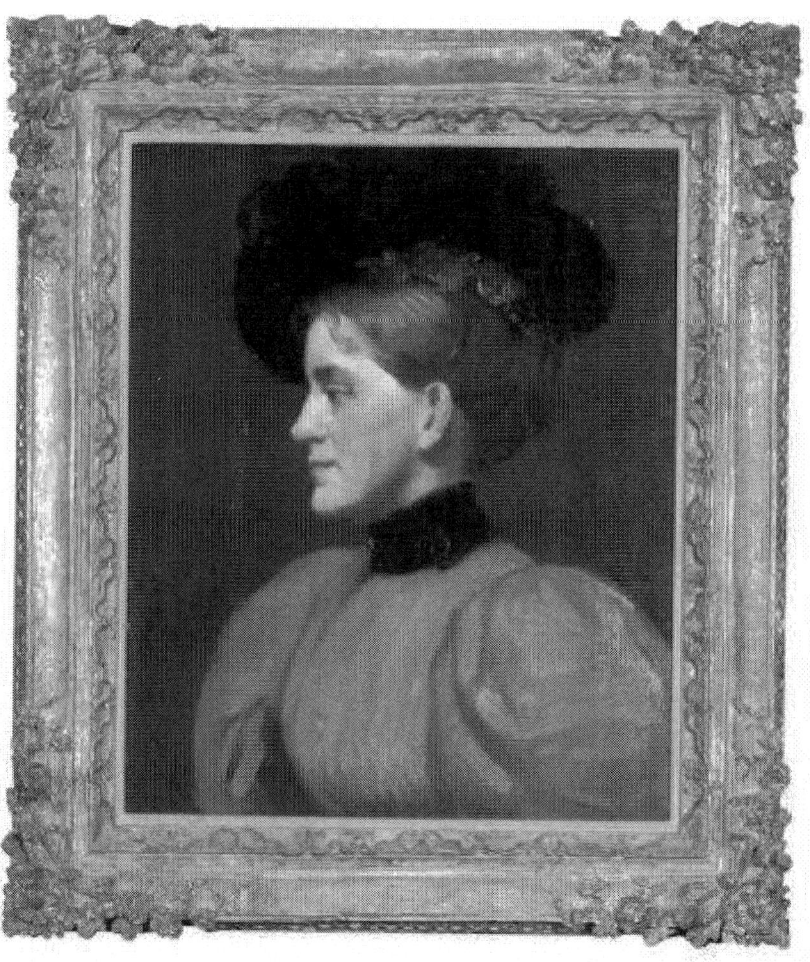

Mollie ,Duveneck, a profile portrait by Frank Duveneck
-Courtesy of the Kenton County Public Library, Covington, Ky.

On an evening in rough-and-tumble Cincinnati, Mollie, Frank's youngest half-sister and his favorite in the family, was seen in the company of a much older man. She was an attractive twenty-six years old, blonde and buxom. The man was nearly fifty, dressed as a business executive with his paunch pulling at his vest. People who saw them said the age difference could easily have mistaken them for father and daughter. But it was just as obvious that their relationship wasn't filial. Mollie was enjoying a night out with Presley J. Forsyth, a coal man from Pittsburgh, and she tried to keep it a secret. When her love affair was revealed, the news was to strike at the Duveneck family with the force of a howling Highland gale.

Mollie's affair came at a particularly difficult time for the Duvenecks in Covington. The U.S economy, if not much of the world's, still flagged from the deep financial depression of 1893. Frank, as an heir of his wife's fortune, was in a position to support his mother, and it's apparent that he did. In January of 1895 Frank was living at 7 rue Scribe in Paris. He was working and preparing to submit the effigy of Elizabeth to the Paris Salon, visiting occasionally with old friends and former students. His friend, the sculptor Clement Barnhorn, then in Paris studying and living a bare bones existence, was his most frequent contact. They dined together, almost weekly, and legend has it, Duveneck picked up the tabs for the impecunious Barnhorn.

"All the boys from Cincinnati live in another part of Paris and quite a distance from my place so of course I see them rarely," he wrote to his brother-in-law, Harry Niehaus in a letter dated January 31. "I have a number [of] old friends within my neighborhood but they are all married so of course they have little times outside of their work and family…" Duveneck's real reason for writing Niehaus was his concerns for the family, particularly the welfare of his mother. In a nice way his letter makes it clear he was putting the bite on Niehaus while he was away. Furthermore, a bit of gossip he had heard from brother, Charlie, had disturbed him.

"I regularly get letters from Charlie but I am in doubt if he would give it quite as well as you could," he wrote to Niehaus in an obvious entreaty for him to see that his mother's needs were being met. "I suppose that Charlie and Mollie make ends meet at home, and John," he added, "of course has always the rough end of it."

The more immediate and sensitive problem lay with his half-brother, Joe, who had fallen on hard times due to gambling debts and had been asking family members and Mother Duveneck for cash to pull him out of his dilemma. In the letter Duveneck advised against bankrolling Joe to repay such debts. "I must say I was most disturbed to hear this. I knew that his father used to be in the habit of paying gambling debts but I thought that he had grown old enough by this time to have more sense and self respect."

Duveneck said he knew that Niehaus and his wife, Josephine, his half-sister, kept close personal relations with Mother Duveneck, and he expressed hope that they would keep him better informed of family matters. He also wrote that he understood the financial pressures on the family had dated to his father, Squire's death. He also knew that the 1893 depression had its impact on his finances as well. "My financial affairs have not been very flourishing since the long business crisis and my expenses are rather heavy here."

Then, at the height of Mollie's spring scandal, another blow fell. Duveneck's letter of April 7, 1895, to the same brother-in-law, Harry Niehaus, tells the sad tale.

My dear Harry

Your cable with the very bad news of Josephine's death has just reached me. I have just been to the telegraph office to send you a few words of sympathy. I am so overcome by this sad news that I do not know what to say to express my sorrow and sympathy. I can hardly make myself believe that truth of it. It is an awful sad blow for you. I know from my own experience of but a few years ago and I am sure that the loss to Mother is unparalleled as you know that Josephine was her favorite. I think that this loss of the whole family would not have been so great a sorrow for her. However, I hope that you will…take this sad blow philosophically as I had to do. My heart and sympathy is with you all.

Believe me, very sincerely yours,

Frank Duveneck

The death of beloved sister Josephine had struck a chord with the artist, recalling the loss of his wife seven years earlier and renewing that pain. The suddeness of Josephine's departure compared with Elizabeth's brief illness and death. And, more was to come to compound Duveneck's grief. Still, he had plans to go to Madrid and notified the bereaved brother-in-law that his letters would be forwarded to 19 Calle Mayor in the Spanish capital. When he arrived in Madrid, he received a letter from Charlie that provided additional details, a clipping from a newspaper regarding the death, and then another letter from Harry Niehaus. The new information allowed him to make an assessment of what had caused her demise. He wrote this to Niehaus:

By this I could make up my mind what may have happened. It is the same story that happens over and over again but women will never learn to know better. I know that medical science is of no avail when such troubles set in. I remember that when my wife was confined she was not allowed to or leave her bed before the end of 40 days and she had to be guarded all this time for fear that she would not obey these orders. However, it is over now and we must content ourselves with events whichever way they come but then [the] blow is a hard one for us all and the conditions surrounding on your side seem to make it especially sad. I am fully appreciative and sympathize with you from my own experience which seems almost identical…

On a personal note Duveneck told of his going to the Prado gallery in Madrid with Charles Forbes, one of the original Duveneck Boys,

185

and with a second artist, possibly the American Indian painter Joseph Henry Sharp, copying the masters of Spanish art. He also had plans to head south and with stops at Gibraltar and later London. He said he was hoping to visit an exhibit in London that featured portraits of children. It's not certain whether he was able to pursue these goals as Mollie's indiscretions during those spring months would bring another family crisis to a head.

Mollie was acting out of character. The youngest female in the family and loved by all, she had eluded the role of home daughter that tradition had asked of her. In that role, she would have devoted herself exclusively to the care of the aging mother and served as the major domo around the house. Instead, perhaps due to the family's financial strains, she had taken a job as sales clerk at the Alms & Doepke department store in Cincinnati on Canal Street, now Central Parkway, which paralleled the Erie Canal. She may have met Forsyth at the department store. Wherever they met, most assuredly she responded to his overture and soon the affair was outed. The gossip was juicy as Forsyth had a wife back in Pittsburgh and was the father of four. Soon, word crossed the Ohio River and passed into Covington's Helentown.

For the coal man on business in Cincinnati spending time with Mollie no doubt injected excitement into a life of fading dreams after three decades or more running offices and beating the drum for contracts. He wrote her that he loved her more than his own life. The roller coaster sequences of the entire affair including Mollie's pledge to Frank that she would forget Forsyth, and her going back on her word, are contained in a cache of letters found behind a brick on a wall of a staircase leading to the Duveneck House attic. Folded carefully in a cigar box, the letters were written by Forsyth, Frank Duveneck and a Boston woman student of his. Also included were several fading photographs and a registered parcel receipt that stands as evidence of Mollie's betrayal. The letters allow the painter to be seen in a new light that broadens the view of him as a decent man motivated by love. Forsyth comes to life in this character-revealing drama the letters disclose. His story, pieced together from interviews and official documents in Pittsburgh, needs some illumination.

Mollie's Man

Forsyth was born in or near Uniontown, Fayette County, Pennsylvania, on September 1, 1845. His name is not among Civil War veterans. He started early in the coal business with a company in Coal Center and ran the firm after the owner died. He was later connected with several coal companies around Pittsburgh and handled payroll in a job he held when he was visiting and writing Mollie. If he at all resembled the Forsyth clans scattered through Pennsylvania, sketched and photographed in county histories, he struck a handsome figure. Of Scottish descent and likely tall and thin-faced, he may have been a novelty to Mollie who inherited the blonde, often golden, look of the northern Europeans and the tendency as they aged toward plumpness.

In the Nineties the coal business was hard for everyone from miner to shipper to salesman. The 1893 depression had wiped out many independent operators who both mined and shipped coal taken from the massive Pittsburgh seam. The independents fielded squads of sales people who managed clients downriver. Once a deal was struck, coal was shipped in specially constructed wood boats and barges pushed by paddlewheel towboats decorated with favored insignia, such as anchors, shields, and in one case, a Maltese cross. On favorable sailing days when the Ohio River was high and flowing—this was before the series of dams were to tame and smooth out the sometimes wild river—boats stretched for a hundred miles heading downstream, fields of black coal heaped in barges. The days of these independents, however, were numbered. Railroads were spreading in the region carrying coal from inland mines in Kentucky and West Virginia to the river cities. By 1911, all maritime independents were gone.

Forsyth was in the middle of this environment. Competition for sales was stiff among surviving independents. He dealt with officials of local companies to obtain contracts for deliveries that necessitated frequent trips from Pittsburgh. Though he was an office man he carried the title, captain, perhaps part of his sales pitch, though the U.S. Coast Guard did not list him as a pilot of a river vessel. He could have earned that title earlier in his career, but there is no way to confirm it. Whether captain, office manager or coal salesman, the Duvenecks didn't want Forsyth seeing Mollie. He was too old for her and was married, which ran contrary to religious beliefs, especially those of the mother. There's no evidence that Mother Duveneck was the chief instigator in the family's campaign against Forsyth, but one can easily detect her hand in what transpired next.

How the word reached the Duveneck House is not clear. It wasn't long afterward that someone, likely the mother, enlisted the help of son Frank, then in Boston, to argue the family's case. Frank dutifully communicated with Mollie. There's an indication in one of Forsyth's letters to her that she may have moved from her home during the affair, but it is not clear and probably unlikely. In any case, it was decided that she should spend the summer with her brother in Gloucester. To Frank, the eldest, fell the responsibility of persuading Mollie to mend her ways and see the light. She was supposed to forget P.J. Forsyth.

Gloucester Exile

When Frank met Mollie at the Boston train station in the summer, the joy of reunion removed any bitterness or embarrassment over Mollie's amours. Assuming that the sister's affair had disquieted him, Frank had the advantage of distance. He had not been involved personally in any daily polemics in the parental home, the kind that serve to widen the emotional breadth, harden positions and destroy any hope of resolution. He probably wanted to hear Mollie's story in person.

Frank and Mollie had a strong foundation to build upon. Their relationship was bolstered by the full magnetism of strong family ties.

He nicknamed her Mollie, though she was christened Mary Catherine. She had a deep respect for his talent and was awed by his connections in New England and his international success. Further, she was sympathetic with his personal losses, the death of his spouse and dislocation of his son, which strengthened these bonds.

Frank's affection for Mollie was expressed in the tone of a letter from Europe dated February 11, 1893, more than two years before the affair.

He wrote:

Dear Sister Mollie,

Your letter of Jan 19th reached me a few days ago with the enclosed letter from Miss Wadsworth.[1] By the same mail came also a long letter from Miss Wadsworth. Miss W- expresses herself much pleased of receiving a good letter from you and, I quite agree with her, that you ought to enjoy writing letters because you write well and with constant practice you would soon make a first class letter writer.
Shortly after Christmas I also received your sole [The letter contains a drawn outline of a shoe sole] and curiously enough I received the same thing from my little boy, I am glad you thought of sending something to my boy who, I hear, was much pleased. Bessie[2] writes me that the cap is too small. You may remember that his head is larger than the average boy of his age. I also received a nice long letter from Mrs. Lyman describing the various presents that baby received on Christmas and of course Mr. Boott writes constantly so I am informed within short intervals of all that goes on in Boston. Mrs. Lyman also writes that Bessie is much more contented since her visit to her home. I was glad to hear that you had some festivities on Christmas but I am very sorry to hear what you have to say about Kate. I heard from Charlie of her illness but he did not make it quite so serious as you do. I am anxious to hear further news and hope she has fully recovered. I should

189

like to hear something about Lizzie? No one has anything
to say about her.
I am glad you gave me some account of many matters at home
which seems to be going pretty good. You don't say whether
your money (that you made at the store) was also used. I hope
not. I hope you will let me know in time when mamma's money
runs out. I should think, that, in case she needs money she
might be able to get a couple of hundred dollars from
Mrs. Ackerman as she has done sometime (sic) ago, but, I should
advise not to take any at the bank at such a high percentage
as they normally charge. I will straighten out her debts when
I get home. I may not get home next autumn as I should like
to stay over for a good summer's work and at the same time I
expect to be on hand to look after my marble cutting if I
can get marble to have the work done during the summer.
My monument for the cemetery is still delayed owing to granite
which has not arrived as yet but the bronze has been finished
some time ago. I am in hopes of having this straightened out
before the first of March and then I shall start off for a
trip to Rome and Naples and possibly cross over to Sicily.
Sicily is an island about 100 miles from Naples. If you will
look on the map you will find it and get some idea of its
location. Sicily is a place I always wanted to see and as I
have a chance of having a friend go with me it can only be
a pleasant trip. I have been considerably troubled with a
cold the last six weeks and I want to get into some warm
climate. We have had quite a cold winter for Florence although
it's not so cold as it is in America but one is apt to feel
the cold here much more because the houses have no stoves. I
read in the papers of the severe winter in America and I was
in hopes of hearing something about (it) from either you or
Charlie but you both have nothing to say about it. Mr. Boott
writes of the severe winter in Boston but says that the little
boy does not seem to mind it. I am afraid Mr. Boott must feel
very gloomy to hear of his many old friends dying over here.
We have just buried one of his most intimate friends

Mrs. Huntington. I also hear that a great friend of his,
Mrs. Green, has just died in Paris.
I may be away from Florence for about two months and then
return here on my way to Venice for a good summer's work. I
am still puzzled to know what to do with all my things. I
think of getting rid of the large pieces and then send off
the rest to America but I am afraid that storage will be
rather high after I get them out there and I have no places
otherwise to put them. Then to send the whole lot over would
be too expensive and I am not making any money now to risk
much expense.
You say nothing about the prospects for Charlie. I suppose
he is about the house looking after chickens. I hope Joe
will try and do something for him in the way of getting a
place for him.
La John is on the move again or, nothing out of the move.
I wish he would keep out of the factory and try and do
something else.
Tell Josephine not to forget to write me again. She started
in well with a couple of letters but it is now some time ago
when I last heard from her.
Hoping that you are well and you will let me hear from you
again. Address the same as before, all letters are forwarded
on to me.

Affectionately your brother
Frank

Her older brother was speaking when he referred to Mollie's ability to write letters and with his comment "with constant practice
you would soon make a first class letter writer." Duveneck realized, too, that Mollie was interested in his work, and he detailed to
her his plans and hopes for the spring and summer. Moreover, he
found in Mollie a correspondent for news of the family.

Duveneck's work and no doubt his desire to see his son, then seven years old, kept him in Boston and nearby Gloucester in the summer of 1895, but his responsibility to the family brought the invitation to Mollie. What was Mollie thinking about when she rode the train through Ohio, possibly through Forsyth's Pittsburgh with its coal barges and smoking stacks, and then through to New York and Boston. The trip filled her with the pleasure of getting away, visiting with Frank, perhaps his wife's family, and his artist friends, and seeing the ocean for the first time. The rhythm of the sea, the warm seaside winds and the limitless horizon were like another world for her. Even though torn at the possible prospect of facing admonishments from her beloved brother, Mollie probably decided to be herself and enjoy the visit wrapped in the security offered by the famous artist. She would love every minute of it because Frank was someone who cared. She dreaded the possibility of admonishments for her behavior, but alternatively she knew that her affair was beneath what was expected of her.

How long Mollie remained and whatever happened in East Gloucester can only be a matter of speculation. Frank had an armful of arguments against Mollie's continued affair with Forsyth, arguments strengthened by her respect. Surely they visited the nearby coves including Folly Cove where Duveneck painted and captured the ferocity of the waves slamming against the rocky shore and strolled through Gloucester harbor, another subject for the painter. The harbor, with its rustic docks, sheds, gleaming sailboats and dories and its fleet of commercial fishing vessels, provided a new setting for her thoughts of what she should do. It's likely that Frank alluded to his own heart-rending courtship problems. In the broad category of courtship issues, they at least had that much in common.

To Mollie, Frank's life was a model. And the tragedies that had beset him with the loss of his wife, his brotherly love and the aura of the new and exciting place and new people must have combined to cast a humbling influence on her. She told Frank at the conclu-

sion of her Gloucester sojourn that she would indeed forget P.J.
Forsyth. The summer over, she departed for home.

All seemed in order

Mollie wrote to Frank in late September.
He responded with his own letter, dated October 2, 1895, from
East Gloucester:

My Dear Sister Mollie,

I felt very thankful to receive your first letter after this long
lapse of time. I cannot help thinking of what has happened since
I last received a letter from you and it will be a long time before
I will get over it and I partly blame myself for having been away
so long for it would have never happened if I had stayed at home.

Fortunately no great harm has been done although I thought differently when we came here and I was very much worried from the
fact that I would not get you to say anything different one way or
another but I was glad when I finally learned that all was right. I do
now hope dear Mollie that your final decisions will hold good and
you will determinently (sic) set your face against this man. It will
not be easy I know perfectly well considering your long association with him and I know your soft heart is easily tempted and he
knows that too perfectly well and will do his best to get you into
his clutches again.

He has had an easy game of it in the face of your brothers and will
try it again. I could not handle him as it was of all and most important to gain your confidence, which you know I tried so hard,
and bring you out of the chance of publicity. I think now that I may
happily say that your promises will stand for good. The rest I will
see to by and by. What I know nobody will ever hear of and what
little those few who know (who helped me in this matter) will be

193

of no blame to you and you will never hear anything about it through them so please do not be worried about that.

You will please excuse my going over this matter again. My mind will not rest and how could it after all my experience. How could it be otherwise when you know how fond I always have been of you and how much I love you and always wanted to do the best that I could for you. I will say no more now and we will hope for the best in the future.

I hope that you will find your place of business pleasant to you and satisfactorily arranged.

I was glad to hear that you found all well at home. After leaving you at the station Saturday morning I took the first train back to Gloucester. I found Mr. Wendel had not called for his letters at the Maitman's[2] so I started off with them for Folly Cove but when I got to the station I met Wendel coming this way. Of course he had not got my postal (sic) and therefore did not know that you had departed which surprised him very much. We returned together to Maitman's and he stayed overnight. Sunday morning we started together for Folly Cove where he wanted me to take wild duck dinner with him which he had previously arranged. There were thousands of ducks flying about at Folly Cove and in the afternoon we started in a dory and provided with all the necessaries to have good shooting but somehow our dory sprang a leak and then a strong wind set in that took us a couple of miles out too far so we had to work a couple of hours hard to get back and of course had no chance at shooting. I came back here in the evening—almost everybody has departed from East Gloucester and with the very cold winds these last few days makes this place very dismal and lonesome. I have been trying to hide myself back of rocks and fences to work in sheltered places from the wind but it is almost too cold to do anything.

I shall probably stay here until Friday when I can go to town and draw some money and will then go back to stay. Mr. Boott worries so much about studios that I had better take that studio we saw the other day together. He seems to be afraid that if I don't find a studio I shall probably run away. I hear from him today that Frankie has a bad cold and also Mrs. Greenough and that his other sister Mrs. Loring is quite sick at the shoals so they could not have their prospective meeting at Cambridge.

Please let me hear from you very soon again.

Your affectionate and loving brother

Frank

I enclose a card which came yesterday.

All had seemed in order for Frank once again. Mollie had pledged to her brother that she would resist Forsyth. Frank alluded to her place of business, indicating perhaps that she had returned to work at Alms & Doepke. It is implied in Frank's letter that he had solicited help in an investigation of Forsyth's background and found damaging personal information. Duveneck presented this information to Mollie, its precise nature unknown. It had the intended effect. He exacted the pledge from Mollie.

A parcel signals a restart

In this new atmosphere of hope, however, Mollie's duplicity is fully bared. She commits herself to a pledge and breaks it almost in the same breath. While still at Gloucester on September 24, 1895, Mollie sent a registered parcel to P.J. Forsyth of Pittsburgh. Was it to have been the last communication between them? Given the evidence was what transpired in the next few weeks, the parcel was taken by Forsyth as a sign that Mollie had withstood the greatest pressure the family could exert against her—the personal force of her famous brother.

The Duveneck family strategy, with Frank as the attacking knight, failed to checkmate Forsyth. On the contrary, he had an open field in which to work. Mollie could resist her family, but not Forsyth. She returned to him in spite of family accusations. Their chief argument, that she was hurting herself and them, bothered her certainly. However they portrayed her affair in moral terms, Mollie pressed these concerns from her mind and ignored her promises. She had found in Forsyth what she had been looking for.

Forsyth played his game well. He knew how to approach Mollie and what to write about in his letters. He signed with his initials, P.J.F., on borrowed stationery from a coal company and used some writing papers from a Pittsburgh hotel, whether out of thrift or elusiveness, it is not known. He wrote her on Halloween night, October 31, that he was glad she was home safe and that she was "happy for that is the most of my trouble & worry about you & Dear it always make me very happy & contented to know these things & anything I can do to keep you happy will be done no matter what it (is). I am so caught up in you that your happiness is a great thing to me."

Rain fell heavily that night and "I hope it will continue until we get a rise in the river & business will commence again," her lover wrote.

Mollie's affair was entering a new and more intense phase. The vacation to Gloucester separated the early stages of Mollie's relationship with Forsyth and this apparently new chapter in which Forsyth confessed that "I am so caught up in you..." The rains came as Forsyth had hoped. The Ohio River swelled and the Port of Pittsburgh came alive with coal boats and barges preparing to head downriver. The first chance he got, Forsyth booked passage to see Mollie. In all likelihood, he rode one of the paddle wheelers en route to Cincinnati pushing a shipment of coal and gave thought of the times ahead with his darling Mollie.

Forsyth and Mollie met in early November in Cincinnati. The word got out, prompting a scolding letter from her brother Frank. Writing on Tavern Club stationery, address, 4 Boylston Place, dated November 12th, 1895, he was brief and demanding.

My Dear Sister Mollie,

There never was a sadder moment for me than yesterday morning
when I received two letters from Cincinnati to tell me that
that man was in Cincinnati and that you had been seen in his
company again.
 I wrote you a few lines at once to give a little expression
of my feeling but I suppose it makes very little difference
to you whether I write a few lines or more or express any
feeling considering the amount of anxiety that I have gone
through and the trouble this affair has given me. I did feel
much encouraged and hopeful since your return home from your
affectionate letter and the favorable account that I had from
Charlie. If there ever was a thoroughly disheartened man in
Boston you could see one today in your brother Frank. I do
not remember when I last felt tears running down my face
except last summer and that was on your account too. I did hope
last summer that when that man's position towards you would
be explained that in time you would feel that he had
no honorable intention towards you that you would come to
your senses and understand it and everybody was willing to put the
blame on the man alone but now this thing looks entirely
different unless you explain yourself.

Of course if you persist in going on in this way I must
make up my mind for the worst and I am about beginning to fear
the worst and I am getting ready for it. I cannot write any more
now but I demand an answer to this by the next mail or I will

take the train home.

Your affectionate brother
Frank

Please write me at once for I feel miserable and an explanation
will ease my mind.

Distance no longer kept Duveneck from an emotional involvement
with Mollie's love affair. She had deceived, and to Frank
Duveneck deception was a greater sin than promiscuity. His own
sister had lied to him and "that man" had bested him in a duel for
her virtue. The news that she "had been seen in his company
again" crushed Duveneck, bringing him to tears. (The ink is
smeared on the original letter, the result perhaps of Duveneck's
tears.) He demanded an answer.

Either Mollie responded to Duveneck's letter convincingly or it
was that other, more pressing responsibilities forced Duveneck to
remain in the Boston area. For one reason or another, Duveneck
didn't return to Covington at this time. But for Mollie and P.J.,
there was still the family to contend with.

A Police Case

Summer indiscretions had metamorphosed into winter's willful-
ness. The family onslaught began days before she had received the
letter from Frank. She had broken her promise and betrayed her
family, that was that, and something had to be done about it. Now
that Frank's intervention had failed, the family was hard pressed
on what to do. They had in their possession one of the letters that
Forsyth wrote to Mollie and had asked her to visit him in Pittsburgh. Believing they had evidence of wrong-doing, they sought
help from the police. They managed an appointment with Colonel
Philip Deitsch, chief of the Cincinnati Police Department.

Deitsch was sympathetic but set them straight on a legal point. The suggestion of a visit was in itself not evidence of wrongdoing. He was willing to help and agreed to send a letter to the Pittsburgh Police Department asking its aid. Deitsch thought there was a remote chance that a bluff might scare Forsyth away. The police in Pittsburgh felt the same way; at least they informed Deitsch they would give it a try.

Meanwhile, Mollie wrote back to Forsyth and told of her troubles, detailing renewed family pressure and exposing Forsyth to the dangers of the affair. Up to this point Mollie had to deal with the day-to-day distresses. Now Forsyth faced opposition in Cincinnati and in Pittsburgh. He wrote Mollie on November 23 saying he was "worried & grieved that you are having such a hard time of it." And, he informed her of what happened to him. The Pittsburgh police chief had summoned Forsyth to his office several days previous. The chief waved a letter from Chief Deitsch and questioned him about his relationship with Mollie.

"He asked me how old you was & if I had called on you. I told
Him I had taken you out to Dinner or Supper & to the Theater
in fact the letter was nothing but a bluff as he said that if I
did not quit I might get into trouble. I said I did not see how
& he said he did not know & that was all there was of it.

Forsyth wrote that he consulted a lawyer who bolstered his confidence that, from a strictly legal standpoint, there was no ground for prosecution. And, he wrote to Mollie that he wanted to come to Cincinnati for a day for the purpose of meeting her, no doubt to commiserate and offer his encouragement. He suggested meeting at Otto Schwind's Café at Corwine and Vine Streets.

In truth the police were helpless without evidence of a violation of the law. Knowing this, Forsyth wouldn't scare away. But his contact with the police served a purpose. It brought him into the fray. He was having his share of other troubles, too; one can only speculate on the discontent he encountered from his wife in nearby Coal Center. Indeed, Mollie had company in her misery and ties to her lover were reinforced.

Forsyth's letter must have read reassuringly in other aspects. He adopted a tone of concern for her. He promised to meet her in Cincinnati if she wanted and needed him, even on Thanksgiving Day, an arrangement having its own implications for Forsyth and his family in Coal Center. He concluded his letter with the pledge: "If I knew you could be happy I think I could give up anything in the world for your sake." The words had to be soothing for Mollie. Furthermore, Forsyth put Mollie on her guard against the family's pressure to quit her job at Alms & Doepke. He realized that Mollie's position gave her that measure of freedom that released her into his hands. She should keep her job at all costs, he told her, for if the family kept her home they would make her life miserable.

It's not known whether Forsyth met Mollie at Schwind's on Thanksgiving, only that Mollie wrote him in mid-December, pouring out her troubles once again.

His reply, written on her twenty-seventh birthday December 18, was short and soul-stirring.

"...I had fully made up my mind to kill myself & end all our troubles for I have been so miserable that I just could not stand it any longer for My Dear I realize that they are going to part us for if they can not (sic) do it one way they will another." He told her of a dream in which his late mother appeared and remonstrated that he would be taking the coward's way out, presumably committing suicide. Then, he wrote that she, Mollie, came into his dream, sat on his lap and put her arms around his neck. In the dream he said to his lover, "I will never desert you or give you up."

This was a crucial time for Forsyth. His life, well into its autumn, had been brightened by a relationship with a young woman and darkened by the prospect of society taking it away. One could offer the interpretation that Forsyth reported his inner conflicts only to impress or to frighten Mollie. He could have done so to receive more attention. Yet of all his available letters this one bears the stamp of sincerity. He moves from the deepest of despair to the heights of resolve. He knew his relationship with Mollie was in danger of ending. Truly, it was heading for a last gasp.

Affair's Last Days

The genial atmosphere of the Christmas season, 1895, in Cincinnati echoed around Mollie, but it could not reach her innermost being. She worked perfunctorily behind an Alms & Doepke counter, offering courteous greetings to customers, her face a mask to the roiling emotions of her psyche. At lunch with her friend, Miss Dreifus, a sales clerk, she could recount her feelings toward Forsyth. Willingly or unwittingly, her friend had served as a go-between for the couple. In one of his letters she was named as a potential messenger who would give Mollie a message from him.

Mollie was betwixt and between. The drumfire of her family against Forsyth had weakened her. She had no defense for her actions. Moreover, the family held certain information about him which she found dismaying. She worried whether he was as vile as they were making out. Was he taking advantage of her? Did she love him? Was the strife worth it? The questions benumbed her, and the affair draining her spirit. Her life had mutated into an emotional roller coaster. Forsyth's visits were irregular and short-lived. Their few more recent hours together found them at the theater or in Vine Street beer halls where they talked over their troubles. For the rest of it, correspondence kept them alive to one another. Mollie's spirits soared each time she opened a letter. Her moments with Forsyth carried the enchantment of romance. Left breathless by these encounters, her reward in due time was solitude, alone with her thoughts in her room, on the streetcar coming home, or in the family garden.

Christmas brought new problems. Her celebration of the season was rooted in her religion. Catholics prepared themselves spiritually for the holy day. They confessed their sins and received Holy Communion. This was the family way of life, yet this Christmas offered a choice, a different kind of life beyond the family. Could she, indeed, love a man in the teeth of the whole world? The holidays were times of great discomfort for Mollie, whichever way her choosing.

Forsyth's holiday posts were delivered by hand in envelopes addressed to Miss Mollie Duveneck. He had developed a personal postal system, with the help of friend, likely another coal man Marshall McDonald, named in his letters. In these letters Mollie's and Forsyth's roles reversed somewhat. As he became a victim, threatening suicide, Mollie moved into the role of comforter. She replied to him just before the holiday, and he replied pathetically.

"…I do not care so much what others say or think of me if I only knew that you do not think I could be what they make me out but if they would tell the truth I could stand that all right."

The letter reflects a turning point. Forsyth was on the defensive against the family's charges, and he feared that the opposition was having an impact. He troubled to make the trip to Cincinnati once again in the days after Christmas and managed to meet her "even if the time was so short…" Within a few days he was writing again from Pittsburgh, advising that they keep their own counsel on their meetings. He had set up a post office box where he directed her to send her letters.

In final communications in early 1896, Forsyth continued to pledge his undying love, but the tide had turned against him. In the cache's last dated letter he referred to the painter Henry Farny, a friend of Duveneck's, famous for his Indian paintings, saying that

"I am not sorry that Farney (sic) did not get the prize nor do I think you are. (not sorry)." In his parting message he wrote:

"I hope Dear when your brother arrives he will not scold you or say any more mean things to you & that you will still be very happy & that things will change for the better for us."

Frank Duveneck returned home in 1896. Mollie's affair was over.

New Directions

The aftermath of Mollie's contretemps appears to have been a period of settling out and settling down for all concerned. Forsyth changed jobs several times, left the coal business and took a post as manager of a saw mill in McKeesport, Pennsylvania. Mollie became the home daughter of tradition, centering her life on the Duveneck House and caring for the aging mother. Frank's life took an inward turn. Except for his routine trips to Boston and Gloucester, he spent most of his time in Cincinnati and Covington. He served as the second president of the Cincinnati Art Club, from 1896 to 1898, for that active group of art-loving people including many of his former students. In this same three-year period, the written record for the painter is slimmest, the lack of information almost mysterious.

What was he thinking about? He was approaching his fiftieth year, a time for introspection for many. His eyesight had failed him. "He had strained his eyes in Venice and Florence working long hours over his etching plates. Now he was forced to wear spectacles. The loss of visual acuity, combined with the remorse over his wife's death, were contributing factors in Duveneck's declining artistic productivity. He shied away from accepting commissions. He realized that the quality of his work had begun to deteriorate. Added to these physical and emotional factors was the absence of any financial need to produce. In Covington, removed from the mainstream

203

of artistic activity, Duveneck was content, for a time, to rest on his hard won laurels." [3]

When he had time he liked to join friends at Nougaret's wine house on Fourth Street in Cincinnati. Barnhorn was there, along with fellow artist and teacher Meakin, F. Hopkinson Smith, and, on occasion, two others who were to become famous, the architect Stanford White and the author Booth Tarkington. In 1906, White made Yellow Press fame as the shooting victim of one Harry Kendall Thaw, the jealous husband of Evelyn Nesbit, the glamour queen of the day with whom White years earlier had had an affair. Tarkington, the young writer from Indianapolis, became famous for winning the Pulitzer Prize for fiction for his novels, *The Magnificent Ambersons* and *Alice Adams.*

We can only speculate on Duveneck's state of mind. He continued to grieve the loss of his wife and was no doubt discontented with the abrogation of his life's promise with her and his son. Commissions were scarce, and he was facing a dry period, in terms of production, perhaps the longest of his entire career, lasting from 1896 through 1899. Chronologies of his life show a gap between 1895 and 1899. Few significant works of his art, among the more than six hundred and fifty located and known pieces of art in his lifetime canon, can be found dated during this period. It's almost as if his painting became a personal affair with himself and himself only.

Duveneck was not lost to the practice of art, however. Starting in 1897 he acted as a critic for a Sunday morning class sponsored by the Cincinnati Art Club. He built a studio in his mother's renovated laundry room that was a dirt-floor attachment to the rear of the living quarters. A northern-facing skylight was installed at one point, and one can see the angled roof there today. He chose a neighbor lady, Maggie Wilson, as his model, using her for six paintings over the next few years. In the summer of 1898 he painted *Profile of Maggie Wilson with Poppies in Her Hair,* and *Maggie Wilson in a*

Red Hat in the 1898-1900 time line. Also in 1898, he painted a portrait of Henry August Barnhorn, the twin brother of his friend, Clement Barnhorn. He also did portraits of family members, his mother (1902), a sister, a brother, and he used Mollie as a model over and again through the years.

Mollie usually accompanied Frank on trips to Boston and Gloucester. They returned to Covington late in the summer nearly every year. He carried a portfolio filled with sketches and paintings so that he could show his students that he had spent the summer "working." Their diversions were simple. Mollie liked playing cards, chatting with friends and taking rides in Charlie's automobile, which the Duvenecks purchased, one of the first automobiles in Covington.

His visits to Gloucester kept vigil of his talent, the Cape Ann region always an exciting place for anyone, the harbor, the wave-lashed coves and fisher folk, especially for a painter. In his many summers at Gloucester, ranging from several weeks to the entire summer season, he produced between sixty and one hundred land and seascapes and harbor views that depict a new turn in his artistic life.

Gloucester Inspires

Duveneck's Gloucester years range from the early 1890s to approximately 1917. His works represent a new style, highly influenced by Impressionism. The canvases are largely *plein air* landscapes such as *Folly Cove* and *Braces Rock*. Human figures are present in occasional portraits and in long views of activities, such as *Dock Works*. The paintings are colorful and vibrant, though not as warm as those of his Italian period, but sharply lighter than the figures of his early works of Realism, which were inspired by Dutch and Spanish master painters, Murillo and Ribera.

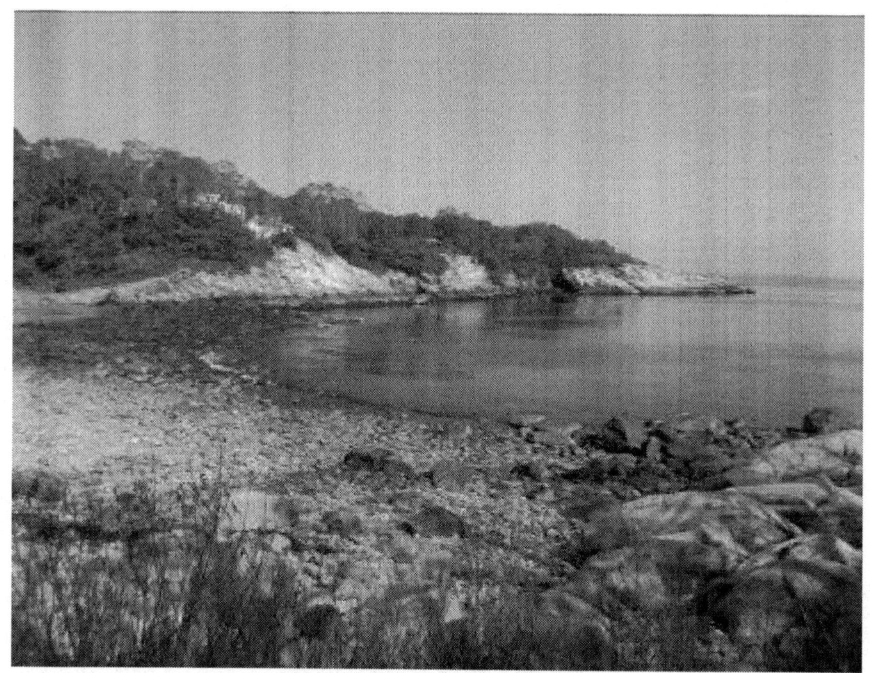

Folly Cove, a Gloucester subject for Duveneck.

"Shepherding his peripatetic classes across the European land-scape, however, he began to grow conscious of the properties of Impressionism, its concern with light, color theory and paint application. By the time he came to Gloucester, his palette had lightened considerably and acquired a blondish hue and he was more concerned with the enveloping atmosphere than with the dramatic effects of his works in the '70s and '80s."[4]

This critic, Robert Taylor of the *Boston Globe*, reviewed a 1987 Duveneck exhibit sponsored by the Cape Ann Historical Society and praised the painter's work from Gloucester's Banner Hill, which overlooks Smith Cove and Rocky Neck. "At their most conventional, these scenes disclose the right overly emphatic compositional framework of Duveneck's academic past; but at their lyrical best, *Moonrise, Tidelands, Gloucester, Dock Sheds at Low Tide,*

206

they have the dappled shimmer, the atmospheric poetry of an In-ness. *Tidelands* reveals Duveneck's success in enlivening surfaces through virtuoso echoes of touch across the composition, the hot sunlight of the greenish yellow foreground, the swift definitions of foliage and the Prussian blue stripe of the ocean against a high and hard-edged horizon. John Twachtman, one of Duveneck's students and represented here by a pearly Gloucester landscape, absorbed the same immediacy of effect. When a Duveneck landscape is wholly successful, the sequences of mobile brush marks integrate subject and effect."

In *Marine Rocks, Gloucester*, Duveneck's effort verges on the ab-stract. "The flat planar tans of the rocks and the interplay between the straight and curved with the ocean serving as a negative sug-gests that had Duveneck wished to take landscape one step further, he might have emerged 20 years ahead of himself. But, as it is, the pictorial relationships of this engrossing small show imply a nine-teenth century artist crossing the bridge into the early twentieth century."[5]

Martha Oaks, curator of the Gloucester exhibit (July 31-November 7, 1987), found an early connection to Impressionist painting in Duveneck's work dating from 1879 through 1888, most of which fell into his Italian period. "...his paintings began to reflect a new interest in the properties of light as well as more careful attention to the application of paint. She cites *Girl with Book* (1880) as dis-playing Duveneck's experimentation with new techniques, later refined by his Gloucester years. Another example is *Marine Rocks, Gloucester* (1893), which is characterized by broad, flat planes of color and an almost abstract rendering of the landscape..."[6]

Duveneck first visited Cape Ann with a group of students in the summer of 1890. This was the same time that he painted the por-trait of *Marie Danforth Page*, a student of Boston artist Helen M. Knowlton. Ms. Knowlton said of Duveneck's students that: "At times, the class work (sic) out of doors from a model, with results that are almost startling in their truth—their absolute freedom from tradition and conventionality."[7] The 1890 visit and subsequent summers in Gloucester have qualified Duveneck as a forerunner and founder of the Cape Ann artists' colony. Local artist Fitz Henry Lane, William Morris Hunt, Lizzie's Boston teacher, and Winslow Homer preceded him at Gloucester, Lane in the 1850s, Hunt in the 1870s and Homer in 1873 and in 1880. Duveneck's visits to Gloucester continued routinely until 1917, making him a pivotal figure in the growth of New England's first art colony in the Cape Ann region.

Son, Frank Jr., accompanied Duveneck in summer, 1892, to vacation at the old Niles farmhouse on Eastern Point. The house was located between the rocky coast and the open ocean on one side and Gloucester harbor on the other. Duveneck rented the idyllic retreat from a group of businessmen known as Eastern Point Associates. In later years, he stayed at Hotel Rockaway, Harbor View, Beachcroft and Hawthorne Inn as the area grew in popularity among artists. In his letter to Mollie he also mentioned Maitman's.

In 1900 Duveneck lived at the Rockaway and attended a concert and art exhibit in August of that year. He exhibited paintings along with students, Edward Potthast, Joseph DeCamp, Charles Abel Corwin and the ever loyal and faithful John Twachtman. Musical numbers were presented by pianist Professor Benjamin Guckenberger, a professor at the Birmingham, Alabama, Conservatory of Music, and his songstress wife, Margaret, a contralto. In appreciation of the event, Duveneck gave his "Study of Braces Rock," to the Guckenbergers. The *Gloucester Daily Times*, August 10, 1900, assessed the event an outstanding success, and Duveneck was accorded the following compliment: "Mr. Duveneck's reputation as an artist and sculptor is too well known to need comment and his presence alone made all happy."

Tradition has it that Duveneck operated two studios in Gloucester, one at Bass Rocks and another on Rocky Neck. The lighting differed between the two, one for the morning and the other for the afternoon. The precise location of these studios is uncertain.

Local artists tell a story about Duveneck that sheds light on his reputation for indolence and his concerns over how students in Cincinnati would view his summer stays at Gloucester. An individual had observed Duveneck as he painted and then offered him $1,500 for the painting. He declined the offer, saying that he had to have something in hand to show his students back home that he had worked, at least for part of the summer. Duveneck carried the painting home and sold it in Cincinnati and gave the proceeds to the Cincinnati Art Club. The local club obviously was a favorite of his, deserving of support.

The turn of the century also brought new direction. In 1899 Duveneck accepted the invitation to serve as a juror for paintings accepted by the Paris Salon, and had to journey to Paris to complete that task. The return to his place of earlier triumph must have had a salutary impact on his artistry. *Girl with a Parasol* painted around this time "he courts Post-Impressionist effects, of a sort, in the green shadows of the face and in the parasol itself, a remarkable abstraction of dragged and scumbled (sic) dry pigment. In the 1900 "Head of a Young Woman" the figure is for once darker than the background and boldly outlined in umber. His numerous studies of nudes done at this time seem to grapple with new problems of *placement*, and these figures interact with space in a more complex and interesting way than in the merely posed early portraits."[8]

In 1900 Duveneck signed on as a faculty member at the Cincinnati Art Academy where he had begun to teach a class as an adjunct professor a decade earlier. From this time on, his life took on a routine. He taught in winter, socialized with friends[9] and relatives and worked on art projects. He trekked annually to Gloucester where he vacationed, spent time with his son, and painted subjects of interest in a refreshingly new way. His friends say that he continued to live with the loss of his wife always in the back of his mind. Grief was part of his life, and he performed at his peak when expressing that terrible emotion.

---

[1] Mollie's correspondent, Miss Adelaide Wadsworth, a friend of Elizabeth Boott Duveneck, was a student of Frank Duveneck's. The painter's biographer, Josephine Whitney Duveneck, wrote: "I think she would have welcomed a greater intimacy but he was not so inclined."

[2] Maitman's was a hotel in Gloucester.

[3] Bill R. Booth, *A Survey of Portraits and Figure Paintings by Frank Duveneck, 1848-1919*, DSS, University of Georgia, 1970

[4] Robert Taylor, "The Gloucester phase of Frank Duveneck," *Boston Globe*, Sunday, August, 16, 1987, p. A8

[5] Ibid, p. A8

[6] Martha Oaks, *Frank Duveneck The Gloucester Years*, catalogue associated with an exhibit, July 31-November 7, 1987, sponsored by the Cape Ann Historical Association, Gloucester, Massachusetts, p. 25

[7] Helen M. Knowlton, "A Home-Colony of Artists" in *The Studio*, July 14, 1890, p.326

[8] John Asbery, "The Indian Summer of Frank Duveneck," *ARTnews*, April, 1972

[9] Duveneck was a baseball fan of both the Cincinnati Reds and the Boston Red Sox. In addition to his membership in the Art Club, he was a member of the Cincinnati Literary Club. He frequently met with friends Clement Barnhorn, Lewis Henry Meakin, a painter and fellow teacher at the Art Academy, and painter Henry Farny. , On occasion others who joined in discussions were the architect Stanford White and author Booth Tarkington.

Chapter Ten

Cathedral Murals: Years in the Making

Covington, Kentucky, March 19, 1905

Starting in 1900 Frank Duveneck's life assumed an interesting routine of leisure, work and commissions. He began teaching at the Cincinnati Art Academy and, at the easel, worked at a steady, somewhat relaxed pace. He acquired property in Ryland, Kentucky, a short train ride south of Covington, alongside the northward-flowing Licking River. His cottage sat on a hillside overlooking one of many spring-fed deep green water ponds that offer the opportunity for a chilled swim even on hot days. He called the place "Little Switzerland."

Duveneck's second home served as the site of picnics for his students. In a photograph of one of those days he is seen holding two large frying pans and standing near a dock. A caption in a newspaper notes that he is calling students to dinner by clanging the pans together. In the other more plausible interpretation, provided by former student Aileen McCarthy, who was present for the photograph, the host was calling on a boatman to row across the pond to collect students for dinner. Ms. McCarthy said Duveneck on that day labeled his second home "Little Venice, as it was easier to get from one place to another by boat in the hilly surroundings served by few roads.

He was still racking up the awards. In 1901 he accepted a silver medal for works exhibited at the Pan-American Exposition in Buffalo, New York, notable as the place where the anarchist Leon Czolgosz shot and killed U.S. President William McKinley on September 6, 1901.

During the summer and on most extended holidays he visited Gloucester and Boston. Francis Boott, his father-in-law, continued to live in retirement in Cambridge watching over his grandson,

Frank's son, young Frankie. The artist and Mr. Boott had grown closer as the years passed. They keenly felt love for their departed Lizzie,, shared in their grief over her loss and delighted in the son and grandson. In his return from European exile Boott had become friendly with William James, a professor at Harvard University who lived nearby. James, the brother of Henry and the diarist Alice James, authored several famous works, *Principles of Psychology* and *The Varieties of Religious Experience*. It was he who had praised Duveneck's artistry on Lizzie's bronze effigy after viewing it in Allori Cemetery in Florence. In the family biography Josephine Duveneck surmised that James's influence brought Duveneck commissions in Boston in the period 1902-1905. During this time the artist completed a sculpture of a seated Ralph Waldo Emerson, destined for Emerson Hall at Harvard, and a bust of Charles Eliot, Harvard's long-time president.

Related to these works, in April, 1904, Duveneck wrote to a friend in Boston,

"I have the Emerson statue under way—that is the second sketch—and the large figure will probably take a year or two and then the church decoration of which you speak is another stumbling block. I have not commenced on the decorations as yet and I am uncertain whether I can do it here or not. I have thought of doing the work abroad, or going abroad for a few months to make studies for it, for in this country I cannot find material for it such as old costumes or old prints. I am anxious to make a good thing of it as it goes into a very handsome church and in my own town."[1]

The handsome church is St. Mary's Cathedral, now the Cathedral Basilica of the Assumption. Of French gothic design, under the management of architect Leon Coquard of Detroit, Michigan, the structure was built over several decades starting at the end of the nineteenth century. Originally, Bishop Camillus Paul Maes [pronounced *Maas*], a native of Belgium, under whose reign the project began, had planned on an interior chapel dedicated to the Blessed Virgin Mary. He changed his mind and designated it the Blessed

Sacrament Chapel. Duveneck's friend, the sculptor Clement Barnhorn, recommended Duveneck for the commission to produce murals on the chapel's east wall following the theme of the Blessed Sacrament; and Maes agreed.

The bishop advised Duveneck in a letter dated September 24, 1903:

My dear Mr. Duveneck:

If you can call tomorrow, I am ready with my suggestions anent your striking sketch for the Chapel of the Blessed Sacrament in my Cathedral:

The central idea is the sacrifice of Jesus Christ on the cross. This is admirably brought out in the central panel; to carry out the idea that before Christ as well as after Him, viz., before He came on earth as well as after the resurrection, that self-same sacrifice is the perpetual oblation in the true Church of God, we will if you please, depict in the smaller panel to the right, the Sovereign High Priest of the Old Law (with attendants if you wish) offering the loaves of bread on the altar of propitiation; in the larger panel to the left, a priest of the New Law (a Bishop with attendant priests (if you like) offering the Holy Sacrifice of the Mass, both facing the crucifixion.

I have some points for suggestion. You may call any time Friday or Saturday Morning; or, if not free then, any time, if you kindly let me know the hour that I may be at home.

With heartfelt thanks for your interest and great kindness,

Devotedly yours in Christ,

+Camillus P. Maes

Bishop of Covington[2]

So in 1903 Duveneck had already roughed out a "sketch," [the bishop's word], for the prelate to review. Bishop Maes accepted the plan for the central panel, the crucifixion, and had some suggestions for the right and left panels. It appears then that the bishop is responsible for the theological underpinnings of the triptych. [*See analyses below*]

In the next few years Duveneck painted at least two smaller-scale versions of the mural paintings, plus studies, to prepare for the final work. One study dated 1904 presents most of the main figures, although it lacks the fine detail that came later. In this version, approximately three feet by five feet, the bishop wears a mitre, the deeply cleft headdress marking his office. In later studies, the bishop wears no mitre and resembles Bishop Maes and his ample gray-white hair. The study was kept by Duveneck and presented as a gift to the Cincinnati Art Museum in 1915. The next larger study, approximating six feet in height across the three panels, lays out the essential picture and story the bishop and he intended. A significant addition in the third panel along the wall is the placement of the scene within the very brown-gray, stone-walled cathedral, with a flash of blue and white representing a window that actually exists.

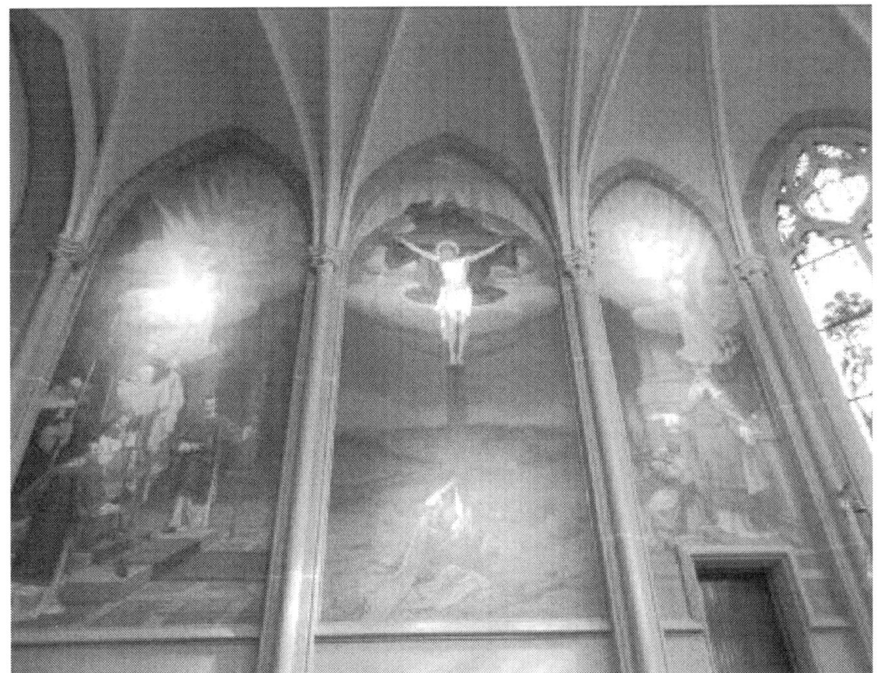

Three panels of Duveneck's Mural at the Cathedral Basilica of the Assumption, Covington.

Duveneck also donated to the museum a copy of a study of the corpus, which was rendered using a live model. The hanging figure in the study, his feet resting on a wedge and his arms stretched in a crucifixion position, hands grasping suspended grips, is approximately five feet high. The final version of the crucifixion corpus is based on this study. Among its more than two hundred and sixty Duveneck works of art, the museum owns two versions of studies of the third panel, in which the bishop raises the monstrance containing the Host. In the cathedral mural, an acolyte is added and a kneeling figure of a deacon replaces a standing one.

The studies were just the beginning of his work on the cathedral project. In 1905 he traveled to Europe to review paintings in galleries and churches, possibly for inspiration as well as information on what he termed "material," such as old costumes and prints. Dur-

215

ing a stop at Assisi Duveneck visited the Church of St. Francis and painted two pictures of the interior of the church. One of these was among donations he made in 1915 to the museum and remains there. Upon his return he began the murals project in earnest, almost certainly confiding in his friend Barnhorn on the progress of the work of art. The two artists had adjoining studios at the art academy, and it is fairly certain that Duveneck worked on his three-panel triptych in a large, high-ceilinged studio now a part of the museum. He spent five years on the project, working on the paintings section by section and rolling up the completed parts. Separately, and later, Duveneck painted a mural that appears high on the west wall of the chapel under the title of *Christ at Emmaus*. It continues the theme of the Blessed Sacrament. At Emmaus the disciples, then in disarray after the death of Our Lord, found peace in the discovery that the stranger among them was Christ himself, known by his breaking of bread.

A Theological Interpretation

Msgr. William Cleves, a priest of the Diocese of Covington and a former rector of the cathedral, has spent hours studying the murals and has come away with an appreciation of the theological understanding of a key element of the Catholic faith.

He wrote:

"The Duveneck Triptych in the Blessed Sacrament Chapel of our Cathedral is profound in its revelation of the paschal mystery, the mystery of Jesus' suffering, death, and resurrection. The middle panel comprises two sections, the bottom one approximately two-thirds of the scene. The viewer sees a woman here, suffering greatly. She kneels in supplication, helpless to save the one whom she loves. She is surrounded by signs of death: skulls and bones. There are few signs of life; a darkened city is in the background, and the few plants are small and scraggly. A cloud blocks her vision of the top one-third of the scene. She sees only her beloved, the crucified. What she does not see is God the Father, dressed in majestic colors and surrounded by angels in glory, lifting up the cross. She does not see the Holy Spirit from who beams of light flow, illuminating the meaning of the paschal mystery.

"The angels connect all three panels, their presence calling to mind God's providence; that the paschal mystery forms part of God's plan for our salvation, a plan conceived before time and governing all times and ages. The theme of this magnificent work of art is expressed well in the words that being the alternate Opening Prayer for the Second Sunday in Ordinary Time: *Almighty and ever-present Father, your watchful care reaches from end to end and orders all things in such power that even the tensions and tragedies of sin cannot frustrate your loving plans.*

"The right panel of the triptych depicts Aaron the priest. His vestments correspond exactly to the description of the priestly vestments in Exodus 28 and elsewhere. At his left hand is a wine cup, and on his right side a plate bearing incense and the bread of offering.

"The leftmost panel of the triptych shows a bishop raising a monstrance for the faithful to adore. The viewer who looks closely at the architecture of the church in the background of this panel realizes that it is the Cathedral itself, and that the Annunciation scene in the church is the stained glass window in the nave of the Cathedral. This panel reminds us that the Eucharist is the commemoration of Jesus' sacrifice on Calvary, and that those who celebrate the Eucharist not only carry the death of Christ in their bodies (see 2 Corinthians 4:10), but must always ally themselves with the poor and suffering. This great mystery is celebrated not just in our Cathedral, but in all the churches and chapels of the diocese.

"This magnificent work of art is to be read from right to left, just as are manuscripts written in biblical Hebrew. It tells us that the sacrifice of Calvary (middle panel), prefigured in the Old Testament (right panel) is celebrated and lived in the Cathedral today (left panel). Duveneck's work also tells us that the view from below is not the same as the view from above. Where human eyes see suffering and pain, divine eyes see quite differently. Where human eyes see suffering and death, divine eyes see the hope of new life and glory.

"The Duveneck Triptych provides us with a way to hold in our hearts the tragedy of September 11, 2001. We do not easily erase the images from our minds and hearts, nor should we. Almost 3,000 people from 115 countries died. Many of us saw the scenes live; those who did not saw the taped footage. How does one respond to such hatred and sinfulness? How are we to interpret the events of those days?

"Like the woman in Duveneck's work, we kneel in supplication, helpless to save the ones we love. Like her, we are sometimes surrounded by images of death. In these moments we need to call to mind that the paschal mystery means that suffering and death are never the last word. Saint Paul tells us (see 1 Corinthians 11;54-55), *Death is swallowed up in victory. Where, O death, is your victory? Where, O death, is your sting?* We need to remind ourselves that in our darkest moments God always offers the possibility of hope, life and joy. Our response must be that of God's, to offer forgiveness and the possibility of reconciliation. Thus we make the ending of the alternate Opening Prayer for the Second Sunday in Ordinary Time ours: *Help us to embrace your will, give us the strength to follow your call, so that your truth may live in our hearts and reflect peace to those who believe in your love. We ask this in the name of Jesus the Lord. Amen.*

After his long study of the murals, Monsignor Cleves, the former president of Thomas More College, Crestview Hills, Kentucky, came to the conclusion that the artist was "working out some terrible grief." First, he had lost his own father to cholera; his foster father passed in 1883; his wife of two years died suddenly in 1888; a sister Josephine in 1895; Mr. Boott in 1904, and his mother in 1905. Perhaps like the woman praying at the foot of the cross, Duveneck himself was likely probing the depths for answers.

Catholics live *sub specie aeternitatis* [under the aspect of eternity]. His work of art portrays the pains of life in the crucifixion scene and the mystery that shrouds our lives. The answer to the mystery is one that faith alone can provide.

Cleves points out a significant relationship between the eyes of the Old Testament figure in the right panel are about the same level as the Host in the monstrance in the left panel. What the ancients had longed for, he said in an interview, has now come true in the sacrifice of the crucifixion and in the sacrificial celebration of the Eucharist. "The mystery of salvation foretold in the Old Testament, happened in the time of Jesus, and now is celebrated sacramentally in this Church."

In his magnificent, expertly drawn triptych Duveneck captures this wonderful idea.

Sources of the Idea

Duveneck's handling of the central panel, the crucifixion of Our Lord, recalls Masaccio's *Trinity*, which hangs in the Basilica of Santa Maria Novella in Florence, a work of art and a church that he was probably familiar while living there. His depiction of the Trinity comprises the crucified Christ, whose cross is held up by the arms of the Creator, and the Holy Spirit is pictured as a dove. Masaccio was by no means alone in selecting this arrangement of figures of the Trinity. The major difference is Duveneck's selection of a woman at the foot of the Cross who implores God's help in a scene of desolation and despair and where she detects only the suffering of Christ. Bishop Maes, in a commentary on the triptych, believed the woman to be representative of the human race, a Magdalen, a sinner, frequently connected to the unnamed woman who washed the feet of Jesus with her hair. The figure, wearing reddish-colored hair in the triptych study, is one with graying hair parted in the middle in the mural. The woman could easily pass for his mother, Katharine Siemers Duveneck. At the base of the left-most panel, Duveneck wrote his dedication of the mural to her, though the proximity of the imploring woman to the dedication is not compelling for identification.

Duveneck loved and respected his mother. Despite childhood hardships, the loss from death of two husbands and more than several of her children, likely some in childbirth, she was a strong woman of faith who put her family first. She experienced a devastating blow in 1895 just about the same time that Mollie's affair became known. A favorite, daughter Josephine Duveneck Niehaus, portrayed by the artist as a woman in white, died suddenly. During this time Duveneck was in Paris participating in the Salon, which honored him for his effigy. He wrote a letter of condolence to Josephine's husband, Harry Niehaus that contained expression of his concerns for his mother: "I know that the loss to mother is irreparable and I fear that some bad effects will come."[3] He encouraged his siblings to dedicate their best efforts on her behalf. Perhaps the precarious status of his mother's life was another reason for his decision to return, for good, to his home.

At some point in this turn-of-the-century period Duveneck sketched concepts for a tomb that would mark his mother's grave. In 1888 he painted a profile of her that captured the wearing effect of years of hardship, clear, somewhat sad blue eyes, straight graying hair parted in the middle and pulled back, and a strong nose and chin. He painted a second portrait in 1902 that was exhibited in Cleveland and displayed at the Louisiana Purchase Exposition in 1904. He also served on the exposition's jury of the International Jury of Awards. His mother accompanied him to the St. Louis event. The story goes that she would linger in the exhibition hall where the painting was hung and cheerfully inform those in the viewing area that she was the subject of the painting and that her son had painted it. When viewers complimented the work she "glowed with pride."[4] The emotional response recalls her habits of years earlier when she and young Frank, on trips to Cincinnati, would see paintings in store windows. She told him then that if he would paint pictures like those, she would be proud of him. At the St. Louis exhibit, her wish had demonstrably come true.

March 19, 1905, was a significant date for Mother Duveneck and her family. After four days of illness, in and out of consciousness and suffering from kidney and heart deficiencies, Kate Duveneck died. She was buried several days later from St. Joseph Church only a city block away from her home. The funeral was an event of note for the people of Covington. Aileen McCarthy, who was to become a student of the painter, recalled more than sixty years later the church bells ringing for Mother Duveneck's funeral. She was then a student at LaSalette Academy in Covington.

Among the pallbearers were a neighbor, George Howell, and Frank Decker, a relative of her first husband, Bernard Decker. Instead of marking her grave with the tomb he had sketched, Duveneck asked Bishop Maes if he could dedicate the murals to his mother. The bishop approved the plan, and Duveneck waived any rights to compensation for the work.[5]

Murals requirements

Any muralist confronts two issues before the work begins. First, the design must be created within a fixed area which is part of an architectural scheme. Secondly, the subject matter should complement the purpose of the building. The Cathedral Basilica of the Assumption is the seat of the Diocese of Covington, the bishop's church identified by the word, cathedral, from the Latin cathedra, chair, from which the bishop teaches. As such it is the main church of the diocese, which, at its founding in 1853, embraced the eastern half of the Commonwealth of Kentucky. The purpose is therefore obvious.

The Blessed Sacrament Chapel is the largest of five chapels that extend from the north to the south transept. The chapel is the only one with a separate sanctuary. It features a gold-plated tabernacle inlaid with semi-precious stones, which sits on a marble altar, the gifts of the people of Ghent, Belgium, to native son Bishop Maes.

The chapel is forty-one feet in length; twenty-six feet in width and twenty-six feet high. It was no small feat to paint mural in three panels, each reaching twenty-four feet in height. The widths of the left and central panels are ten feet; the right panel is smaller at six feet, ten inches wide. As in other areas of the cathedral, rich colors burst forth from stained-glass windows, leaving a gorgeous palette on the interior even as the day passes.

"Perhaps most challenging is the task of designing not only a personal expression, but also imagery intended for the edification and universal enjoyment of the wider public," artist Carl Samson wrote. "Such challenges and restrictions require the possession of a specific set of skills—strong draftsmanship, a fine sense of perspective and decorative pattern, a literary mind, research proficiency, and probably a good measure of diplomacy as well."[6]

Duveneck had early training under the Benedictine church artists. He painted his first mural in 1868 as an assistant to Wilhelm Lamprecht in the interior of St.-Romuald-d'Etchemin Church in New Liverpool near Quebec City. On a trip to Canada years later, he criticized his work as an immature and flawed effort. In 1874 he painted a fifteen-foot-high figure of St. Peter receiving the Keys of the Kingdom from Jesus amidst a flock of sheep in a chapel of Trinity Church in Cincinnati. Unfortunately, the fresco was destroyed during a rebuilding of the church. He worked on a fresco at the Villa Castellani in the first months of his marriage to Lizzie.

Equipped with this early training, his talent broadened by life experiences and exposure to new methods, meeting demands of works in other media, the artist picked up his brush. Fortified with a concept of faith and living with the imposed and accepted restrictions, he summoned his feelings and let them loose on the canvas that bears the majestic sweep of the theology bolstered by an understanding of the human condition.

One study, approximating six feet in height for the three panels, lays out the essential picture and story he and the bishop intended.

The triptych, encased in a gold-painted wood frame, occupies a wall in the board room of Good Samaritan Hospital in Cincinnati. Duveneck gave the study to his friend, Clement Barnhorn, who in turn donated it to the hospital.

Evaluations

The triptych in the confines of the Blessed Sacrament Chapel is interesting for its historical perspective and theological statement, and definitely, for its composition. It is a creation of the mind and heart, something seen and understood in the figures, the ideas and beliefs coming across, fortified by the unusual design, and correct and creative compositions of people. The colors, after a 2003 cleaning, were revived to a more vivid state, yet they fall in the lower value ranges typical of a mural in keeping with its role to decorate and contribute to the architecture of a space. Artist Carl Samson makes this judgment:

"There are challenges for an artist doing a mural on a flat surface, as opposed to easel paintings. It must be kept flat and simple and the architecture and the integrity of the room respected. That was done very successfully here." In the layout of figures and things, Duveneck established diagonal lines in composing the pictures that direct attention to key elements of the paintings, God the Father holding up the Cross. He created expressive and beautiful shapes in the panels, which the artist refers to as "a remarkable piece of painting for our country and the world."

After viewing the study triptych in the hospital board room, Artist Linda Crank, a student of Samson's, wrote her opinion on the Facebook page which she manages, *Frank Duveneck and the Cincinnati School.* She believes the study contains many lessons for the student. Duveneck, she wrote, valued:

-Excellence in drawing
-Making clear statement with light, shadow and edges
-Stating things in their broadest terms

223

-Making each plane, even the smallest, very clear while keeping them in their worlds of light or shadow
-Excellence in composition
-Seeing the image as a whole
-Use of color to draw the eye around
-Putting meaning into the images.

In the family biography, Josephine Whitney Duveneck spent less than a page on the murals and referred only to one study. She took note of Duveneck's European tour for additional "material," as he had put it, and said: "The work was accomplished with great difficulty, as the canvas was so long that it had to be rolled up and painted in sections. The original sketch, set in a decorative Italian frame (in Good Samaritan Hospital), has more vitality and life than the large finished triptych."[7]

The lesser color values in the cathedral paintings are, however, in keeping with traditional standards for a mural, complementing the purpose of the building and decorating rather than dominating.

In his dissertation, art historian Bill R. Booth, expressed a different opinion.

He wrote:

"The Crucifixion is treated in a dry, static and thoroughly academic manner. Duveneck followed a program established by Camillus P. Maes, Bishop of Covington. The artist reverted to a technique, style and approach which he had used as an apprentice with Schmitt* (also frequently spelled Schmidt) and Lamprecht in their murals. When a comparison is made between the large decorations of Schmitt and this group of panels, it is apparent that Schmitt indoctrinated his student in the 'proper' method of executing a mural. Duveneck's panels bear an extremely close resemblance to the works of Schmitt. This is not meant to condemn them."

He continued:

"Schmidt [Schmitt] was a thoroughly competent painter, and his works are included in many fine religious collections including the Vatican's. The fact that Duveneck would go back to his youth for his stylistic and technical ideas, however, is inconceivable. He seems to have sacrificed his artistic integrity in these examples. As a final opus these works are extremely weak. If there is a positive remark that can be made concerning these works, it is that Duveneck does demonstrate his ability to handle the figure. Although all the figures do not have great emotional force, they are competently drawn. The single most expressive figure in the group is the Magdalen. The color today is dark and somber, and the paint which was applied in flat areas is lifeless and dull. Duveneck could use paint expressively and handle the figure convincingly, so it is lamentable that he did not have the freedom or the inclination to produce a more inspiring example of religious art.

"When the artist dealt with the High Priest of the Old law he followed the Scripture related to the description of the high priest which is found in Leviticus, Chapter seven, Verses 7-9. Perhaps these descriptive restrictions limited the artist, but the results are ample proof that a successful career does not insurance a great final work.

"In Sacrifice of the New Law there is a fine realization of space and a convincing grouping of figures, but again they lack the sense of inner vitality that this artist in his younger years could give to his subjects. The last and weakest work in the series of panels is Christ at Emmaus."

Booth admires Duveneck as a portrait painter. He contends that his strength lay in painting single figures and studies and concludes that he was less successful as a painter of large canvases. The late critic Mahonri Sharp Young took another tack in an August, 1972, criticism aimed at Duveneck's final foray at a large and complicat-

225

ed work: "The murals which he painted in St. Mary's Cathedral in Covington in honour of his mother are a deplorable return to church art of journeyman days."

Samson argues that mural paintings have purposes that differ from easel painting and that any criticism that compares murals with easel paintings is unfounded. He believes that Duveneck correctly adhered to the dictums of mural painting and that his performance was masterful in giving conscious extra effort in all aspects of the work. In his view the talent to do the extra effort makes the difference between a master and a conventional artist. "I believe the panels are a most worthy final effort. Much thought and preparation went into every aspect of their execution--Hardly a 'sacrifice of artistic integrity!' They are noble, dignified works that, in my view, are a national treasure."

Crank makes a valid point: restrictions on an artist are not necessarily limiting. "Sometimes they can lead to greater creativity than someone may have had otherwise." She believes the bishop's suggestions were more likely a positive than a negative. The suggestions clearly put Duveneck on a definite path to a theological truth. Furthermore, his talent and his sincere intentions equipped him to complete the work in masterly style. He also was motivated by the prospect that it would be displayed in the cathedral in his hometown. Another powerful incentive was his dedication of the work to his beloved mother.

Lastly, Young's criticism using the term, deplorable, as applied to Duveneck's return to "church decoration," seems crabbed and undefined. What is so deplorable about an artist working in a genre that gave him his start?

In the extant, superb studies in storage at the Cincinnati museum, it is clear that Duveneck took pains to carefully prepare for the final version. None of these rely on his style of earlier years of church decoration. If anything, they show that he evolved as an artist, particularly in his presentation of the figures, a point that

Booth also makes in his dissertation. Duveneck's figures are unlike the figures of his earlier "religious" paintings. They are more human and lifelike, reflecting his evolution as a craftsman and a person who understood human nature.

The murals by Duveneck have long divided the art world on their worth.

In 1915, Anna Seaton-Schmidt, a writer and art critic, wrote:

"Until quite recently no one thought of him as a mural painter, now he stands among the first in America. Desiring to erect a monument in memory of his beloved mother, he felt that the decoration of a chapel in the newly erected Gothic Cathedral at her old home, Covington, Ky., would be more in accordance with her wishes than an expensive tombstone in an unfrequented cemetery, and to his profound reverence for her religious beliefs the world owes a magnificent series of paintings wherein he has proved himself a master of mural decoration. But admirable as is the handling and combination of color, the spacing and arrangement of his figures, one loses sight of all this in the noble and original conception which reveals him as a great creative artist. Studying this work I am haunted by the words of one of our best critics: 'There is no art so elevated as that which, to the end of producing a profound impression, illustrates a lofty idea.' The old, old story of man's redemption is here told in poignant language; the story is old but is revealed to us through the vision of a great modern artist. No written works and no reproductions can do justice to such a masterpiece. As Wagner's music should be heard and not described, so these superb religious paintings must be seen in order to be appreciated."[8]

A year after the mural had been completed and dedicated, Duveneck's later academy colleague, L.H. Meakin, wrote: "This is a very serious and dignified piece of work and presents Duveneck in a new light."[9]

[1] *Frank Duveneck, Painter-Teacher*, Josephine Whitney Duveneck, John Howell—Books, San Francisco, 1970, p.136-137

[2] A Guide for the Cathedral, under pastorate of Rt. Rev. Msgr. Walter A. Freiberg, 1947

[3] Letter to Harry Niehaus, brother-in-law, contained in the Duveneck Family archive, Archives of American Art, Smithsonian Institution, Washington, D.C.

[4] *Frank Duveneck, Painter-Teacher*, Op. Cit., p.135

[5] *Cincinnati Times-Star*, 22 March, 1905

[6] *Cincinnati Report: Herman Wessel, Salon America Journal*, 2004

[7] Op. Cit., *Frank Duveneck, Painter-Teacher*, p.137

[8] Anna Seaton-Schmidt, Frank Duveneck: Artist and Teacher, Art and Progress, Volume VI, Number 11, September, 1915, pp. 393-394, http://www.jstor.org/stable/20561522

[9] Meakin, L.H., "Duveneck, A Teacher of Artists," *Arts and Decoration*, July, 1911, pp.382-384.

Chapter Eleven

'Men of his Caliber appear only at great intervals'

San Francisco, California, late spring, 1915

Making his way through the flower-bedecked lanes of the Panama Pacific International Exposition, Duveneck entered a wonderland of light and color that had put attendees in thrall since February of 1915. Spotlights beamed various hues at a vast assembly of buildings stretched across the Exposition's six hundred and thirty-five acres, part of an illumination scheme set up by General Electric (GE). In San Francisco Bay, a barge billed as a "Scintilator," using forty-eight searchlights, projected seven colors into the sky that reflected on roiling billows of steam generated by a locomotive.[1]

Visitors were further awed by the sight and fresh scent of some thirty-thousand trees and bushes and some seventy-thousand blooming rhododendron carefully displayed under a plan by John McLaren, designer of Golden Gate Park. The Tower of Jewels, standing forty-three stories high, dominated the extravagant scene. Breezes from the Pacific Ocean caused the jewels to dance and reflect light from the many sources. On viewing the massive display, author Laura Ingalls Wilder commented, "I have never imagined anything so beautiful."

Three years earlier U.S. President William Howard Taft had selected the City of San Francisco for the site of the 1915 World's Fair over a rival bid from New Orleans. The city fathers linked the fair's theme to the recently opened Panama Canal, which served as a godsend to navigation and commerce. The broadly based theme gave the City on the Bay an opportunity to demonstrate its rebound from the 1906 earthquake and fire that destroyed eighty per cent of the city and killed some three thousand people. An inspired group of city fathers labored creatively and smartly to establish a fair that set a high bar for future exhibitions.

During this nearly year-long celebration, February 20 through December 4, America's inventions, ingenuity and talent, specifically in art, were displayed and honored. It was here that Frank Duveneck received his greatest recognition, as a master artist and as a founding father in America's artistic pantheon. Two years before, in August of 1913, Duveneck had received a letter from John E.D. Trask, commissioner of the Exhibition's Department of Fine Arts, inviting him to exhibit his work and serve as a member of the jury. The source behind the invitation was artist Edmund Tarbell. He had advised the officials on the artist's importance, and the advisory was quoted in the invitation letter:

"Mr. Duveneck seems to be the one man who started the present era of American painting and I hope that it can be brought about that recognition can be shown him so that he may have the benefit of knowing that he is appreciated."

Atypical of him, Duveneck who for years had zealously avoided opportunities to gain renown was openly delighted by Trask's gracious invitation, if not the fully accurate assessment of him and his work by Tarbell. He gratefully accepted the invitation and asked colleagues at the Cincinnati museum to help assemble a representative group of paintings, etchings, pastels, water colors and sculptures for the exhibition. Museum officials eagerly put together art works in the museum's possession, Duveneck's own cache, and interceded with private owners for others. Contributions came from museums in New York, Philadelphia and Boston.

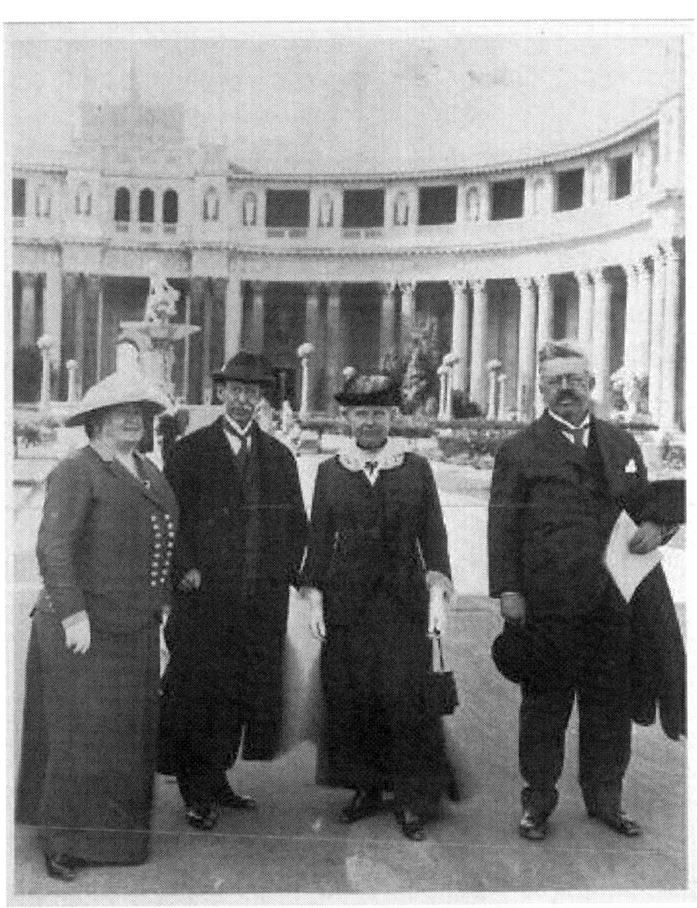

Mollie , Duveneck, left, joins Duveneck, far right, and friends in San Francisco

Exhibition officials assigned Gallery 87 in the Fine Arts Palace, just to the left of the Main East Entrance, for Duveneck's one-man show. On display were thirty oil paintings, twelve Venetian etchings and one Florentine, and a replica of the memorial to Lizzie. His works were in good company. Other one-man galleries were dedicated to paintings by his friend, William Merritt Chase, former student John Twachtman, and other colleagues, Childe Hassam,

John Singer Sargent, James Abbott McNeill Whistler, and E.W. Redfield, a realistic painter of outdoors. As if to compare Duveneck's works with a master of the past, a painting, said to have been done by Velazquez, was added to Gallery 87. The painting was Duveneck's, given to him by Bishop Maes.

Duveneck's works stole the show. A fellow artist and writer, Eugen Neuhaus, author of program notes to prepare visitors for the experience, singled out Duveneck's gallery as the place to visit and dispensed compliments that exceeded in praise all others.

He wrote:

"Paradoxical as it may seem, Duveneck's art is carried by the same painter-qualities found in Redfield [another painter whose works were in the exhibit]. From his dark colour it is self-evident that he belongs to an older German School—a school which has been superseded in the affection of Americans by French methods. We know relatively little, entirely too little, about the generous methods of the best men of the Munich school, of which Duveneck is so conspicuous a member. His importance in the history of art can hardly be set too high, for the soundness of his methods alone. Only the greatest ever attain the capacity for direct painting which characterizes this astonishing collection of his pictures. Juiciness is the only word which will adequately express the result of his brush. The pictures here are most interesting for the reason that they were all done while he was not yet twenty-five and while he lived in an atmosphere of workers of whom Leibl was probably the most famous. There are few paintings – and then only the greatest – which give one the same satisfaction at a big distance as well as at close range as Duveneck's do. Men of his caliber appear only at great intervals. This Duveneck collection, if brought together permanently, as we are fortunate enough to see it temporarily here in San Francisco, would become the Mecca of all painters who want to refresh their memory as to what constitutes real painting. Unfortunately these canvases are owned by different people, and to think that they will all have to be scattered again among individual owners is a shocking thought. The uniformity of excellence in the Duveneck room forbids any attempt at picking out individual works; however, Duveneck's equally great accomplishments on another wall, in the field of etching, are apt to be easily overlooked. The sarcophagus of his wife, done by his versatile hand, increases the admiration that we, must hold for this liberal genius. Duveneck's art, no matter how much it is rooted in foreign soil, will forever make its influence felt for the best of American art."

Most of the works on display were completed by Duveneck in his most productive years spanning the Munich and Florence periods—into the 1890s with the memorial to Lizzie and at least one later painting from Gloucester. The jurors recognized the value of the works and, without the artist's knowledge they decided that he deserved something special.

The jurors issued a brief statement recommending that a special Medal of Honor be struck for him:

"We, the representatives of foreign countries acting upon the international jury of awards in the Department of Fine Arts, do hereby ask your kind consideration of the following recommendation unanimously adopted by us in a meeting specially called for this purpose. 'Whereas, the comprehensive retrospective collection of Frank Duveneck's works in oils, etchings and sculpture has astonished and delighted all those hitherto unacquainted with his life work, while confirming the opinion of those few who have long held him in the highest esteem, both as an artist and as a man, we, the foreign jurors on the international jury of award, feel that some special recognition of his distinguished contributions to American art should be awarded Frank Duveneck, and we herewith recommend that a special medal of honor be struck in his honor and awarded him.'"

The surprise award came at the final session of the international jury, and it caught Duveneck unawares. Signers included jurors from the Netherlands, Japan, Cuba, Italy, Portugal, China, Argen-

233

tina, Sweden and Norway. Dr. Albrecht von Mogelas said that Duveneck and his pioneering work in Munich had changed direction of art history and was deserving of recognition.

He wrote:

"This step was decided upon to proclaim before his native country and before the world what American art owes to this one man. When Duveneck was born and when he was in his early twenties, American painting was entirely under the influence of the Dusseldorf school—This microscopic and painfully detailed way of handling the drawing and painting of pictures did not appeal to Duveneck...his paintings created a sensation for their broad and bold handling which upset all academic traditions of the Dusseldorfers. From that moment dates the modern development of American art."

His daughter-in-law affirmed.

"He was overwhelmed and had difficulty to control his emotions to reply in acceptance. It is hard to overestimate the deep satisfaction he derived from such recognition."

Duveneck told his colleagues:

"This came from the foremost artists of the world, and this is what is most important."

More than anyone, the artist understood that his status in the art world had become obscured by the overwhelming triumph of the French school of Impressionism painting. It had brushed aside, temporarily, much of the work of the Munich School, those works from his Italian period, and the more recent work at Gloucester. His daughter-in-law, Josephine Duveneck, who no doubt loved and respected him, complained as did others that Duveneck himself was responsible for this diminished standing as an artist. "Duveneck was well known among art students as a great teacher but not as a creative artist," she wrote. "This disregard was accentuated by his own (sic) indifference to publicity. A revealing instance of this may be seen in a standard encyclopedia of American art which mentions his name, with the caption, 'No answer to circular.'"

Duveneck's Surprise

The Exhibition occasioned an outburst of generosity all around. When Duveneck returned to Cincinnati from his travels, the trip to San Francisco and his annual sojourn to Gloucester, he and his fellow teacher L.H. Meakin entered together the office of the Cincinnati museum's chief librarian Elizabeth R. Kellogg.[2] She was accustomed to seeing Duveneck after his annual visit to the Boston area. He would tell her of the highlights of the summer there. She in turn offered local news and "a bit of light gossip."

Duveneck carried with him the Medal of Honor and proudly showed it to her. She was delighted that his Gallery 87 "had proved to be the real surprise of the whole American section." Ms. Kellogg ranked this honor "as startling as Sargent's remark at a Henry James dinner party in London that 'after all's said, Frank Duveneck is the greatest talent of the brush of this generation.'"

Viewing the medal she described for him the "excitement this had caused in Cincinnati and at the Museum." After hearing her rendition, Duveneck turned his cool blue-grey eyes on his colleague Meakin.

He said:

"This might as well be the moment for me to present my pictures to the Museum."

Startled at his offer and having an idea of the size of the collection, she queried, "All of them?"

Duveneck issued a characteristic grunt and said, "That is, if you want them all."

235

The librarian joyfully spread word of the gift. First to hear the news was J.R. Gest, director of the Cincinnati Art Museum and a founder and director at Rookwood Pottery, a close friend and colleague of Duveneck's. He promptly assigned Ms. Kellogg to catalogue the art works, many oil paintings and including certain copies, *After Velasquez*, and water colors, pastels and etchings, totaling one hundred and forty two pieces. Duveneck had donated his most famous work, Whistling Boy (1872) to the Cincinnati museum in 1904.

Former Duveneck art student Mary Alexander, then a columnist with the *Cincinnati Times-Star*, wrote that the gift to the museum provided an explanation for the artist's puzzling attitude toward his own works. He could have sold many paintings at high value prices, but he didn't. Instead, he often searched out and located works and re-acquired them.

"Those who knew of this peculiarity have wondered at it, but now we can understand that it was because of his desire to have them remain here, in the museum…"

The columnist remarked to Duveneck:

"That is, indeed, a princely gift; think of the value of even one picture."

"Why sell them just for money? Money isn't everything," Duveneck replied.

There followed several parties "for the now social-minded lion," the librarian wrote. At a gala held at the Art Academy, a stairway was decorated with a strand of gold medals strung across the top. Each student stepped up to Duveneck and presented him with a rose. Receptions in Duveneck's honor followed at various art clubs. Ms. Kellogg capped the events by writing a play with tableaux vivant commemorating the event.

In a July letter to his friend, Barnhorn, he had called the heap of praise he was receiving "lots of taffy."

A final tribute was held November 20 at San Francisco, a dinner in Duveneck's honor. The supper featured Minestra Milanese, Roast Larded Tenderloin of Beef, Potatoes Albert and Green Peas, with salad and dessert. "Dinner Lunch & Big Beer 10 cts."

The honors were not to end for Frank Duveneck. In May of 1917 while he and Mr. Gest traveled to New York City to review a collection of Chase's, paintings for sale at an auction, the Senate of the University of Cincinnati recommended that the university bestow the honorary degree of Doctor of Laws upon the artist.

"Someone must have taken Duveneck in hand and made him answer this communication—promptly in the bargain," Josephine Duveneck wrote.

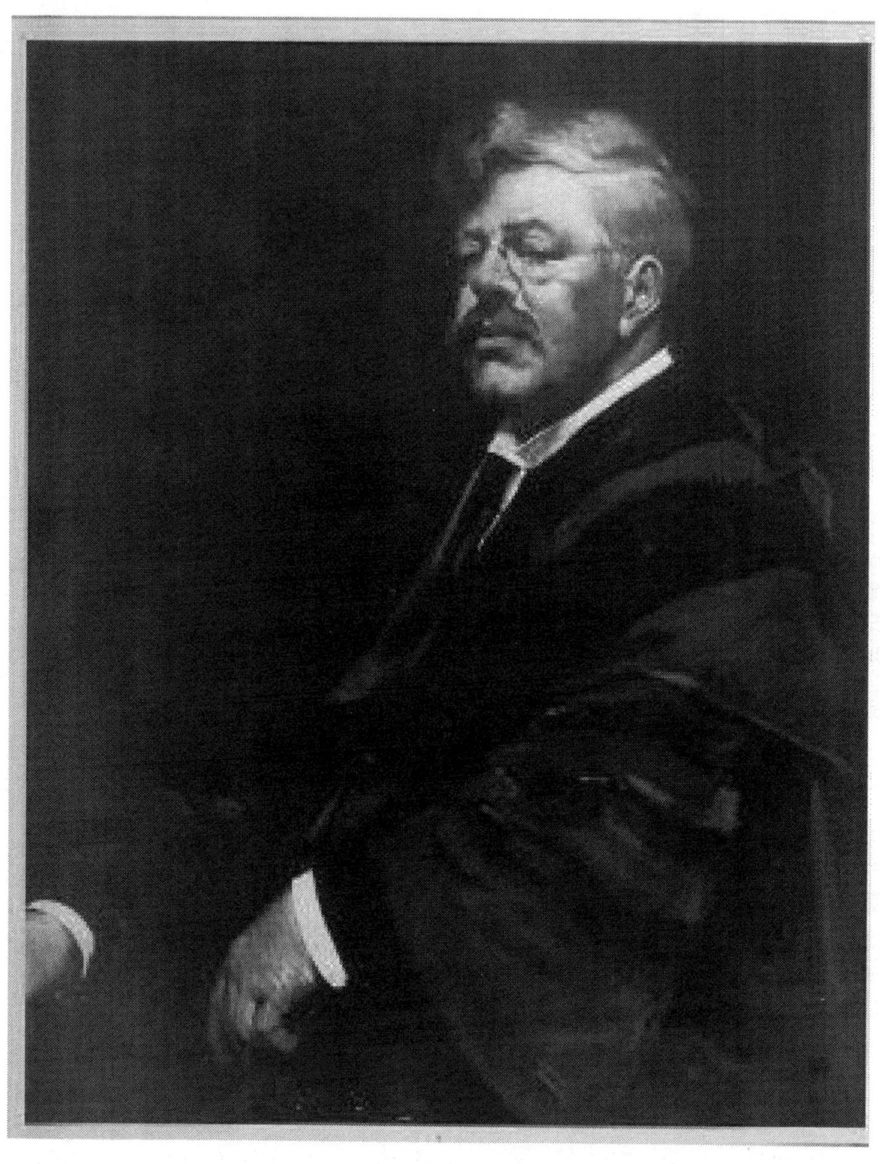

A portrait of Frank Duveneck by his former student, Dixie Selden

-Courtesy of the Kenton County Public Library, Covington, Ky.

Duveneck responded thusly to the university's letter of invitation:[3]

"It is hard to express in words my appreciation—that a professional should be chosen by the University of his home as the recipient of this distinction is to him the highest tribute of his fellow citizens. What is however uppermost in my mind at this time is the recognition you are pleased to give to my profession in itself, rather than to any personal achievement of my-self as an artist. This seems to me full of encouragement to other artists whose efforts are usually devoted to public service in a profession whose seriousness is sometimes not altogether understood.

"I shall be very glad indeed to be present at commencement on the 16th of June."

Duveneck informed his daughter-in-law of the honor.[3] He had been in New York, he said, and upon his return was surprised by a letter from the University Senate extending the invitation. He was impressed because the honor was thought to be the first presented to an artist by a university not on the East Coast. He wrote to her that he expected he would look quite handsome in an L.L.D. gown.

The commencement came off as scheduled. Charles W. Dabney, university president, presented the award. The artist reveled in the new honor and took pride as he marched in the procession with the faculty and administrators. With a satisfied smile he posed for photographs and thoroughly enjoyed donning the mortar board cap and impressive doctoral gown. To accommodate Duveneck's large head and thick bushy hair, the mortar board was a special order. The aviator Orville Wright from nearby Dayton, Ohio, joined the artist on the dais to receive the degree of Doctor of Science.

The university cogently had honored two of the country's great men that day—Duveneck, for launching American art into a new age both as a practitioner and for helping to form that age as a gifted teacher, all along opening our eyes to beauty and truth, and Wright, who with his brother, the late Wilbur, for creating a new

239

form of transportation, powered flight, at last freeing man from the primeval bonds that had chained him to the Earth since Adam.

---

[1]Brochure for the exposition maintained by the de Young museum at www.sfmuseum.org and www.sfpl.org

[2]*Frank Duveneck, His Gifts of His Work to the Art Museum, Cincinnati*, published by the Cincinnati Art Museum Association, 1929, and "The Duveneck Story," a brochure, available in the Frank Duveneck files at the Cincinnati Art Museum library

[3]*Frank Duveneck, Painter-Teacher*, John Howell Books, San Francisco, 1970, p. 160

Chapter Twelve

Jesu, Maria—I am near to death, And Thou art calling me

The Dream of Gerontius

   --John Henry Cardinal Newman

Cincinnati, January 3, 1919

At a time when Frank Duveneck enjoyed full honors of recognition by his peers and from the academic community, the catastrophe of war scarred his final years.

Recalling his dreaded experiences from the Civil War in the United States—and his proximity to the Franco-Prussian War during his studies in Munich, Duveneck said, "People don't understand what war is, and this will be bad for the Germans in this country."[1]

He lost sleep over it and "could hardly speak of anything else," his daughter-in-law, Josephine, remembered. In 1913 she and Duveneck's son, Frank Jr., were living in Cincinnati. Son Frank, a Harvard University graduate who had earned a master's degree in engineering, was looking for employment. The young couple shared their father's abhorrence for war. The only jobs open to Frank Jr. involved development of war materiel even in 1913, a year before World War I began in Europe. So they left the city for Lowell, Massachusetts, where the young engineer gained a post at one of the Lyman textile mills. Before long, however, eager to be on their own, the young Duveneck family moved to California in the area around Carmel. They were familiar with it from a visit with Josephine's sister in Santa Barbara. The former New Englanders felt a deep appreciation for the temperate climate of California and the unusual coastal flora and fauna.

Duveneck was correct in predicting German-Americans would suffer from prejudice. Fantasies of the marauding Hun ran rampant from coast to coast, breeding mistrust. Some German-Americans were harassed by fellow citizens and attacked physically. To avoid antagonisms Teutonic family names were anglicized: Schmidt became Smith; Grunwald, Green. In Cincinnati and elsewhere, Germanic-sounding street titles were abandoned in favor of patriotic names such as Liberty Street.

While he eagerly discussed the war, Duveneck avoided arguments over it. Coming from German-born parents and having much affection for the land where he had studied, for Italy and France, he held ambivalent feelings toward each of the European nations involved. Like her mother, Josephine, granddaughter Hope Duveneck Williams surmised that the force of the artist's sympathetic and humane personality precluded him from arguing with others over any thing.

"He wouldn't challenge them even though he might not agree with them," said Hope.[2]

Then, in April, 1917, when the United States entered the war against Germany on the side of Great Britain and France, issues became even more personal. Social pressures to serve in some manner grew with reports of German atrocities. The American press portrayed Kaiser Wilhelm as a hell-bent, authoritarian monarch, reckless in his pursuit of European domination.

As Josephine put it in her autobiography:

"It became more and more apparent that our whole civilization was threatened by the German war machine, and we would no longer remain passive in the face of this catastrophe."

Frank Jr., at thirty years of age and the main breadwinner of a family, probably could have avoided the draft. Yet, he apparently wanted to serve in some way. Hearing of the formation of an all-California regiment, the 322nd Field Signal Battalion, he enlisted as a private. Antiviolence at heart, he assumed that by serving in a communications unit he could be a noncombatant and avoid personal conflict.[3]

"He felt he could contribute his technical skill without being involved in shooting his fellow men," wrote Josephine.

After training at Fort Lewis, Washington, Frank Jr. passed a test to become a master sergeant electrician. Then, his unit was sent to a base near a harbor in the New York area for embarkation to France.

Frank, his sister Mollie and brother, Charlie, traveled to New York to visit with Frank Jr. They spent an afternoon and evening together with son and nephew, and planned to see one another again the next day. But that was the last meeting for father and son. The next day the soldier boarded a convoy ship for Europe.

Frank Jr. lived through intense war. His Signal Corps unit was engaged in most of all major campaigns conducted by United States forces on the Western Front.

When the war ended on November 11, 1918, Frank Jr. had already separated from his unit while he was preparing to join the officer corps. With the cease fire, however, the plan for promotion was abandoned, and he was assigned to occupational duty.

For that reason Frank Jr. was unable to be with his ailing father in the painter's last days.

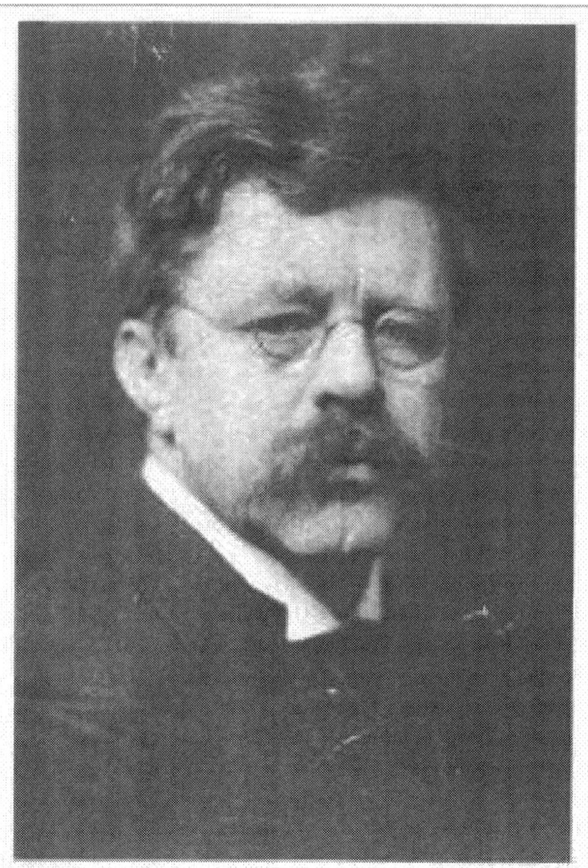

Frank Duveneck in later years

-Courtesy of the Kenton County Public Library, Covington. Ky.

Meanwhile, Frank Sr. was intending to spend much of the summer of 1918 on a visit with Josephine and the children in California. He was looking forward to it, especially as the family was growing. Hope, born the day before her father's embarkation, had become his fourth grandchild. He wrote to his daughter-in-law in February that Mollie and his friend, Clement Barnhorn, would likely be in the traveling party.

The California trip was not in his future. Frank had a sore in his mouth and a dental examination regarded it as suspicious, especially since the artist was a heavy tobacco user from his youth. He cancelled his plans for California and traveled to Philadelphia to visit a specialist. Further examination showed the sore was a manifestation of cancer.

In a letter to Josephine, he wrote from Gloucester about his recent visit to the doctor in Philadelphia:

I underwent another three or four days torture but the Doctor tells me that I am getting on fine but of course he says my case will take a long time treatment possibly a whole year and that he wants me to be in Philadelphia three or four days every month."[4]

An operation conducted shortly thereafter at a Philadelphia hospital was not successful. Frank started extended treatments requiring daily visits to the hospital. He and Mollie took up lodgings in a hotel. At one point brother Charlie must have visited. His concern over Frank's condition prompted him to contact Josephine in Carmel. He asked her to come to Philadelphia, very likely to make a case for returning him home.

Because of their mutual respect Josephine may have been one of the few people who could take Frank Sr. in hand.

"She was very fond of him, and he of her," said granddaughter, Hope.

Leaving her family in charge of a trusted friend, she traveled to Philadelphia. By this time, it was the middle of September.

She wrote:

"There I found Father Duveneck very ill, and the hotel arrangements were thoroughly inappropriate. I conferred with his sister and brother, consulted the doctors, and got him moved into a hospital."[5]

Hospital beds were already scarce as the epidemic of influenza (1918-1919) was beginning to strike, taxing medical facilities everywhere. Once Frank was settled in at a hospital, Josephine took a room in a boarding house. It was there, after supper the first night:

"I was seized with nausea, a terrible headache and a raging fever. I had not yet heard about the flu epidemic, so I had no idea what had hit me."[6]

The care-giver had become the sufferer, but one of a different kind.

Josephine was so very ill that she feared she was at death's door. Desperately worried since she knew no one in Philadelphia, alarmed at what might happen to her children and her ailing father-in-law, Josephine felt indescribably alone and powerless as she lay stricken in her boarding house room. A strange transformation came about that she describes so well.

She wrote:

"I was determined not to leave my loved ones in the lurch. I made a supernatural effort of will—a declaration to myself that I was going to live and a sort of declaratory prayer to fate and to the great Unknown, asserting my independence of choice. I believe—and have seen my belief confirmed more than once—that there is a Power in the Universe that can be evoked when the need is great, that if one has faith, healing will take place and the seemingly impossible is vouchsafed."[7]

By 7 a.m. the following morning, the fever passed. Josephine recovered, spending the entire day in bed while quickly regaining her strength. On her feet the next day she made arrangements for an ambulance to take Frank Sr. to a train station and bought tickets for a railroad trip to Cincinnati. A room was found for him in Good Samaritan Hospital in Cincinnati's Clifton area where he was admitted on October 18, 1918. He was seventy years old on October 8.

With Frank Sr. in good hands, Josephine took the opportunity while on the East Coast to briefly visit relatives in Boston. On her return trip across country she stopped in Cincinnati and called on Father Frank lying abed in the hospital.

"The nuns were very kind to him. He was as comfortable as it was possible for him to be. He could not talk but he wrote me several tender little notes. I reassured him about Frank and told him about his grandchildren. I hated to leave, but there was nothing further I could do for him. I felt I had been gone from my precious kids, who were my first concern, much too long already. As I went down in the hospital elevator, I could not restrain my tears. As I got out, the elevator man patted my shoulder and said, "Don't take it so hard, Miss. We all have to go sometime."[8]

Upon her arrival by train in San Francisco, she found Market Street in pandemonium. The war was over.

Frank Duveneck was to last on this earth for more than two and a half months, all the time a patient in Good Sam, as the hospital is affectionately called. Nurses and religious women from the Sisters of Charity congregation attended to Duveneck. A visitor who came as often as she could was Sr. Ernestine Foskey, assistant Mother in the congregation. She was a former student of Duveneck's and a friend. She taught art in several schools in the Archdiocese of Cincinnati.

In the archives of the Sisters of Charity there is a book by Norbert Leo Heermann, titled *Frank Duveneck*, New York: Houghton Mifflin, 1918. Inscribed is this dedication:

To Sr. Ernestine

In memory of the pleasant student days at the Cincinnati Art Academy

Frank Duveneck Nov. 15, 1918

With a good probability of accuracy one can speculate that Sr. Ernestine and the other religious women distressed over Duveneck's physical and spiritual states. He was unable to speak and in pain, knowing the end was near. Disguising the attempts at the cheerful banter of the sick room, a feeling of angst for him must have hovered like a mist clinging to the nearby Kentucky hills. [10]

Sister Ernestine came in one day holding a crucifix, a representation of Christ on the cross, and placed it at the foot of his bed so that Duveneck might see it.

No, no, he said, a crucifix belongs on the wall, above the patient's head.

She saw to it that that the crucifix was hung as directed.

His sister Mollie was the most frequent visitor, rarely leaving her brother's bedside while there. Among visitors were brothers John and Charlie, his former students and close friends, in particular Clement Barnhorn. A daily communicant, he would have been equally concerned, as were the religious women, for Duveneck's physical and spiritual wellbeing. Barnhorn no doubt wanted to do all he could for his friend.

Prayer was the only answer.

Final Days

Duveneck lingered through Thanksgiving and the Advent season, the weeks just prior to Christmas, unable to speak, miserable with his pain. To those who visited, it was said, he faced his sufferings with fortitude.

Similar to Cardinal Newman's Gerontius, he could say:

I can no more; for now it comes again
That sense of ruin, which is worse than pain,

That masterful negation and collapse
Of all that makes me man; as though I bent
Over the dizzy brink
Of some sheer infinite descent;
Or worse, as though
Down, down forever I was falling through
And needs must sink and sink
Into the vast abyss. And, crueler still,
A fierce and restless fright begins to fill
The mansion of my soul. And, worse and worse
Some bodily form of ill
Floats on the wind, with many a loathsome curse
Tainting the hallow'd air, and laughs, and flaps
Its hideous wings,
And makes me wild with horror and dismay.
O Jesu, help! Pray for me, Mary, pray!

Aware of his personal struggles, Sr. Ernestine gave Duveneck a copy of a book, titled *What Is Worthwhile?*, written by Rev. Martin Scott. It is not known whether he read the book, but it is likely that he did. It's legendary in the Catholic community that Sr. Ernestine was a strong influence that contributed to Duveneck's formal return to the Church.

What is known is that Duveneck signaled his resolve by drawing a circle on a piece of paper, indicating to the sisters that he desired to receive the Holy Eucharist, which comes in the form of a round host of unleavened bread. One can say with certainty that this humble effort, possibly his last work of art, was met with great joy.

To receive the host, the Body of Christ, Duveneck would need to confess his sins and express his sorrow. He would have known of this requirement from the instructions he received in his youth.

Then and now, priests are trained to deal with penitents who are ill. If a patient is *in extremis,* the priest asks whether the person is sorry for his or her sins, and he would look for some kind of affirmation, a squeeze of the hand or even a purposeful nod of the head. The process could be more elaborate depending on the circumstances. The priest could run down the list of the Ten Commandments and those of the Church and look for affirmation in the penitent.

Duveneck had to indicate in some way sorrow for his sins. He must have done so and then was able to receive absolution from the priest, cleansing his soul and freeing him to receive the sacrament.

Ego te absolve in nomine Patris...

Duveneck did in fact ask for a ceremony that would recall for him his First Holy Communion some sixty years earlier at St. Joseph Church. The sisters called together a group of flower girls who led a procession of religious women carrying lighted candles. They processed into the hospital chapel, where Duveneck waited in a wheelchair. Duveneck received communion from the priest, followed by his sister Mollie, who joined him in returning to the fold. Barnhorn, the daily communicant, was there, receiving, and so was brother, Charlie.

There is no way of telling on what day this triumphal return to the Church occurred. Advent, the weeks before Christmas, is a time set aside by the Church for believers to make an extra effort to dwell with Jesus. During this time Duveneck would have received the last rites of the Church, holy oils applied to his body and special prayers offered to arm him against last temptations and, most of all, to prepare for meeting his savior.

Like Gerontius, Duveneck was breathing his last:

I hear no more the busy beat of time,
No, nor my fluttering breath, nor struggling pulse;
Nor does one moment differ from the next.
I had a dream; yes:-- some one softly said
"He's gone;" and then a sigh went round the room.

His Singular Greatness

Duveneck's death, expected for months, still came as a shock to the community especially for his students. In the next day's *Times-Star* Mary Alexander wrote:

"He has been for over twenty years the magnet that held together the artistic world of Cincinnati. What will happen now?"

The same newspaper carried an article, which stated:

"Miss Mary Duveneck, the sister of the late Frank Duveneck, has the deepest sympathy of a wide circle of friends in his passing, which she, perhaps of all of his family surviving, feels keenest of all. Miss Duveneck always has been her brother's confidant, has traveled with him always, kept his home and been his almost constant companion all his life, save the few years of his married life, cut short so sadly and suddenly on the death of his wife."

The Cincinnati Enquirer, with perhaps a touch of prescience, that, "although suffering from illness due to the shock of her brother's death, Miss Mary Duveneck, with whom the painter resided in Covington, joined the family group of mourners, which included the artist's two brothers, Charles and John Duveneck."

Devastated by his passing, members of the Cincinnati Art Club and the Women's Art Club maintained a vigil at the Sullivan mortuary chapel at 235 East Fourth Street in Cincinnati, where his body lay. On January 7 they joined mourners filling the Cathedral Basilica of the Assumption for a Solemn Requiem High Mass. Very Reverend Joseph Flynn, vicar general of the Covington diocese, served as celebrant. Local Catholic hierarchy took places of honor in the chancel choir. Henry Moeller, bishop of the Archdiocese of Cincinnati, occupied a chair for a visiting prelate. Since it was his cathedral, Ferdinand Brossart, Bishop Maes's successor as bishop of

251

Covington, sat in the episcopal chair that identified him as the diocese's religious leader.[11]

During the Mass Duveneck's coffin was rolled to a place in the transept in front of the altar and railing. A blanket of oak leaves, a gift of the art academy, lay as a cover and a tribute to his singular greatness. The academy's gift provided a personal touch. Atop the bier in the middle lay a facsimile of his *FD* signature. Mourners sitting in front seats could view his greatest known tangible gift to his Church, the murals dedicated to his mother, to the right in the Blessed Sacrament Chapel.

As the choir sang the *Dies Irae*, the obligatory [at that period] thirteenth century music of the Mass for the Dead, the finality of Duveneck's passing came all too clear. In those days black was the color of the day, for the ministers at Mass and many of the mourners. Sister Mollie, had arisen that morning from a sick bed to attend the Mass, joined by her brothers, other relatives and friends. Sadly, Frank Jr., in Cloblenz, Germany, with the U.S. Army of Occupation, was unable to attend. A cablegram went unanswered, likely lost in the confusion reigning at the end of World War I.

Charles P. Taft, son of former U.S. president Howard Taft, sat in front, representing himself and the Cincinnati Art Club as president. The Taft family owned at least one Duveneck painting, the *Cobbler's Apprentice*.

Broken-hearted members of the Art Club passed a resolution on January 10, which reads:

"In his passing, our Club loses one of its strongest supporters. His loss to this Club, to this community, and all of the organizations in which he was active, and to all within reach of his influence, is irreparable.

It is a well-known fact that among all who knew him, there was a feeling of sincere affection, as well as abiding esteem for this great artist and man.

Frank Duveneck was of the best type of what we term 'a Father to all interested in art.' He knew hard work in his early days, and it did not narrow him; he knew sorrow, but it did not embitter him; his judgment always of the best; he was gifted with wonderful vision.

He had marvelous power, which was easily transmitted to those with whom he came in contact, but his thoughts were not grooved in a channel, and his interests always universal. There will be many who shall miss the steady strength which flowed from him, and the sincere kindness so unfailingly shown, the wise council (sic) so freely given.

In the infinitely greater sorrow of his family and those closely allied with him in his work, in his far reaching benevolences, in his labors for art, we ask to extend our condolences, and to lay our tribute upon the bier of this fine man, who has been called to his reward."

A former art museum official set the tone for the day, "We shall miss him beyond expression."

Perhaps the most poignant condolence came from the etcher Joseph Pennell. He wrote to Charles Duveneck this brief note:

"Your brother has gone, but he has left name and fame. In the future he will live with the few—the very few—artists of the United States. There are some of us still living who knew this."[11]

Mollie's Surprise

Duveneck designated Mollie as the primary beneficiary of his will, the homestead and "all the books, pictures, ornaments, furniture and all household furnishings and supplies of every nature belonging to me and being in said house at the time of my death…" More substantially, Mollie was to receive during her life the interest produced by investment of the remainder of his estate.

The *Times-Star* reported later that Duveneck had inherited $600,000 in 1888 at the death of his wife. His estate in 1919 was valued at $50,000 and stood as a "testament to his generosity" over the years.

Mollie was not to receive this last gift from her brother. His death was a catastrophe for her, now on her own, without duties, for the first time in twenty-three years. She had Charlie to look after, but he was not the great artist, the older brother and protector that Frank was. The public ordeal over, Mollie returned to the homestead. Without Frank the house was empty. His paintings, his second floor office, and his studio were as museum pieces. At fifty years old, grossly overweight and feeling unloved and not needed, her will to live was shaken.

Within several days of the funeral Mollie suffered an attack diagnosed as appendicitis. She was removed to Bethesda Hospital in Cincinnati, but after recovering somewhat, was taken to Scarlet Oaks Sanitorium. A neighbor visited her there and returned to Helentown with the hopeful news that Mollie was recuperating though still ill. The neighbor, a Mrs. Aufdemwasser, had news that Helentowners received joyously. Mollie had indeed returned to the Church. She confided to her neighbor that Frank had asked her to rejoin with him. He had told her that he felt responsible for her falling away. In his laxity, he said, he had not set a good example.

Mollie's condition worsened. A deadly infection had set in— peritonitis, inflammation of the membrane lining the abdominal wall. The morning of January 15 brought shocking news. Mollie had died alone in her room. A nurse found the body as she made rounds. The resident physician, E.W. Mitchell, signed the death certificate, finding the cause to have been peritonitis, appendicitis as a complication.

Dr. L.E. Bunker, a Covington physician who attended to Mollie, told the *Kentucky Post* that the death of the noted artist had caused weakening of his sister's vitality.

Ten days after Duveneck's funeral, a requiem Mass was sung for Mollie in the Cathedral Basilica. Mollie died intestate, leaving her affairs in disorder and for her brother, John, to straighten out. John and Charlie shared in Mollie's $18,000 estate, after taxes, following a provision in Frank's will. Order after order was recorded in the Kenton County Probate Court to clarify who were to be the inheritors and to settle claims by the Commonwealth of Kentucky and local businesses.

The surviving brothers found a realtor to dispose of the Duveneck homestead. He had no difficulty finding a buyer. A neighbor, Mrs. George Howell, always admired the Duveneck Garden, and she wanted a larger house to accommodate her growing family. In an interview in 1973, her daughter, Annette, or Nettie, recalled that:

"The place was a shambles when we walked in. Charlie was there. There were also two large pictures of the older Mr. and Mrs. Duveneck in big, thick gold frames with velvet mats…and another painting, *Lady with a Cat*. Then, Charlie slashed the painting with a knife. I guess he didn't want anyone else to have it, and he left the pictures of the Duvenecks.

"We didn't know what to do with them, so I put them on top of a little loft, above the door near the kitchen. And they stayed there until we sold the house. We just felt that they weren't our property, and we didn't know what to do with them."

Later, the Howells found what has been referred to as a plaster of Paris facsimile of the death mask of Lizzie. That mask, whether an actual death mask or a sculpted face, and a pair of cameo earrings and a pin, believed to be Elizabeth Boott Duveneck's, were for years in the hands of descendants.

Upon moving into the Duveneck house, the Howells proceeded to remove unwanted articles from the attic.

"There were all kinds of clothes: riding clothes, dresses, jodphurs," she remembered.

None of it useable to them, the Howells started a bonfire in the side yard, and piece by piece the clothes burned away. In Mollie's rooms the front and middle rooms of the second floor, a large pile of letters lay on the floor.

"It looked like they had been dumped out of the dresser drawers," said Nettie, whose married name was Kipfer. "They were piled about a foot high, and about two feet in diameter. My father looked at me and said, 'What do you think we should do with these letters?' Well, I said they were private correspondence, and none of our business. And he said, 'Yes, I feel the same way,' so we took them outside to the fire and burned them."

Mollie's body was buried in a grave adjacent to her brother's in Mother of God Cemetery in Covington.

---

[1] *Frank Duveneck—Parent, Teacher,* John Howell—Books, San Francisco, California, 1970, p. 162

[2] Interview by the author with Hope Duveneck Williams, November 20, 2013, in Monterey, California

[3] Ibid, Josephine Duveneck became a Quaker after World War I. The anti-war feelings and non-violent trends ran high in the Duveneck family. One of Frank Jr. and Josephine's sons was a conscientious objector during World War II and a second served in the armed forces but in a noncombatant role.

[4] *Annals of American Art,* Smithsonian Institution, Washington, D.C., letters file.

[5] *Life on Two Levels,* Josephine Whitney Duveneck, Trust for Hidden Villa, Los Altos Hills, California, p. 110

[6] Ibid, p. 110

[7] Ibid, p.110-111

[8] Ibid, p. 111

[9] *The Underlying Catholicity of Duveneck,* Mary Leocadia Wilde, O.S.B., Notre Dame University, 1938

[10]Ibid [Sister Mary Leocadia's account of Frank Duveneck's last days came from contact with former students Herman Wessel, Leon Lippert, Mary Alexander and Brother John Duveneck, who had spoken with nurse Lelia Burkart.]
[11]Diocesan clergy assisting at the Mass included Rev. Alfred Hanses and Rev. Herbert Egbring. Rev. Herbert Hillenmeyer, later chancellor of the diocese and long-time pastor of St. Thomas Church in Fort Thomas, Kentucky, served as master of ceremonies.
[12]*Annals of American Art, Smithsonian Institution*, Washington, among newspaper clippings in the Duveneck file.
[13]*Frank Duveneck—Painter, Teacher*, Josephine W. Duveneck, John Howell—Books, San Francisco, California, 1970, p. 162

Chapter Thirteen

The Red Monument

Fort Wright, Kentucky, 1919

Mother of God Cemetery occupies rolling fields in the valley of Banklick Creek, an area ringed and shouldered by glacier-formed hills thousands of years old. It is partly in Covington and partly in the suburban town of Fort Wright. Madison Avenue runs along the fenced northwestern side. It is also known as Kentucky 17, or Three L, because since pioneer days it has squirrelled its way southward to connect the Covington suburb of Latonia with Lexington and Louisville. It became the final resting place for artist Frank Duveneck.

As in any cemetery, headstones spread brokenly over grassy fields. In one large section the ground is punctuated by closely arranged Teutonic-styled iron crosses that bear the names of Benedictine nuns. On headstones throughout the plot German names predominate. Here and there, a pillar or statue reaches high. A bronze figure of St. Francis stands over the grave of one of Duveneck's first teachers, Johann Schmitt whose works grace the colorful interior of the parish church of Mother of God in Covington. , On a plinth, the legend is written in German just as if the grave were sunk somewhere in Munich. Superintendent Phil Zumdick understands the importance of Schmitt to the Duveneck story and therefore the historical value. He watches carefully that a small hole near the base of the St. Francis statue does not widen and cause problems.

Duveneck's is the most impressive monument for an individual. The name, spelled out in fine Roman typeface, fills the facing front side of the red granite monument mined in Wausau, Wisconsin.[1] The monument dominates the family plot. Headstones mark only a scattered handful of the eighteen grave sites.

To Clement Barnhorn fell the sad duty of creating the cemetery memorial to Duveneck. He knew of Duveneck's previous sketches for a memorial dedicated to his mother since the two artists had worked on the concept together. The artists were close friends and consulted one another on many projects dating to the early 1890s, most significantly for the design and crafting of the tomb effigy of Lizzie Boott Duveneck.

If Barnhorn wasn't responsible for locating the sketches, surely he was among the first to see them. He knew that the cemetery memorial project had been put on hold as Duveneck faced difficulties obtaining proper stone. And then, the plan was abandoned after Duveneck chose to honor his mother in another way by dedicating the cathedral murals to her.

Whatever the facts, family and friends sifting through the artist's sketchbooks after his death, reviewed the recovered sketches. With the family's approval, Barnhorn decided to follow the master's concept. He marked each of four corners of a rectangular shaped monument with statues of winged angels, three of which carry symbols of the Christian theological virtues of faith, hope and charity. An angel of resurrection occupies the fourth corner.

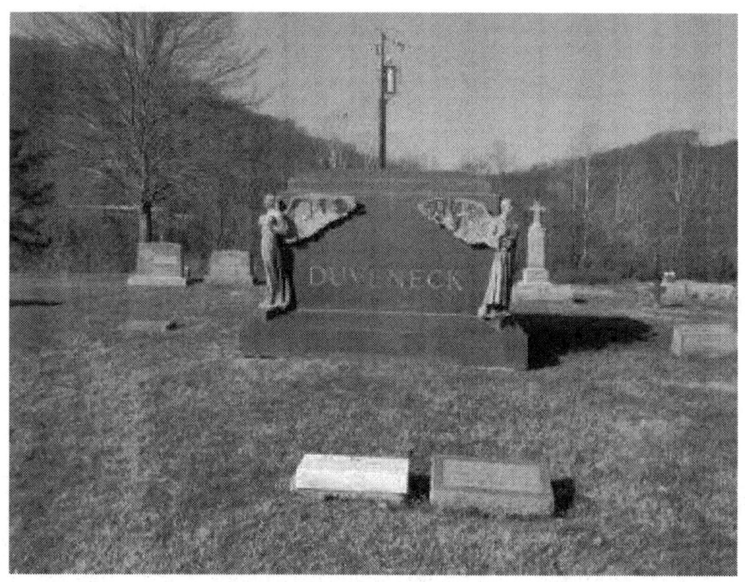

The Duveneck Tomb in Mother of God Cemetery.

Artist and teacher Mary Leocadia Wilde, O.S.B., believed that the idea for the memorial originated "in the mind of Duveneck.… The entire work proves that Duveneck was a Catholic at heart and that he clung to the Catholic philosophy of life."[2]

Duveneck's concept was further described:

"The outspread wings are emblematic of the speed and willingness to carry out God's Commands.

"Faith holds a disk, symbol of eternity, and the Sacred Host on which we find the Greek figures Chi Rho; Hope is represented as peering into the distance; Charity, the figure of a woman, holds in her hand the emblem of love—the heart; the Resurrection represents the mummy, not swathed in bandages as was the custom among the Egyptians, but in flowing draperies acclaiming the joy of the Christian Ideal."[3]

The Duveneck family plot lies near an interior road and roundabout. Standing high in the center of the circle is one of Barnhorn's finest works. *I am the Resurrection and the Life* represents a faith statement for those buried there, a crucifixion grouping of the dying Christ on the cross and three mourning figures at its foot.

William Fay[4] served as the model for Christ as Barnhorn worked in the academy studio. In an interview during the 1970s, Fay observed:

"Duveneck sat there and smoked, whether reading or watching Barnhorn. He did not have much to say while I was there. He would go to sleep. Barnhorn and I would keep up the conversation. Barnhorn was young with ideas, and he got along well with the students. He could talk about anything, what was going on in public, or classical things, and he would understand."

Duveneck "made his hangout in Barnhorn's studio. It was the only comfortable place to sit, and he would smoke and maybe dream of the past, not thinking much about the future at that time in his life. One day, he came over and was watching. He made a few gestures while he smoked—he always had a cigarette in his holder—and pointed to the arms.

'The arms are too heavy.' [He said to Barnhorn].

'Darn you, Duveneck, yesterday, you told me that they're not heavy enough.'

"Duveneck sat down, and said,

'I'd bet he never even touched them.'"

Barnhorn was paid handsomely for the Crucifixion Group work, $10,000, on a commission from the Mother of God Cemetery As-

261

sociation. The sculpture was dedicated in 1915, the year Duveneck was honored in San Francisco at the Panama Pacific Exhibition.

The crucifixion sculpture and the nearby Duveneck memorial constitute a personal link, among many, between the two artists. Their studios at the Cincinnati Art Academy were side by side. They enjoyed each other's company and shared their love of art and treasured techniques that they accumulated by experience and learned by study.

Barnhorn relayed several telling stories that reflect on the character and style of Duveneck. In a conversation[5] with the painter's daughter-in-law Josephine, he said:

"Duveneck never seemed to think along the lines of other humans. He had a vocabulary all his own. It took me a long time to appreciate this and even then I could not always follow his line of thought. I was very busy on a clay figure one day when Duveneck strolled in. I could see in an instant that there was something on his mind that was bothering him. He slouched into a chair and sat scowling at my clay figure.

"'There is something wrong with that face,' he declared.

"'Yes,' I partly admitted, 'but what's wrong with it?'

"'Make the features regular.'

"'Make the features regular' I retorted, but those are E's features. How are you going to make them any more regular than they are?'

"'I know those are E's features but make them regular.'

"'Well, then if you want them regular, you do it, for I can't for the life of me see what you are driving at.'

"With that Duveneck got up from his seat and in a moment had changed the features to a shapeless mass. From this he broadened the forehead and worked the clay down to the shape of the nose. It was the old formula for modeling (that Barnhorn had taught him). What he meant by 'regular' was that I should follow the accepted rule. I protested that it was fallacy to do a thing wrong in the beginning and then correct it to the satisfaction of the creator, but he held to it doggedly that things should be done 'regular' and that was the way it had to be."[5]

Barnhorn was nearly always the understudy to the great painter whose strong physical presence could be intimidating, his quiet ways as a man of few words adding even more *gravitas* to his person. When the Cincinnati Museum Association asked him to create a bust of Duveneck, he moved with caution. Accordingly, Duveneck took advantage of Barnhorn's discretion and became something of a dictator.

"I think there was a certain hidden vanity in the 'Old Man' for I know in his youth he was a handsome fellow with a great shock of blond hair and when he came to be perpetuated in bronze he wanted to look young."

"'Don't make me look old,' he would bellow from his seat on the stand, 'make my eyes big.'

"He would button up his coat and look as important as a statesman or a victorious general. As the hours passed, however, he would get bored and slump. So up and down he would go, sometimes solemn and important, sometimes sleepy-looking with all muscles relaxed. He of all men should have known how to pose, but for him to be on the other end of the business was a novel experience."[6]

Duveneck got what he wanted, a solemn and younger-looking image of himself.

Naturally, Barnhorn was ambivalent towards Duveneck's habit of coming by the studio and commenting on his work. At times, criticism was welcome, and on occasion, disturbing. The sculptor found a solution. He acquired the most comfortable chair he could

263

find and outfitted a corner of his studio with a table, an ash tray and a package of cigarettes.

Duveneck came by the studio and asked where the chair had come from. Vague about its origin, Barnhorn asked him to "try it." The artist sat down and quickly slipped into a nap. From that day onward, a nap in the chair was a daily exercise for Duveneck. He fell into Barnhorn's trap. Criticism was muted. The artist's daily "siesta" took precedence.

After Duveneck's death, Barnhorn disassembled the furniture setting and shifted the chair face-forward toward a wall. He piled papers and other items on it so that no one could sit there.

"I sit in it occasionally just to remember," Barnhorn said.[7] "I think of him every day. He was a delightful man."

The Cemetery's Puzzle

If Barnhorn were living he could probably solve a puzzle confronting anyone who reviews grave site records at Mother of God Cemetery. Thirteen graves in the family plot are occupied by Duvenecks, the last buried in 1974. The name, Decker, the artist's birth patronymic, is given for two graves. A common marker next to the artist's bears the title, Frank Decker, giving rise to the puzzle.

The cemetery's index card file states that Frank and Charles Duveneck co-owned the family plot. The card file orients the list of grave holders in their relationship to Frank Duveneck. After his name, the title, *artist,* is penciled in, with parentheses. Next is Miss Mollie, identified as *sister*. Mrs. Elizabeth Duveneck Kesting is also identified as *sister*. The fourth entry is Frank Decker, titled *father*. Next is Mr. Joe Duveneck, also titled *father,* followed by Mrs. "Cath" Duveneck, *mother*.

A note under a column for each entry labelled "Church" typically lists the church from which the person was buried. In the case of

Frank Decker, it says the remains were removed in March, 1925, from the St. Joseph parish cemetery in the old Buena Vista area of Covington, to the Duveneck family site in Mother of God cemetery. Graves of his mother, Catherine, and his foster father, Joseph, also were moved there from old St. Joseph's.

The question remains: Who was Frank Decker? The orientation suggests that Frank Decker was the artist's blood father. However, the family biography lists Frank Decker as the artist's uncle for whom Frank was named at birth. Recall that Bernard Duveneck died in the cholera epidemic of 1848 and that widow Catherine married for the second time to Joseph Duveneck. A possible explanation is that someone made a mistake in making a notation and applied the name Frank to his blood father's last name. But the tombstone bears the name, Frank Decker.

The cemetery superintendent says that the notations as to relationship are likely inaccurate. The truth as to identity of Frank Decker, whether he was the uncle, parent or other relative of Frank Duveneck, probably will not be known in this lifetime.

---

[1]Previous commentators have referred to the red granite as Warsaw, an obvious mistake

[2] *The Underlying Catholicity of Duveneck*, Sr. Leocadia Wilde, O.S.B., paper, Notre Dame University, 1938, p. 66

[3]Article, *Cincinnati Post*, Nov. 28, 1934, quoted in Wilde

[4]William Fay was a student of Frank Duveneck who worked in commercial art in Cincinnati. The author interviewed him April 27, 1973

[5]*Frank Duveneck, Painter-Teacher*, Josephine W. Duveneck, John Howell Books—San Francisco, 1970, p.144-145

[6]Ibid, p. 145

[7]*Kentucky Post*, March, 28, 1934, John E. Murphy

Chapter Fourteen

An Appreciation of Duveneck I

Frank Duveneck's life and his art drew much praise and some criticism. Assessments of his art nearly always yield an historical perspective. He was a leader of the Munich school and later experimented with light and color in an Italian period and later in a Gloucester period. His Munich style, and perhaps the Italian one, has taken a sideline position against the rise of Impressionism and the other, more modern schools which followed.

One may evaluate a work of art as either good or bad, perhaps even inexplicable as Ruskin did with a work by Whistler. Behind each grading, there should be some kind of reason and understanding. How one approaches a work of art, what he or she brings to the table, is important. Therefore, a critique of art appreciation is helpful in a discussion of Frank Duveneck's life, his art, and the praise and criticism that entailed.

First, the basics:

Dominican cleric and medieval interpreter of Aristotle, St. Thomas Aquinas (1225-1274), defined as beautiful anything that gives pleasure on its being seen (pulchra enim dicuntur quae visa placent]. Jacques Maritain, the twentieth century Aquinas authority, ably assisted by Eric Gill, the Dominican tertiary, said the Angelic Doctor assigned three conditions to the creation of a beautiful thing. These thoughts from Maritain were wonderful, and are presented here with clarifying author's punctuation, recognizing that, in explaining them, Maritain or his interpreter, did use the word, "like," far too often.

"The work must have:

-**integrity,** *[perfection]* because the mind likes being *[and not ugliness]*;

-**proportion**, because the mind likes order and likes unity;

-(and) lastly, and above all

brightness or clarity, because the mind likes light and intelligibility."

Another point Maritain offers is that ancients of the western world affirmed the essential character of beauty is "a certain splendor,"[1] defined as a great and dazzling brightness or brilliance.

It's interesting how the idea of light, which enables knowledge and understanding—and unfortunately at times, to the contrary—comes into play.

A work is beautiful and therefore good because of its integrity, or it is mean and debased. Art is created by a skilled person, enabled by apprenticeship that enriches a natural talent. Granted there may be degrees of success in any work of art. Composition may be true, color excellent, and theme agreeable. The central issue deals with the subject matter and how it is handled. It's the performance by the author that counts. The presentation cannot be a distortion. A piece of ecclesiastical art must be, by its nature, theologically correct for it to achieve truth. The Victorian critic, John Ruskin, the first Slade professor of Fine Art at Oxford University, would agree.

Sir Kenneth Clark, a later Slade professor and the famous narrator of the televised series, *Civilisation,* counted Ruskin as one of his chief influences. One can't help but agree with what he wrote in summarizing Ruskin's thinking:

"Art is not a matter of taste, but involves the whole man. Whether in making or perceiving a work of art, we bring to bear on it feeling, intellect, morals, knowledge, memory, and every other human capacity, all focused in a flash on a single point. Aesthetic man is a concept as false and dehumanizing as economic man.

267

"Even the most superior mind and the most powerful imagination must found itself on facts, which must be recognized for what they are. The imagination will often reshape them in a way which the prosaic mind cannot understand; but this recreation will be based on facts, not on formulas or illusions."[2]

British philosopher Alfred North Whitehead adopted a more general, almost neutral approach. "Art is the imposing of a pattern on experience, and our aesthetic enjoyment is recognition of the pattern."

From the Christian perspective, a work must display the character of this essentially rational and humanistic view of life. Anyone, of any faith or persuasion, can accomplish this, and they frequently do. Maritain said this Christian view is "to be found in its subject and its spirit. It is the art of humanity redeemed. It is implanted in the Christian soul, by the side of running waters, under the sky of the theological virtues,[3] amid the breaths of the seven gifts of the Spirit. It is natural for it to bear Christian fruit."

Maritain does not mean that an artist must be a saint to do such work. He quotes Goethe, speaking in the broader sense: "That is the whole secret. To be able *to do* something, you must *be* something." Leonardo da Vinci said it succinctly, "Every characteristic of painting is a characteristic of the painter." In a general sense, Oscar Wilde captured the obverse side with his phrase, "The highest art rejects the burden of the human spirit." It somehow succeeds, even triumphs.

Ruskin wrote that honest work aids mankind and, in it, he found strong elements of religion:

"God appoints to every one of his creatures a separate mission, and if they discharge it honourably—there will assuredly come of it such burning as, in its appointed mode and measure, shall shine before men, and be of service constant and holy!"

One could say that Ruskin had artists such as Duveneck in mind when he wrote this.

A Real Talent

Duveneck was no saint during much of his life. He was a man of many good and solid virtues: generous, loving and caring, in many respects, a decent and sincere person towards other people, his family and his friends. Even though he distanced himself from his religion and the accepted route to sanctity, he retained his basic Christian self, and it is revealed in his work. His subjects were ordinary people. He portrayed them as they were. None of his works challenge what he understood as being true. His approach was honest. He brought integrity to his works that penetrates beyond surface material, whether a portrait, a landscape or a religious article, a sculpture or an etching. Nothing he did is contrary to natural law.

Norbert Heermann, former Duveneck student and author, captured this spirit.

"His compelling interest is in the normal aspects of man and nature; the subjects he chooses are everyday types; he conceives them in an unpretentious spirit, but transmits them endowed with quiet power. There is in his work a certain finality of grasp with a dignity, a calm, which to the connoisseur is akin to the serenity of the Greek, which to the multitude it may appear actually commonplace."[4]

In an article[5] on Herman Wessel, one of Duveneck's finest and most accomplished students, by Carl Samson and Carol Cyran, the point is made that Duveneck's training in Munich "was based on truth to nature, using subjects from ordinary life, and a solid three-dimensional interpretation of form. Duveneck was, however, careful not to lead his students into a perilous effort to emulate his own bravura brushwork, instead insisting on a methodical and disciplined regimen of highly finished charcoal drawings, painted figures, and portraits."

Further, the article specifies a component of his work, as applied to his student, Wessel, which made it unique:

"Under Duveneck's instruction, Wessel learned the critical importance of constructing the head with a clear understanding of the demarcation between its front, side, top and bottom planes – even to sense the back of the head. Perceiving where these plane changes occur, and giving each its appropriate degree of emphasis, encourages a nearly sculptural understanding of how the painter can interpret and suggest three-dimensional form on the flat surface of his canvas."

Duveneck was one of at least three portraitists who used the concept of planes in structuring images that suggest three-dimensional form. It is a technique he learned from studying Frans Hals. Not alone in its use, he was joined by his contemporary, John Singer Sargent.

A former Duveneck student, Henry C. Loughmiller, took a similar view. He wrote that the artist emphasized "the representation of the figure as a solid object broadly sculptured by natural light...its detail simplified in terms of its major planes, the hair and costume, by subdued tonal contrast and reduced modeling, subordinated to the face, the whole defined by a single unified light and a single unified dark—to the end of producing an ordered oneness of total effect."[6]

Duveneck's Apprenticeship

Our subject, Duveneck, was no one-trick pony. He painted portraits and landscapes, completed etchings, sculpted and painted murals, in addition to having the ability to teach. He learned his craft much like a medieval apprentice—from scratch while in the studios of the Benedictine-founded Catholic Altar Building Stock Company under Brother Cosmas Wolf, the artist trained in Germany. His painting of the *Our Lady of the Immaculate Conception* in the Latrobe Archabbey, completed when he was fifteen years old, and the *Madonna and Child* in St. Walburg's monastery in the Nazarene, also known as Pre-Raphaelite style, reveal a depth of understanding and a strong faith.

A recent finding from the archives at St. Vincent Archabbey is informative:

"From Br. Cosmas he learned how to use tools, carve wood, model figures, and design friezes, as well as to gild. From Johann Schmitt he learned how to mix pigments, clean brushes, paint floral borders, and paint on canvas and make wall murals. His painting skills were quickly recognized [as superior], and he began to receive painting instruction and assignments."[7]

In 1867 Duveneck assisted Wilhelm Lamprecht in producing ten murals based on designs by Br. Cosmas. The next year he was in Quebec working on the church of St.-Romuald d'Etchemin near Quebec City, now designated by the provincial minister of culture a historic monument. During this time Lamprecht permitted him to work on larger areas of the church murals.

Frank Duveneck later spoke to his daughter-in-law about his instructor, and she wrote that Lamprecht:

"...was a strict task master. Every morning before breakfast he made Frank draw two or three eyes until he found out how to do it with skill and dispatch. This discipline stood him in good stead in later years, for nearly all of the Duveneck portraits look out of their frames with startlingly life-like eyes."[8]

European Training

As the 1860s drew to a close, Duveneck was given the advantage of a European education. He learned techniques from the Dutch masters through his Munich training, and he applied the same pattern of clarity, unity and depth of understanding with even greater skill to his raw subjects. He had vision of who they were. His ordinary people-subjects come to life as real and true even as the models themselves were real.

His paintings won more than awards. They caused stupendous responses. Consider this from the *Records of William M. Hunt,* a third-person account of the European-trained Bostonian who had awakened artistic interests in New England and was among the first in America to discover Duveneck:

"The portrait called *The Old Professor,* of Duveneck, interested him exceedingly. He took it in his lap and fondled it for a half hour or more even while talking of other matters. A few evenings later he begged us to lend it to him for a short time; he wished to see how it looked in his studio; so he carried it off under his arm, frame and all refusing to have it sent round to him in the morning. He also showed us a very friendly letter from Duveneck, in response to an invitation from him to remain and paint in Boston. So far from feeling jealous of Duveneck's talent, as had been alleged, he would gladly have had him live in Boston, and would have done all he could to help him to get orders. Later in the year, when Duveneck was in Boston, Mr. Hunt expressed great regret at not meeting him."[9]

In another reference in the memoir:

"Mr. Duveneck's appearance in Boston fluttered the dove-cotes there to some purpose, and nothing that we know of in the recent history of our art world seems to me as interesting as the cordial enthusiasm his pictures excited among the younger members of the Art Club,—an enthusiasm which took the practical shape of an invitation to the artist to come and settle in Boston, where, it was hoped, he might give efficient help in the opposition that was making itself felt to certain arrogant and dogmatic claims beginning to be unbearable. Mr. Duveneck did not accept the invitation, but his pictures worked powerfully in the desired direction, and greatly strengthened the hands of the rising school."[10]

Hunt was joined by others who praised the artist and his works. "Here at last was a personality that spoke a definite, a beautifully and powerfully definite language," Norbert Heermann wrote years later. "The opening of a new era in American art was proclaimed." The new era was more officially launched in 1877 when Duveneck and other painters of the Munich school presented canvasses at the National Academy Exhibition in New York, followed by another at the Kurtz Gallery in New York.

"The younger men among the American painters had been brought into contact with a vital influence from outside and had been taught to respect their own reaction to it," wrote Heermann. "In speaking of Duveneck I would emphasize the powerful effect of his own work at the outset of our era. What he accomplished after that, while not less surely, was more quietly done."

Heermann pointed to how Duveneck broadened his artistic reach in this period, citing the school in Florence, his Italian paintings, Venetian and Florentine etchings and later his sculptures. He argued that Duveneck was a strong and fundamental figure in the establishment of American art; his role "as adviser has been of inestimable value, the story of his life affording a natural bridge by which to pass from our early period to the present day."

A later commentator, Richard J. Boyle, author of the art biography, *Twachtman,* wrote of Duveneck:

"The essence of Duveneck's painting and the secret of its popularity lay in his exceptional combination of the direct attack on the canvas, using a bold 'modern' brush work carried out in the mellow tones of an Old Master—a combination that was hard to beat."[11]

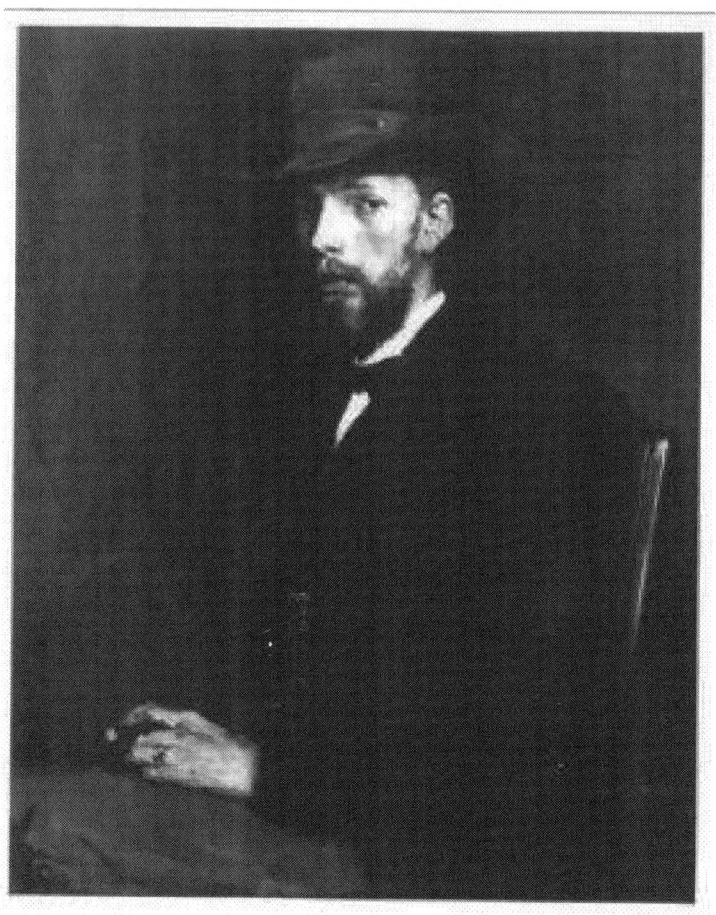

Duveneck's portrait of Professor Ludwig Loefftz

Boyle singled out the portrait of Ludwig Loefftz, which he called masterly. "The relaxed pose and calm, steady gaze of the sitter are in contrast to the directness and vigor of its presentation. Fresh, intense, and technically impressive in execution, the figure emerges from a dark background, producing an illusion of what Henry

274

James called 'palpable reality.' This is the Munich style at its best…"[12]

Maturation of an Artist

No stranger to honors and criticism, Frank Duveneck matured under task masters who were not afraid of new things. He had a knack for artistic expression. He learned the basics of his trade from painters of religious works. Then he became a student of the new and evolving Munich school influenced by nature and the Dutch masters. Duveneck's teachers, Wilhelm Leibl, and Wilhelm von Diez, launched the new Munich school under the concurrent inspiration of France's Gustave Courbet whose late 1860s' exhibit in Munich brought a fresh and outside influence to the city's artists. The author Emile Zola became a spokesman for the new movement that was sweeping Europe, with his comment, "Une oeuvre d'art est un coin de la nature vu a travers un temperament." [A work of art is a fragment of nature seen through a temperament.] After his studies Duveneck became a leading exponent of the Munich style.

Heermann, the artist, critic and former Duveneck student, said that Duveneck had an affinity for the naturalists. "Given immediately the close contact with a mood and method so absolutely suited to him, and remembering also the technical skill which he had already gained, especially through his free handling of paint in the work of church decoration in American, we can more easily understand the rapid progress of this newcomer in the stimulating art world of Munich,--this blond, vigorous and single-hearted young giant with the 'eye of a hawk,' fresh from a new world and conscious of his own power."[13]

These early paintings of Duveneck's broke new ground in American art in the nineteenth century, eclipsing the broad nature scenes of the Hudson River school that had dominated previously. In his lifetime Duveneck mastered other modes of etching, of sculpture and of mural painting. A testament to the level of his production,

275

more than six hundred and fifty of his works have been located and identified. An unknown number of other works from his first and second European periods, when it was his practice to casually part with paintings, are likely in attics somewhere. He was omnivorous as a painter, doing portraits of anyone who came along and asking for twenty marks' compensation. For example, he is known to have painted the portrait of the suffragette Susan B. Anthony while in Austria. There are also references to Duveneck's completing a portrait of a United States Supreme Court Justice and of the Covington, orchard owner who visited with Duveneck in Florence. The whereabouts of these paintings, likely representative of a much larger number, is not known.

Many of Duveneck's works are signed and easily identified. A good number are not, including unsigned and unfinished paintings, even some with fake monograms, says Cincinnati Art Museum curator Aronson. Therefore, "lots of confusion exists between his work and his students," making authentication difficult. During his teaching years Duveneck would demonstrate by adding brush strokes to a student's canvas. Still, the case can be made: the actual production number of Duveneck works should rise significantly beyond the six hundred and fifty, not a poor canon of works for a professional artist.

Dear wife Lizzie is responsible for labeling Duveneck as lazy. She referred to him in this way early in their relationship. Her friend and his nemesis, Henry James, built on the suggestion, as he followed Duveneck's career from his highly respectful review of Duveneck's Boston Art Club exhibition in 1875 through the years even to the mixed, on-and-off reviews he offered of Lizzie's effigy. His close friendly relationship with Lizzie and, doubtless, the lack of a strong personal connection to Duveneck, interfered in later years with his evaluation of the artist and his work.

Without question, in the period after Lizzie's death in 1888, Duveneck's production declined. Not to provide excuses, the artist was then in his fourth decade. He was belabored by his personal

276

loss and, given the artistic, sensitive nature for which he is known, it is likely that he dwelt on the loss and scrutinized its meaning. However, the decade of the 1890s provided him with the satisfaction of the effigy's triumphant success, honored by the Paris Salon in 1895. Yet a shadow followed Duveneck as he traveled abroad, copied paintings, became involved in critical family issues, and spent time reconstituting his life. Still, there was recognition. Officials of the Paris Salon in 1899 asked him to serve on the jury of paintings for the 1900 Salon. Some later paintings from this period, of his mother for example, are interesting and demonstrate that the spark of old was still ignitable. He continued to be known as a father of American Realism.

Kimberly Allen-Kattus, professor of art history at Northern Kentucky University, has drawn an interesting comparison between Duveneck's early paintings of his mother and a later one completed in 1902. None of the several paintings of his mother present an idealized subject. "They offer straightforward likeness that reveals a serious, hardworking, and intelligent woman. But the 1902 portrait differs from the earlier portraits in some significant ways. Duveneck's earlier portraits are busts; the 1902 painting is a three-quarter length portrait. Katherine is seated regally in her chair, in a pose and garbed as a woman of gentility. Her headpiece, kerchief and pose are oddly reminiscent of contemporary portraits of Queen Victoria. [Curiously, the British monarch had died only a year earlier.] The painting offers a shallow space and thinly applied pigments recalling Duveneck's portrait of his wife and his earlier adoption of the salon style."[14]

In the new century, then in his fifties, where did he turn? He became again a teacher, and by doing so, effectively kept his hand in his career field. He continued an active life outside the classroom. He made several transatlantic voyages in this turn-of-the-century period. Recall that he made first contact with Gloucester in 1890. He returned there most every summer from 1900 onwards, more than fifteen summers of three to four months each. More than sixty paintings have been located from those Gloucester summers, many reflecting his dabbling in the Impressionism trend. He worked, albeit at a leisurely pace, always defensive that he was serious about his commitment. He always said it was important to show his students examples of his work, that his summer holidays were not wasted in playtime. As the Gloucester period clearly demonstrates, he took an interest in new ideas and approaches.

An unknown writer for the Cincinnati *Commercial Tribune* must have had access to Duveneck and watched him work, likely at the end of the academic year in 1914. He observed Duveneck using his thumb to move paint around and wrote in the June 14th edition:

"…with a sweep or two (the artist would) pull an otherwise bit of wet painting into beautiful harmonious masses; then would come those broad brush strokes of modeling which gave new structure and a finer relation of masses; at the end came the blending; all of which seemed too easy when the pupils saw Duveneck do it; but it was in reality magic."

Duveneck's philosophy of art was simple and true:

"Art is not an imitation but a sublimation of Nature. Nature presented you with a faulty copy; it must be edited to become Art. Lights and shadows could not be indiscriminately transcribed as they chance to appear; a very dark upper lip, in Nature, would on canvas destroy the unity of the mouth; a deep shadow under the lower lip, if so rendered would be given a force which belonged only to the features. Even character lines must be treated judiciously. If one cuts across a major form, it must be so subdued as not to destroy the integrity of that form. 'Nature can afford to do that; you can't was Duveneck's classic admonition to one who had recorded a literal fact to the detriment of an artistic value. Where paint handling was concerned, he appears to have been very careful not to encourage his students to emulate his own style, but allowed each to work in his own way. The only advice he was said to have given along these lines was to 'paint in little planes' –an exhortation to crisp handling."[15]

After sweeping prizes as a student at the Munich Academy, he won recognition from author and then critic Henry James. This connection was the beginning of a rare and revisionist relationship that lasted more than a decade. As an artist of the word, James pierced the minds of his literary characters and laid them bare. Duveneck, an artist of the brush, probed their souls in his paintings. In other aspects the two men differed from each other in high contrast: Duveneck, a quiet, bold and creative painter, friend to many; James, a clever, introspective, opinionated, superior outsider, friend to a few outside of his family.

When he reviewed Duveneck's paintings in Boston from the artist's first Munich tour, James had only recently returned to New England from lengthy sojourns in Europe. He had found his American home culturally arid. His verbal gifts were bolstered by a strong visual sense. He had what artist John La Farge called "'the painter's eye,' a rare and great virtue in a man of letters. In Henry there was a capacity to look with great intentness at the world around him, to see a landscape or a street entire. Through the wedding of his visual sense and his verbal power he dominated and used his other senses."[16]

The Boston Art Club's exhibit in 1875 in which Duveneck showed five portraits was a cultural oasis, for the critic most assuredly. James noted that the paintings differed from the smoothly finished courses of Dusseldorf and the Hudson River School. He generalized with the comment that the paintings offered "the excitement of adventure and the certitude of repose." Given James's descriptions, the portraits were: *William Adams*, which Lizzie and her father acquired; the masterly *Professor Ludwig Loefftz*; and another of a professor. He also commented on three other paintings, *The Lady with a Fan; Head of an Old Man in a Fur Cap*, and *The Bohemian* that were on display at Doll & Richards gallery. By today's standards, the subjects are by no means "ugly," as James referred to them. They were and are refreshingly honest depictions of the people in a style that was new.

"The discovery of an unsuspected man of genius is always an interesting event…" he wrote for *The Nation*. He described the paintings in this way, "There are no accessories, the handling is of the broadest and freest, the color ranges through only two or three variations of black or grey, but the relief, the vigor, the frankness, the comprehensive simplicity are most striking." Completeness was a word he used to contrast Duveneck's work with other Americans' paintings he had seen in Boston and in New York. He regarded Duveneck's work as strong and brilliant, "the most highly developed phenomenon in the way of a painter that the U.S.A. has given birth to."

Learning that Duveneck was planning to return to Europe for additional studies, James observed: "We confess that as things stand today, almost any young artist of promise is likely to do better out of America than in it."[17]

Duveneck's return to Europe was marked by a series of artistic successes. He learned and mastered the art of etching. He was held in such respect even in his twenties that he founded a popular school in Munich and continued the practice of art. His landscapes from around Polling are particularly and artfully beautiful. In this period James shifted from art critic to full-time writer and novelist, an author neither American nor British, yet claimed by both nations' literary establishments. His attitude towards Duveneck, who had won the hand of his friend, Lizzie, evolved from awed public critic to fault-finding opponent in private. James was, however, a discerning critic who expressed strong opinions about works of art and choices of subject. To his credit he was close with artists and the arts community. He seemed to have an aversion to a painter's narratives that explored "the ugliness of things," and criticized portraitists Singer Sargent and Julian Story for demonstrating this view. He belittled as ugly some of Duveneck's choices of subjects from his Munich period. That is a fair criticism. But as art historian

Allen-Kattus points out, Duveneck's self-portrait from this time, depicting a rough neck effusively mouthing his outrage, can be compared to the *Bitter Draught by* the Dutch artist Adriaen Brouwer. The Dutch style was one that he was pursuing, emulating and performing well.

James praised Duveneck's work and always looked for something more, expressing doubts later that he would do anything great. He was unduly harping and critical of the artist's personality, at least as that personality was expressed in James's company. In his worst moments James even had the audacity to disparage the effigy of Lizzie, suggesting that his critical abilities were eroded by personal feelings. He later recanted when it became clear that Duveneck had scored a major triumph.

Branching Out

Before long, still in Europe and under twin influences of his talented and clever wife and the environment of Italy, Duveneck launched into a new and brighter style. He presented Italian maidens and sunny courtyards, scenes from Florence and Venice, frequently where waters and rivers play roles. His rendition in oil of the Villa Castellani views a peaceful fortress exuding the history of Bellosguardo, the wonders of nature, and the significance of a place.

Carol M. Osborne, former curator of the Stanford University Museum, captured the change that had taken place with these words:

"In Duveneck's work, qualities of extreme naturalism grew subdued in the years that followed his Bohemian Munich days. During the Italian stay of the 1880s…his palette grew lighter [than it had been], and his brushwork smoother and more finished. Moving to France at Lizzie's suggestion, he set to work on a painting for the Paris Salon of 1888 with his wife as the model."[18]

Having branched out in subject matter and style, Duveneck returned to his natural media, painting and portraiture. He completed

281

the full-length portrait of his wife, in her wedding dress. It is one of his great achievements. Today, Elizabeth Otis Lyman Boott Duveneck shines from that Victorian canvas as a modern Madonna—feminine, enormously capable, intelligent and beautiful. He used such restraint in his presentation that you can feel the quiet power coming forth, you nearly expect her to move. His great love, Lizzie, inspired him in her life and, tragically, in her death. His sculptured effigy of her is another great artistic achievement, which will stand the test of time.

He applied his talents to etching, and he succeeded in this medium, new to him and highly technical. His *Riva degli Schiavoni* in Venice is a masterpiece. When James Abbott McNeill Whistler saw Duveneck's version, he responded in the third person: "Whistler must do the Riva also."

Nearly forty years later, a *New York Times* critic[19] contrasted the two works, saying that Whistler's was:

"a daintier, more fastidious little scene that says to the imagination: 'This Venice, Bridge of the Sea, is, after all, a small place in comparison with the great world that stretches in all directions beyond it. Why, then, exaggerate it? Why make much of it? Why not accept it as a perfect small thing, exquisite in its detail and noble in its proportions and worthy of the most loving and patient interpretation with the finest needle and the most exigently selective vision?'"

"Duveneck's 'Riva,' several times repeated with variations, conveys a more robust message and fills the mind with hints of the maritime splendor of the past, of the sturdy, adventurous race of sailors by whom the city was founded, of the swarming life with which it is still quick after many historic Italian cities have sunk into apathy."

Further, the critic wrote:

"In the plate, called 'Shipping Opposite the Piazzetta,' Duveneck's ability to suggest the animation of nature without letting it degenerate to restlessness is especially noteworthy…What holds the imagination, however, is the stir of the foreground water, a stir that goes deeper than the ripples and dimples of the surface and reveals that movement of the whole mass which may be felt even in these quiet channels. Echoing the curiously stimulating movement of the water is a more agitated movement of the clouds above the little buildings in the distance, emphasizing their stability and ponderable substance and, adding to the whole composition a degree of dramatic intensity.

"The honesty of his work is refreshing after an impartial survey of the etchings of the nineteenth century, with their frequent excursions into a region of rather cheap mystery where blurs of tone and impenetrable shadows leave the friendly imagination to impute a meaning of some sort."

The master etcher Joseph Pennell, in his 1919 work *Etchers and Etching*, commented on Duveneck's etchings that "no one has approached him in beauty and meaning of line." Specifically, on his work, *Rialto*, Pennell observed: "It is a genuine etching, every line is vital, the point of view is personal, and the arrangement individual, (sic) and this is the case with all the rest. Only in one or two, so far as I remember, is there in composition any similarity to Whistler's work. Those are of the *Riva*, and I am not sure that Duveneck did not make his plates before Whistler came to Venice; at any rate he showed them before Whistler exhisited his. Duveneck, so far as I know, only worked for a short period in Florence and Venice at etching, but this *Rialto* and his *Desdemona's House* and the *Ca' d'Oro* are masterpieces. He too discovered the beauty of the flag poles in front of St. Mark's, with their floating, flaming banners swung up on a festa. There are two Rivas by each artist, similar as I have said, in being take (sic) from an upper window, the window of the rooms where both artists lived, and which gave on that wonderful, ever changing, ever moving life of the city. A few by Duveneck were done on the Zattere, and by the Dogana, and one or two in Florence, they are masterpieces."

High praise this was, indeed, for Duveneck, trained as a painter.

Duveneck and Obscurity

So what happened?

Art history says that Impressionism eclipsed Duveneck's Realism, but other forces were at work. As the nineteenth century was closing, in the wake of colorful Impressionism, R.H. Ives Gammell says a schism split the arts community. The nature of art itself, he contends, began to transform. The division among artists caused dissension that resulted in the wholesale degrading of historic and essential preparations and practices "on which the survival of painting as a fine art depends."[20] Instruction in the basics was condemned as "academic," and this critical component for maturation in art was launched on a long and steady decline. The harsh consequence has been the loss of techniques and expertise, on one hand, and the rise of popularity of artless expressionism, the work of schoolchildren and bored adults "who had not the slightest understanding of the noble but inaccessible art they were unconsciously and blissfully caricaturing."

Gammell has praised the endurance of the Boston School of artists in his posthumously published book, *The Boston Painters: 1900-1930*. They emerged as polished workmen of the age, inheritors of such American antecedents as John Singleton Copley, John LaFarge, William Morris Hunt and Frank Duveneck. It was Duveneck whom Gammell regarded as the most eminent among those who influenced Boston painters and specifically, his students Frederic Porter Vinton and Joseph DeCamp. Duveneck's reputation, Gammell wrote, has never declined. His works have survived the rise of the Ash Can School, which came to fame early in the twentieth century and again during the 'thirties as the focus of art turned relentlessly on the fate of the downtrodden.

Of Duveneck's durability, Gammell wrote:

"He was one of the scant four or five previously celebrated American painters of genuine distinction whose reputation survived during the esthetic revolution of the nineteen-thirties when our tastemakers decreed that pictures should be rated by the degree of 'social consciousness' manifested in their subject matter and in inverse ratio to the European influence detectable in their execution."

In his earlier work, *Twilight of Painting*, Gammell forecast that trained artists eventually would recognize the great loss perpetrated on society and rediscover the artists whose training and capabilities produced truly great art works, such as Duveneck.

Since the turn of the century through today, the rediscovery is manifested in comments on Facebook, on blogs and other Internet media. Frank Duveneck and the Cincinnati School is a popular Facebook page. Landscape artist Stapleton Kearns recorded his views in his blog and illustrated them with a reproduction of a forest scene from Polling. He offered his thoughts on what the art world owed Frank Duveneck. The artist, he wrote, took an ordinary corner of nature as his subject. The Polling landscape he chose focuses on several trees and avoids broad scenic views of huge expanses –a focus that broke new ground. Kearns wrote: "His students' broad style of expressive painting brought a new kind of painting to America that ended the Hudson River School and ushered in an era of ... moody and dramatic landscapes."[20] Duveneck, he wrote, "was a hinge upon which the painting of America turned."

The revolution in American art launched by the next generation of American painters came about because of this man's influence.

The *New York Times* critic John Canaday recognized Duveneck's genius and expected what he termed "an overdue Duveneck revival."[21] He was impressed by the painter's sixteen works on exhibit at a show, "The Triumph of Realism," in 1967 in the Brooklyn Museum. Realism, he wrote, was a "successful revolution against

285

both the classical and the romantic idealism, dedicated to the idea that the world around us everywhere, even in its commonest aspect, was worth the painter's attention." Courbet had launched the period in France, he wrote, and the Ash Can School closed it out in America. In between the trend of Impressionism came on with such speed and authority that the practitioners of "Realism became the squares" of the art world.

Perhaps the most encouraging turn of events is the trend at art schools towards a return to the basics as a preparation for fine art. In defense of the basics, Gammell wrote: "A painter's execution bears the stamp of his personality at every point and his emotional expression is strictly limited and shaped by his technical equipment."[22] In a caption under a photograph of *The Old Professor*, Gammell wrote: "Duveneck's extraordinary gift for handling paint to create beautiful and expressive surfaces has, in conjunction with his other qualities, given him a position unique in American art, and in the art of the world for that matter. It is notable that his brilliant manipulation always expresses and enhances the structure of what he painted and never loses control of the form."

---

[1]*Art et Scolastique*, Jacques Maritain, translated by J.F. Scanlan, "Art and Beauty," p. 19, and *Summa Theologica*, Thomas Aquinas, I, q. 39, a

[2]Kenneth Clark, "A Note on Ruskin's Writings on Art and Architecture," *Ruskin Today* (John Murray, 1964), also, *Selected Writings* (Penguin, 1991, pp. 133-134)

[3]Faith, Hope and Charity

[4]Arbiter, Petronius, *Art World & Decoration*, 1918, quoted in Wilde, Mary Leocadia, O.S.B., "The Underlying Catholicity of Duveneck," Notre Dame University, 1938. Arbiter is a name adopted by Norbert Heermann, author of a brief biography, *Frank Duveneck*, 1918. Arbiter is the name of the Roman writer, likely author of the *Satyricon*.

[5] "Cincinnati Report, Herman Wessel," *Salon America Journal*, 2004.

[6] "I Studied with Frank Duveneck,"*American Artist*, March 1965

[7]*Br. Cosmas Wolf, monk architect sculptor designer*, Br. Nathan Cochran, O.S.B., The Saint Vincent Gallery, Latrobe, Pennsylvania, p.14, quoting *Frank Duveneck, Painter-Teacher*, p.29, and Billy Ray Booth, "A Survey of Portraits and Figure Paintings by Frank Duveneck, 1848-19119," (University of Georgia, Ph.D. dissertation, 1970), p. 11

[8]*Frank Duveneck, Painter-Teacher*, p. 29

[9]*Records of William M. Hunt* by Henry C. Angell, Boston, James R. Osgood and Company, 1881, p. 23-24

[10]Ibid, p. 77; [Hunt had been under fire from New York critics for having what was termed a "monopoly in the art world" that was leading to stagnation of the Boston art scene.]

[11]*John Twachtman*, Richard J. Boyle, *Watson, Guptill Publications*, New York, 1988, p.11.

[12]Ibid, p. 13

[13]Norbert Heermann, Frank Duveneck, Houghton Miofflin Company, The Riverside Press Cambridge, 1918, p. 21

[14]*Frank Duveneck*, by Kimberley Allen-Kattus, Copyright 2009, a paper prepared for a Duveneck exhibit at Northern Kentucky University, Highland Heights, Kentucky

[15]*Cincinnati Past and Present*, Carl Samson, Classic Realism Quarterly, Volume VI, No. 3, p. 19.

[16]*Henry James, The Conquest of London: 1870-1881*, Leon Edel, Discus Books, Avon, p.54

[17]John Asbery, "The Indian Summer of Frank Duveneck," *ARTnews,* April, 1972, quoting James in *The Nation,* 1875

[18]*Frank Duveneck & Elizabeth Boott paintings, drawings, prints, and memorabilia,* catalogue, Stanford Art Gallery, Stanford University, an exhibit, September 29-November 22, 1981

[19]"The Etched Work of Frank Duveneck," *The New York Times Magazine*, September 7, 1919

[20]Stapletonkearns.blogspot.com/2009/09/frank-duveneck

[21]The (Temporary) Triumph of Realism, John Canaday, October 4, 1967, *New York Times*

[22]*The Twilight of Painting,* R.H. Ives Gammell, Putnam Sons, New York, 1946, p.10

Chapter Fifteen

Duveneck Appreciation II

Even a tiny painting by Frank Duveneck, in this case a rendering smaller than a postage stamp, served as the main attraction in a scheme put forth by an anonymous clever member of the Cincinnati Art Club. The year was 1897, and the club member and his friends came up with the word, tambola, to name the scheme. A strange word, it sounds like a terpsichorean activity of the South Seas, like a dance in grass skirts and lei—exotic-sounding whether the accent falls on the first or second syllable. Cincinnati, even then known for its own slow and measured pace of living and a healthy appetite for pork, had banned gambling, raffles and auctions. The name, tambola, provided a slim but effective cover for an illegal raffle.

The scheme was designed to turn a profit for the club's benefit. In the 1897 version of the so-named raffle, Duveneck and twenty-eight other artists painted small portraits and scenes on a canvas called a Panel. Duveneck's contribution of a woman's profile took center stage. Beneath the deftly painted face is an American Indian scene by his friend, Henry Farny. There are miniatures by luminaries from Cincinnati such as Edward Potthast, the other Cincinnati-rooted Indian painter J.H. Sharp, the Rettigs, John and Martin, Otto Beck, W.J. Baer and Robert Blum. The Rookwood artist, Japan-born Shirayamadani, known as Shiri, was among them.

Lawrence Poland, a Duveneck student, acquired the panel in an auction. His descendants in the Verkamp family have loaned it to the Cincinnati Art Museum. The Poland-Verkamp tambola is one of a few that have surfaced. [A small version of a tambola[1] was sold in Cincinnati in recent years.] In those early days artists collaborated to raise funds in other ways. They painted small pictures and pasted them on calendars. These were sold and proceeds directed to the club's coffers.

The 1897 tambola panel, which hangs in the Cincinnati museum, evidences the towering strength of the arts community of the day. "The tambola is a reminder to me of a time when there were universally accepted standards by which a work of art could be judged," the portrait painter, Carl Samson, told me. "As artists strove to meet those standards, it fostered a very strong sense of camaraderie. They were all in it together, striving for excellence in an exceedingly difficult art."

Come forward sixty-seven years to an assembly of Cincinnati artists [2] at the residence of Mr. and Mrs. Joseph A. Verkamp, 2776 Baker Place on October 19, 1964. Several in the party had had close personal contact with Duveneck and offered interesting and offbeat comments about the money-making schemes and artists of that late Nineties era. Herman Wessel, one of Duveneck's most successful students, observed:

"… I don't know if you will find as many artists who can do that sort of a thing as well now as they could then. One reason for this was that a good many artists were working in lithography day after day. They had to keep drawing all the time. Drawing was their basic quality to a picture. They believed if a picture was well drawn they could have any scheme of color on it."

As the evening wore on, the subject turned to the almost magical potency of Duveneck's influence. Reginald L. Grooms, artist and teacher, observed that he saw Duveneck only several times while a student at the Art Academy yet his presence was felt deeply and served to magnify his authority, for him, it was an ennobling of the time and place. "Yes, indeed," Wessel chimed in. "When he said anything it was just a few words—that's all. You would never get a long sentence out of him. He would not talk for a long time. He would not sit and talk like we are now doing. He would run away."

Another former Duveneck student, Ernest Haswell, offered this:

"…Duveneck was not a great teacher in the sense that we think of teaching today. The mere contact with Duveneck was what meant so much. It had nothing to do with teaching, but that certain something was there."

Then Haswell told an odd tale of how one student tried to avoid Duveneck.

"Now think of this," he said, "John Carroll came all the way from California to study with Duveneck. He was at the Art Academy for two years. Never in all that time did he appear in Duveneck's class for a criticism of his own painting. He always walked out of the class when Duveneck came close to this easel."

The reason for this strange reaction had more to do with a transformation of Carroll's appreciation of certain colors than anything else, Haswell offered. He happened to meet the artist years later at one of Carroll's New York shows and the one-time student talked as if he had "studied with Duveneck for ten or fifteen years." He learned that Carroll at that later point in his career was "advocating browns[,] which was the color that he had absolute contempt for when he was a student and [he chose] getting out of Duveneck's way, so Duveneck could not give him a criticism."

Wessel told a character-revealing story of a time when he served alongside of Duveneck as a member of the Art Academy faculty. "He came to my class one day and told me there were too many 'extras' in his class, and, [he said] 'I want you to tell them to get out and never go back into my class again.' You see, Duveneck would not tell them to leave his class, but I had to do it. Of course, it was not so hard for me to do because it was not my class."

What does this say about Duveneck?

Perhaps he was too timid to address the extras directly. Possibly he felt that he might do an inadequate job of turning them away, hurt their feelings or by rejecting them, stifle their personal plans. It is clear, however, that he didn't want to do it and that he was personally close to Wessel in whom he had confidence to rectify the situation. His attitude is in keeping with his sensitive character. He wanted to avoid a scene, and he stepped aside from what could have been a confrontation. After all, it may have been Duveneck who was the first to understand the impact of his personality on others.

"Even when he was sixty-five the sound of his heavy footsteps flurried and fluttered the female members of his portrait class..."[3]

Student Recollections

While an art student William Fay[4] served as the model for the corpus in Barnhorn's Crucifixion Group installed at Mother of God Cemetery. Later a commercial artist in Cincinnati, he was a student of Duveneck's and recalled fondly his days at the academy.

"It was an exceptional time to study, for Duveneck at that time was dean of the American painters. It was a period that existed between the old and the new, the Open Air School and the Ash Can School and all of those deviations, which began to occur in America. They were just showing up and people were talking about the broken techniques being used to represent light and shade...

"Meakin," he said, with some emphasis, referring to L.H. Meakin, a faculty member at the academy. "He painted in the broken style that indicates atmosphere in the mountains, most of them he painted in British Columbia, and I have since visited that area, Kicking Horse Valley, and the majestic mountains on all sides were just simply tremendous. I very much admired Meakin's style, from the first.

"The old painters," Fay said, bringing up his subject with the same emphasis as before. "They believed in painting hands and character in the heads. Mr. Duveneck was remarkably accurate in his painting of heads. [He looked for] good draftsmen and [advised] not to make caricatures of anything. If a wart was growing on a face, it

292

could be easily removed. It's better to take them out, and character shown by expression of the eyes and the mouth than anything else."

Fay knew of Duveneck's half-sister, Mollie, but had no personal recollections of her. He understood that she was a frequent subject of his portraits. "I do know that he destroyed lots of his work himself, when he moved from one studio to another. He had the idea that people should have destroyed many more things than they keep, because the stuff that builds up in an artist's studio, usually the result of sloth and negligence, and it's good to throw away some of the useless stuff."

The loyal former student could not accept that Duveneck was a true Bohemian in the generally accepted meaning of the term. "No, I don't think he was a Bohemian. I think he was just a good solid Dutch type who believed in friendship." He said Duveneck was among "the most sincere and fair people I have ever talked to…and this was near the end of his life…and at no time did he treat me as a useless impediment."

Duveneck spoke in a baritone voice, he was "never a tenor type," Fay said. He tended to speak fast and took time to sort out what he wanted to say. "It was sort of guttural…[from] inside of himself. He spoke with a great deal of ease. No broken words."

Aileen McCarthy[5] studied art with Sr. Josenia, a member of the Sisters of Charity of Nazareth at LaSalette Academy in Covington, a religious woman who had taken private lessons from an art academy professor. After completing studies at LaSalette, she was admitted to the art academy in 1907. In her last two years, she studied with Duveneck under a scholarship that, she believed, he had paid.

"He did like my work," she recalled with joy. She remembered vividly his words of encouragement, "I can see that you are going to be a fine artist."

293

Duveneck conducted separate classes for men and for women, though photographs indicate that some or many were integrated. Ms. McCarthy recalled that her classes averaged twenty-seven-to-thirty students. These included international students who had come to Cincinnati and registered to study under Duveneck. The class convened in a spacious room at the art academy equipped with a skylight. She also remembered Duveneck showing kindness to the models. During breaks he would distribute chewing gum to them. If the "boys would get smart with the models," she said, Duveneck would intervene.

One day, Ms. McCarthy recalled, she was riding a street car to Mount Adams for her class and Duveneck happened to be on board. The car stopped at a corner and a woman got on, followed by several children. The driver closed the doors and, unknowingly, left a young child on the sidewalk. Duveneck saw that the child was stranded, rose and shouted that the toddler was alone out there! The driver opened the door again and the child was reunited with the family.

"He was a great humanitarian," the former student said.

Aileen McCarthy befriended another student, Bessie Hoover, who married fellow student Herman Wessel. The ceremony took place in Gloucester, Massachusetts, while the couple was visiting with Duveneck. The Wessels grew close to the painter and often spent long weekends at the seaside with him during the summer. Bessie and Herman Wessel acquired a residence on Alpine Place on the hillside just above the Krohn Conservatory in Eden Park. They built a studio in the rear of the house. In it were some treasures including Duveneck's easel, and many of his brushes clustered in open-topped cups. The residence was later bought by painter Carl Samson, and is now used exclusively as a studio and a setting for gatherings.

Paul Sawyier, a Kentucky artist who studied with Duveneck in 1891, remembered his teacher as one who seldom sang the praises of his students. "He had, however, a way of nodding his head backward toward…his left shoulder and winking his eye, then indicating some pupil who he regarded as doing exceptionally fine work and this gesture he frequently employed with respect to PS—Paul Sawyier."

Sawyier also studied with William Merritt Chase. He told another Duveneck student, Martin Rettig, that, "I like Frank Duveneck (FD) better." The reason: he learned more about overall composition from Duveneck. Further, he liked the master's style of instruction. He did not pressure students into following his personal painting style. Rather, he emphasized the need for good work habits and development of individual talents."[6]

Henry C. Loughmiller, a later student of Duveneck's, recalled the artist's physical characteristics especially his "lordly lionesque head…his thick, carelessly tossed sandy-gray hair, the broadly blocked virile face, with its flowing mustache, full lips, determined jaw, and moodily reflective eyes." His quiet unaffected manner conferred a sovereign dignity on the artist, Loughmiller wrote. "Our respect for him amounted to reverence." He would enter the studio, offering a courteous "Good Morning" to the class. And, the room would fall into the quiet of anticipation."[7]

As Duveneck strolled through the thicket of easels students on occasion would hear him say, "not bad, not bad at all." Recommendations would follow.

"He had the unique power of the great teacher, of keeping a student keyed up to the highest pitch of endeavor with the struggles of earnest effort, he was endlessly patient—losing grace only when he (wrathfully) noted some departure from the path of his guidance. He strove painstakingly, tirelessly to develop in us—the least gifted of us—the painter's clarifying vision of nature, and the ability to render it soundly, effectively, in paint."

295

Loughmiller was present when Duveneck, on the infrequent occasion, dropped his reserve and would offer an amusing anecdote from the life of Henry James, John Singer Sargent or James Abbott McNeill Whistler. He liked to talk about the art of painting, but he didn't like being questioned by students about painting. They were aware of his friendship with his colleagues Clement Barnhorn and L.H. Meakin, but none of the students in Loughmiller's recollection could be called a personal friend. (The Wessels are a likely exception.) He described Duveneck as a "rather isolated figure, like a monarch is introverted, self-contained, not deeply involved in personal relationships…apart from the world of affairs."

Students would tip their hats to him when they met him off campus, on the streets of Covington or Cincinnati.

Among the first scholars to recognize Duveneck's genius was Charles Henry Caffin, the Oxford-educated aesthete whose written works broadened the horizons of art appreciation for many in the Victorian and Edwardian ages. He wrote a series of books about painting, sculpture, architecture and photography. An early supporter of modern art, popular rather than scholarly, he grasped the essence of Duveneck's method. In a 1907 work, *The Story of American Painting,* Caffin wrote:

"He [Duveneck] taught a method by which the canvas was promptly covered with color and locking in large masses of the subject; afterward, superimposing the various succeeding planes to produce the modeling."[8]

Royal Cortissoz may have been the first critic to proclaim Duveneck "as the founder of a new movement in American Art."[8] He had seen Duveneck's work at the 1915 exhibit of the Panama Pacific Exposition in San Francisco and wrote lavishly on the works he had seen there and in American museums. Duveneck, he affirmed in a *Scribner's* article in 1927, was the leading cause behind the American tradition that had sprung from Munich. He marveled at the painter's ability to apply sensitivity in required areas of an otherwise powerful performance. He had seen his portrait of William Gedney Bunce, many years after its completion in 1878, and said the experience was still like an encounter with an old friend.

"There you come close to another of Duveneck's secrets, his powerful grip on life."[9]

The Encyclopedia Britannia recognized Duveneck's achievements with a fact-based account of his life and contributions. In today's electronic version of the famous book, the information on Duveneck continues in the same form as decades ago In 1930, the *Dictionary of American Biography*, contained these words of appreciation for the painter:

"It may well be that in the final appraisal of his achievements his most valuable contribution …will be found in his personal influence as a leader of his 'boys." Their doings have become a legend and a tradition, not to be omitted in any history of American art."[10]

After Duveneck's death in 1919, an editorial writer for *The Cincinnati Enquirer* offered an acute observation, rooted in knowledge of the artist's personal history.

"He was one of those rare and happily endowed men who seem to be born for their profession."

Truly, art dominated his life. He had to create—it was in his blood—and he chose well the painting in oils' medium, and he mastered several media during his lifetime. His relationships helped to mold his character. He started with close ties to his family, his Church and his early absorption in the craft of art. He grew under his professors' guidance in Munich. He matured and learned from colleagues in Venice and Florence. His dealings with his own students, in Europe and in America, became legendary. He became a husband and father. He suffered great personal losses during his life, which stifled him. But, he endured, becoming a generous,

297

rock-solid friend and mentor to many. In the end, in the most important relationship of all, he reconciled with his God.

---

[1]Strangely, the word, tambola, is used widely around the world as a synonym for bingo, or housey, as the British call the game. In India an electronic version of tambola is played on computers known as "etambola."

[2]Participants included Herman H. Wessel and another Duveneck student, Ernest B. Haswell, Reginald L. Grooms, art teacher, Norman H. Doane, and members of the Verkamp family.

[3]Mahonri Sharp Young, "Duveneck and Henry James: A Study in Contrasts," p. 213, Duveneck papers, Archives of American Art, Smithsonian Institution, Washington, D.C.

[4]The late William Fay, a commercial artist in Cincinnati, lived in the suburb of Terrace Park, Ohio. The author interviewed him for an article on Mollie Duveneck.

[5]Aileen McCarthy taught art at LaSalette Academy and gave private lessons from her residence and studio in Covington.

[6]*Sawyier, The Art of Paul Sawyier*, Arthur F. Jones, *The University of Kentucky Press*, 1976.

[7]Henry C. Loughmiller, *American Artist*, March, 1965

[8]*The Story of Painting, the Evolution of Painting in America*, 1907, Charles H. Caffin, p. 114

[9]"The Field of Art," *Scribner's*, February, 1927, pp. 216-225

[10]*Dictionary of American Biography*, 1930, p. 559

Epilogue

One day in the early 1970s Frank B. Duveneck Jr. and Josephine Whitney Duveneck called their two sons and two daughters to Hidden Villa, a two-thousand-acre ranch off Moody Road in California's Los Altos Hills, which had been the family home since the nineteen twenties. Josephine had sifted through family art treasures, drawings, water colors, sketches and paintings by Frank and Elizabeth Boott Duveneck, and she, daughter-in-law to that famous couple, was in mood to share them. She said it was high time for the art works to be seen and not hidden away.

The foursome, Elizabeth Dana, Hope Williams, and Francis and Bernard Duveneck, examined with an awe mixed with family pride the profusion of colorful works that lay about them. Some had been seen before in various exhibitions, others were new. Each of the siblings had spent their early years at Hidden Villa. They farmed, cared for animals and rode horses on hilly, winding trails near Black Mountain through the moist coastal fauna of mossy trees, redwoods and waterfalls. The olive trees planted by Franciscan missionaries continue to thrive in the valley occupied by the farm, the first footprint of charity and caring for others that honors this place.

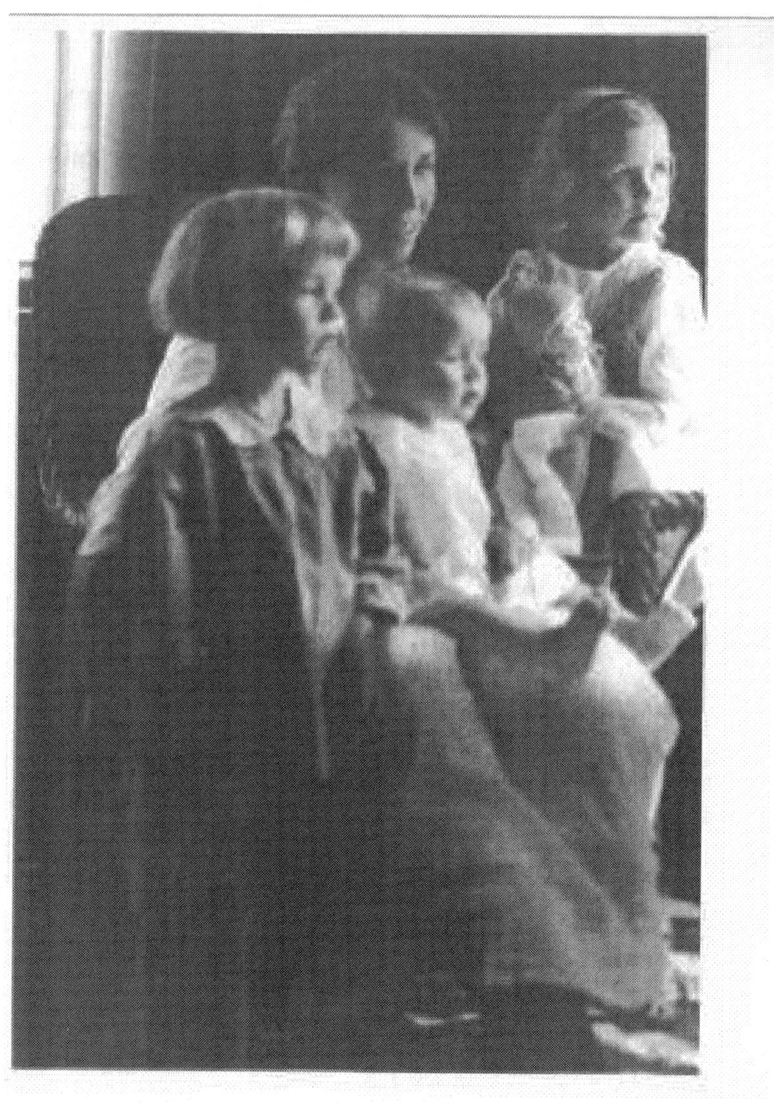

Josephine Whitney Duveneck and three of her children

-Courtesy of the Kenton County Public Library, Covington, Ky.

Mrs. Duveneck wanted to be fair about the apportioning of these treasures and had landed on a method of distribution. She set out a deck of playing cards and instructed each of the four to pick up one

300

card. The holder of the highest card then had first choice to select from the cache. The second highest card holder took a turn, followed by the next highest. After this first round, cards were selected again and again, multiple times, with the highest card holder having first choice, until all items were taken.

Hope Williams, youngest of the siblings, selected pieces that reflected the several periods in her grandfather's art history and an assortment of interesting works of her grandmother's. She favored *Girl in a Boat*, a 1912 Frank Duveneck painting in Impressionist style of a young woman leaning on a railing. She wears a high-collared white blouse and a wind-blown straw hat. A red bow tie matches the color of a fluttering band on her hat. The sunburned face carried through the dashing bright color. The harbor at Gloucester, Massachusetts, serves as a backdrop to the portrayal of this vivacious young woman.

The Cape Ann Historical Association reproduced *Girl on a Boat* for the cover of a catalogue for its exhibition, *Frank Duveneck, The Gloucester Years*, July 31-November 7, 1987. The exhibition demonstrated that Duveneck, who had experimented during the 1880s with the properties of light under the then new influence of Impressionism, refined these techniques with his Gloucester paintings. The exhibit, designed by Martha Oaks, curator, identified more than sixty paintings from the Gloucester years and cast a new light on the later days of the artist.

Hope also chose a rendering of *Brace's Rock*, a well-known natural breakwater that shields Gloucester harbor. In an interview in November, 2013, Hope, then ninety-five years old, said that she liked to think the painting, which appears unfinished, was an exercise in her grandfather's teaching methods that demonstrated to students where to focus attention—to the rock itself. Duveneck and many other artists have admired the variety of ever-changing colors at Brace's Rock and the intensity of tides and the crashing sea.

Other works in Hope's collection reflected the several different periods in Duveneck's artistic history. She liked the face he had painted of a professor from his student days in Munich; a sailing ship in the harbor of Venice, and the life drawing of the female figure, completed probably in the late 1890s. A portrait of an Italian child by Elizabeth Boott Duveneck and many of her grandmother's sketches were among her other selections. Since that time of redistribution, the family has allowed works to become part of special exhibitions and generously donated dozens of paintings.

Every Duveneck painting, perhaps every subject of his art, has a story to tell. Take for example Brace's Rock. A *Study of Brace's Rock* by Duveneck is part of the Cape Ann Historical Association Collection. Gloucester personage Walter L. Molina gave it to the association in 1986. Duveneck had painted the study around 1893, and presented it in August, 1900, to Molina's grandparents, Professor Benjamin and Margaret Guckenberger of Birmingham, Alabama, in appreciation of a musical performance during a program at the Hotel Rockaway in East Gloucester.

Duveneck was the important guest at that event and an active participant. A news article about the occasion effused:

"Mr. Duveneck's reputation as an artist and sculptor is too well known to need comment and his presence alone made all happy."[1]

The newspaper account has the power to transport a reader back to that turn of the century year to the sun-tanned and delighted faces, the women in fine white dresses and straw hats, the men dressed a bit more formally than usual just for the occasion. That evening, Mrs. Guckenberger, a contralto, sang, *Swallow, Swallow, Flying South* by Arthur Foote, and professor Guckenberger, a faculty member of the Birmingham Conservatory of Music, performed Chopin's *Valse, E. Minor* and Dvorak's *Slavonic Dances* on the piano. The program featured an exhibit of paintings by Duveneck and other visiting artists, among them, former students DeCamp Potthast and Twachtman. After the musical performances, "the art-

302

ists and musicians repaired to the dining hall and enjoyed a supper in only the way artists can."

Such stories are family heirlooms of memory for Hope Williams and other members of the Duveneck family in California. They are familiar with Duveneck legends from conversations among family members and in part from their mother's two books: the biography of the artist and her autobiography, *Life on Two Levels*. Josephine had kept notes from lengthy discussions with her father-in-law while she and her husband, Frank Jr., lived in Cincinnati before World War I, and used them to build her story about the painter and his art.

"She was very fond of him, and he, of her," Hope said.

While the marriage of Frank and Lizzie Boott is historically distant to her, Hope has definite opinions about the difficulties her parents faced when they first were engaged around 1880. The opposition of the father, Francis Boott, was rooted in his concern for his daughter and the class difference between the two, a concern shared by novelist Henry James, and likely other fatherly worries.

"Henry James was a snob," she said, in the belief that the author was in love with Lizzie and found in Duveneck a strong competitor. "It's just a feeling."

Hope knew and loved her uncle, Charlie Duveneck, the last surviving sibling from the Covington, Greenup Street family. After Frank's 1919 death, Charlie at first visited and then later moved to Hidden Villa. Hope said she was his undoubted favorite. They visited San Francisco and relished in attending events such as the thoroughbred horse races. She enjoyed examining horses on parade in the paddock with Uncle Charlie at her side. They reviewed the histories of the horses before laying bets, usually $2.50.

"We never made any money," Hope recalled, but she had lots of fun.

Charlie did not resemble his famous, physically robust brother and likely favored his thin and angular mother. In the artist's letters to the family from abroad Charlie emerges as a kind of beloved character, the youngest in the family.

"He spoiled me and I loved it," she said.

Hope recalls her mother, on horseback, leading a second horse along the trails toward a rail stop where she would meet Frank Jr., who was working at the time as an engineer in the San Francisco area. He also taught college-level courses in engineering that took him away from Hidden Villa. Josephine Duveneck found time beyond farm work and her family to take a leading role in community service, which is detailed in her autobiography.

Having lived and worked at Hidden Villa is a source of pride for the Duvenecks. David Duveneck, an Oakland landscaper and great grandson of the artists, lived there from age three to eighteen. He recalls his grandmother as a Force of Nature "who did what she thought was right. She had enormous energy, a deep reservoir of spiritual energy." Josephine Whitney Duveneck was imbued with a sense of justice and possessed an acute awareness of inequities and outright discrimination that afflict the human family. She and Frank Jr. started the first interracial summer camp in the 1940s. In the World War II period Hidden Villa became a haven for refugees from Nazism. When the Nisei Japanese were forced into various depots awaiting transportation to camps, Mrs. Duveneck appeared in person distributing food from the farm and books as a "statement" against ironhanded rule. After their war-time internments, Japanese-Americans received assistance at Hidden Villa. The family cooperated with the American Indian Council and the American Friends Service Committee, and became a meeting place for Cesar Chavez's farm workers' union.

Reflecting their mother's dedication to Quaker principles of non-aggression—and possibly their grandfather's abhorrence for war—Bernard Duveneck registered as a conscientious objector and worked on a farm for the duration of World War II. Francis also declared himself a conscientious objector but served in the Army as a noncombatant.

David Duveneck has saved Christmas letters that Josephine wrote to family and friends dating from 1927 to the 1970s. "She would talk about her children, giving them a page apiece, and it was so interesting to see what she noticed and observed of these individuals." Each showed artistic interest, perhaps an inherited trait. Hope became a potter and created sculptures from pottery, particularly of animals and birds. Elizabeth Dana was fond of drawing and became an architect. Bernard was an excavating contractor. David's father, Francis, a high school teacher and counselor, could repair any mechanical device, and was interested in the power of steam. He fashioned sculptures from metal and wood that "made you laugh."

In the summer of 1962, when David was fourteen years old and his older brother, Peter, eighteen, they bicycled across the United States, from Vermont to California, an experience perhaps more adventurous than their great-grandfather's first trip to Europe in 1869-70. "I'm proud of Dad to let me," David said. He, the father, was criticized by the superintendent of the school where he taught for letting his sons "do something so dangerous." The motivation behind the trip was simply just to do something adventurous. Peter had been attending school in Vermont. David joined him there and they pedaled towards Maine and the coast and then turned southward to Washington, D.C. They headed west and followed U.S. 50, stopping for a few days in Cincinnati. They visited the Cincinnati Art Museum to see their great-grandfather's art collection and looked up his gravestone monument at Mother of God Cemetery in Covington before pushing on. Residences of relations and friends along the route served as temporary refuges. They were required to telephone home every Wednesday evening. People they met were friendly. David doesn't recall any close calls. "We were lads on bikes. At the end of the day we would ask a farmer, or whoever it was, if we could spend the night on the property, and they would say, yes." The journey continued across the center of the country, to Denver and Salt Lake City, and it consumed all of the summer that year.

The Duveneck legacy in California is largely represented by Hidden Villa and its history of support for just causes, summer camps for the disadvantaged in society, and its contemporary mission as a non-profit educational organization dedicated to conservation and ecology. As to his extended family, David Duveneck said, "If I could make a generalization, they are outgoing, gregarious and proactive. There is a set of unwritten rules that are followed, natural laws, being kind and considerate, industrious, hardworking."

In the Duveneck biography, Josephine Whitney Duveneck issued a sweeping indictment of the Covington Duvenecks. She referred to them as "un-enterprising," sliding from one crisis to another, haunted incessantly by the four horsemen of the luckless: poverty, ill health, improvidence and irresponsibility. She drew this conclusion even as she was unaware of Mollie's indiscretions, which might have added to the opprobrium.

The indictment was general; no one individual was cited. Still, the criticism seems harsh from someone who otherwise possessed a keen sense of compassion for the underprivileged. She was a strong personality, a doer, who came from a privileged background. Hard luck may not have been an adequate excuse for her. It's also possible that some Covington Duvenecks deserved the censure. Her comment may help explain the limited association with that side of the family. She, Josephine, wrote in the biography that she didn't understand why Frank Jr. had no connection with the Covington family in his youth. He never met his grandmother. There is an unconfirmed story that when he first viewed a painting of her by his father he broke into tears of regret that he had never met that formidable pioneer woman.

Like many immigrant families, the Duvenecks were among the many millions of people who lived on the edge in nineteenth century America. In the uneven economic times of post-Civil War America, the family was likely better off financially than most. In the 1880 United States census the family numbered nine at home, Father Joseph, 56, Mother, Catherina, [so spelled in the census report] 50, Lizzie, 27, Joseph, 25, John, 23, Kate, 20, Josephina, 13, Mary or Mollie, 11, and Charley, eight years old. Father Squire, the main breadwinner, died in 1883. By the end of the decade, the older five had moved out of the house to marry and were employed. Only half-sister Mollie and the youngest half-brother, Charlie were living in the family home when the painter returned using Duveneck House as a base again in the 1890s.

Males in the family were not as philoprogenitive as their parents. One was well known as a Covington city fireman. But since the 1950s the Duveneck name has disappeared from the local telephone book while some descendants, still local, may have come down along the female lines.

The Decker family in greater Cincinnati has thrived and remained strong in number. Recall that Frank Duveneck's blood father's name was Bernard Decker, who died in the 1849 cholera epidemic in the Cincinnati area. Bernard's older brother, Frank, had married previously and fathered a family. His son, also named Frank Decker, born in 1854, lived in Covington. It is most likely that he is the Frank Decker who became known as Frank Decker Senior, a cousin of Frank Duveneck.

From him there followed Frank Decker, Jr. , (1895-1946) and two daughters, Edna and Clara Decker. Neither was married. Edna was a professor at the University of Cincinnati. Clara made and sold hats in a shop in Norwood, the small city that exists within the confines of the City of Cincinnati. Frank Decker Jr.'s son, Frank Decker III, lives in Fort Mitchell, Kentucky. He is a retired drug salesman, a graduate of Covington Latin School and the Covington Diocese's institution of higher education, Thomas More College in Crestview Hills, Kentucky. In keeping with the family tradition of serving others and especially the disadvantaged in society, Frank

III maintains the food pantry at Blessed Sacrament Church in Fort Mitchell and frequently serves needy families with home visits as a member of the Society of St. Vincent de Paul.

Finally

The artist and critic Ives Gammell observed that Duveneck's reputation has never faded. His paintings, too, have maintained value. Many of the best known and highly regarded paintings are owned by the Cincinnati Art Museum and still others of high quality have found their way to other public museums. The number of privately owned works is, therefore, limited. Still, many good and representative works are available in the art marketplace. Doug Eisele of the Eisele Gallery of Fine Art in Cincinnati's Fairfax section deals routinely with as many as sixty owners of Duveneck works. Highest known recent sale of a Duveneck work is $750,000. This amount was paid by an individual in the purchase of one of three Italian *Siesta* paintings by Duveneck. The transaction was confirmed by Randy Sandler of the Downtown-based Cincinnati Art Galleries, LLC.

The etcher Pennell summed up Duveneck's life and work this way: "Duveneck found it easier to teach, than to paint or etch... Duveneck for years did little and showed less—fell out of sight in this country—lived his own life, in his own city, in his own way, beloved and respected by all who knew him—and then just before his death found himself a great man—to the little men in American art, as he always had been to those who knew."

Pennell captured the unique character of Duveneck. He was "just an artist who had done what he wanted in his own way and for his own pleasure."

---

[1]*Gloucester Daily Times*, August 10, 1900

Profiles: Their Later Lives

Clement Barnhorn (1857-1935), born a twin in Cincinnati, was more of a colleague to Frank Duveneck than a student. He met the artist upon his return to Cincinnati from studies in Munich. After Duveneck's wife, Lizzie, died in 1888 and he returned to Cincinnati, the two resumed a friendly and often collegial relationship. Barnhorn, a woodworker and sculptor, advised Duveneck for the effigy to his wife. In the 1890s he studied under William-Adolphe Bouguereau in France and won an honorable mention from the Paris Salon of 1895 for his sculpture, *Magdalen,* and a silver medal from the 1900 Paris exhibition for another *Magdalen.* Barnhorn joined the faculty of the Cincinnati Art Academy and served as Duveneck's close confidante and friend for the next twenty years. Barnhorn created the Crucifixion Group in Mother of God Cemetery near Duveneck's memorial tomb and a Madonna and Child statue at the Cathedral Basilica of the Assumption.

Otto Bacher (1856-1909), one of the Duveneck Boys, studied with Frank Duveneck in Munich and Florence. A native of Cleveland, Ohio, he studied art locally and worked as a decorator for Lake Erie vessels and city residences. He was among the founders of the Art Club in the city. In Germany he obtained a printing press and learned the art of etching. While in Italy he befriended the artist James Abbott McNeill Whistler, who used Bacher's press to produce his famous works as did Frank Duveneck. Bacher returned to teach art in Cleveland, married a local artist and moved to New York where he wrote a series for *Century* Magazine on his life with Whistler.

Francis Boott (1813-1904) spent his final years in Cambridge, Massachusetts, an honored figure as the oldest living graduate of Harvard College. At age ninety he led the procession at the Harvard commencement, the orchestra performing *Viva Italia,* one of his many compositions. He was likely instrumental in Frank Duveneck obtaining commissions in Boston, including the sculptures of Ralph Waldo Emerson and former Harvard president Charles Eliot. In his later years he befriended the psychologist and philosopher William James, brother of the author Henry. In a tribute after his death, James wrote of his devotion to his daughter, Elizabeth, and his contributions to music. "Tender hearted he was and faithful as few men are, in friendship." He and his son-in-law, Duveneck, developed strong ties of family and friendship.

Lady Colin Campbell (1857-1911) was a student of Frank Duveneck and a friend of Lizzie Boott. She was born in Dublin, christened Gertrude Elizabeth Blood. The family owned estates in County Clare. She became engaged to marry the son of the eighth Duke of Argyll after a three-day stay together at the home of a family friend in Scotland. The Campells regarded her as beneath him socially and proposed a prenuptial agreement. In spite of these obstacles, the marriage took place in 1881. She maintained that her husband infected her with syphilis. In 1884 she was granted a judicial separation. However, she lost her case for divorce after a two-years-long trial. The Campbell defense accused her of immoral behavior. Ostracized by society, she became a popular London journalist, a favorite of writers and artists. Henry James visited her, and she exchanged insults with Oscar Wilde. The Boldini portrait of her hangs in Britain's National Portrait Gallery. Her final years were difficult as she suffered crippling effects from the disease.

William Merritt Chase (1849-1916), born and reared in Indiana, studied in Munich with support of St. Louis patrons and there met his long-time friend, Frank Duveneck. He found success, as Duveneck did, in Boston, but his first break to fame came with a painting, *"Keeping Up" –the Court Jester* in Philadelphia. He joined Duveneck on a second tour of Europe in 1877, spending time largely in Venice. Known as an Impressionist, a friend of many famous artists, he painted portraits, landscapes and still life renderings. A flamboyant dresser he became something a cult figure in New York. Chase founded the Shinnecock Hills Summer School on Long Island and later the Chase School of Art, which became the New York School of Art. He led students on painting expeditions to Europe in the early twentieth century. At the time of his death he was hailed as one of the great American artists.

Joseph Rodefer DeCamp (1858-1923), born in Cincinnati, studied under Frank Duveneck in his birth city and in Munich. He took classes from Willem von Diez and joined with the Duveneck Boys at Polling, Bavaria. Like Duveneck he began his career as a follower of Realism and shifted later to Impressionism. A famous work is a portrait of *Theodore Roosevelt,* commissioned by Roosevelt's former classmates at Harvard University. He is known for portraiture, nude paintings and landscapes. He later settled in Boston and is regarded as a primary member of the Boston School of Painters. His paintings are exhibited in leading museums in the United States.

William Dean Howells (1837-1920), known as the Dean of American Letters at the turn of the nineteenth century, referred to the Duveneck Boys as the Inglehart Boys in his novel, *Indian Summer.* His note to a Cincinnati Art Museum staff member in 1919 confirmed that the Inglehart appellation came just by chance to him as he was writing about the characters he had met in Florence. Howells, a native of Martin's Ferry, Ohio, served as an editor for the Ohio State Journal in Columbus before heading to Boston and fame as editor of the *Atlantic Monthly.* Among his many works was *The Rise of Silas Lapham,* one of the first American novels about a businessman. He was friends with the major nineteenth century writers including Henry James.

William Morris Hunt (1824-1879), a New England-born Romantic painter, was the first among American artists to have discovered Frank Duveneck. After studying at Harvard University, he migrated to France during the 1850s and became an advocate of the Barbizon School, studying under Thomas Couture and Jean-Francois Millet. Upon his return to the United States, he established a school in Rhode Island and later moved it to Boston. Elizabeth Boott, then on her first visit to America, became one of his students. Hunt came in contact with Frank Duveneck's paintings from his first Munich period. These were displayed to acclaim in Boston in 1875. Hunt was instrumental in establishing a culture of the visual arts in Boston. He wrote a book that has become a classic, *Talks on Art,* in 1878, the same year he completed a painting, *Niagara Falls.*

Henry James (1843-1916), a major figure in transatlantic literature, was a close friend of Lizzie Boott Duveneck. He adapted his relationship with the Boott family as a basis for two, perhaps three novels. James wrote in a style that has been compared to Impressionism in painting, by creating characters revealed largely by their thoughts and perceptions. Though born in New York, James spent most of his life abroad and became a British citizen. He was a successful literary and art critic and heralded during his lifetime as a great writer by a comparatively small but highly educated public. He is memorialized with a stone in Poet's Corner in the Abbey Church in London.

William James (1842-1910), one of America's great philosophers of the nineteenth and early twentieth centuries, wrote the kindest remarks about Lizzie Boott upon first meeting her in the late 1860s. By that time he was already a graduate of Harvard Medical School. He began teaching at Harvard at the request of the president, Charles Eliot. An original thinker, James produced a large number of works including *The Varieties of Religious Experience.* His pragmatism philosophy strongly influenced the work of others in America as well as the writings of the European philosopher Ludwig Wittgenstein. He was a close friend of Lizzie's father, Francis Boott.

Wilhelm Lamprecht (1838-1922), born in Altenschoenbach, studied at the Munich Royal Academy of Art during the 1860s. He was hired by Boniface Wimmer, O.S.B., abbot of the St. Vincent in Latrobe, Pennsylvania, after Wimmer's visit to Germany. Lamprecht worked at a Benedictine monastery in Newark, New Jersey, before joining the staff of the Covington Altar Stock Building Company in 1867. Lamprecht was a disciplinarian who is said to have taught young Frank Duveneck the importance of painting eyes. Under Lamprecht Duveneck also learned how to paint murals. The young painter joined with Lamprecht to paint at the Church of St. Romuald d'Etchemin in Quebec. Lamprecht was influential in persuading Frank Duveneck's parents to finance their son's studies in Munich.

Bishop Camillus Paul Maes (1846-1915), born in the Flemish city of Courtrai in West Flanders, served as the third bishop of the Covington Diocese from 1885 to his death in 1915. Drawn early to the priesthood he had a desire to serve the American missions. He studied at a minor seminary in Bruges and met Bishop Peter P. LeFevre, coadjutor of the Diocese of Detroit who encouraged him to come to America. Father Maes served in the Detroit area for fifteen years. In 1882 he was assigned as a theologian at the Provincial Council at Cincinnati across the Ohio River from Covington. During his term as the Covington prelate he supported the foundation of The Catholic University of America in Washington, District of Columbia, and was a leading figure at the 1895 Eucharistic Congress in Washington. He is best known as the builder of the Cathedral Basilica of the Assumption where Duveneck's murals can be found.

Aileen McCarthy (1886-1982) of Covington owed her opportunity for academic work in art to Duveneck's generosity. She learned that he paid her tuition so that she could continue studying with him at the Cincinnati Art Academy. One of her best known portraits was of Duveneck. She also studied with Clement Barnhorn, artist George Elmer Browne and landscape artist Emile Gruppe of Gloucester, Massachusetts. Her early training came as a student of Sister Josina Whitehead of the Sisters of Charity of Nazareth at LaSalette Academy in Covington. After her graduation and completing her studies at the academy, she taught at LaSalette from 1915 to 1923 and opened her own studio at her residence. Among her students was Covington-born Bernard L. Schmidt Jr., a painter and sculptor, who became chairman of the Art Departments at Thomas More College, Crestview Hills, Kentucky, and later at Xavier University in Cincinnati, Ohio. She continued to draw in her retirement and died at age 96 at St. Charles Care Center in Fort Wright, Kentucky.

Elizabeth Robins Pennell (1855-1936), born in Philadelphia and reared in a convent through the age of seventeen after her mother's death, wrote chiefly from her base in London. An uncle and writer, Charles Godfrey Leland, encouraged her to pursue a career as a scribe. She began writing for periodicals and authored a popular biography of Mary Wollstonecraft. After wedding artist and etcher Joseph Pennell, together they produced a series of publications on their cycling journeys in Europe and numerous other books comprising her essays and his etchings. Among her books of memoirs is *Nights: Rome & Venice in the Aesthetic Eighties,* in which she described Frank Duveneck as the toast of Venice. She also wrote extensively on cooking, travel and art, and was friendly with Whistler and Lady Colin Campbell. ,

Joseph Pennell (1857-1926) was also Philadelphia born and worked with his wife, Elizabeth, in London. Their home became a salon for writers and artists. He is known today largely for his etchings and lithography and for his illustrations. He taught at Oxford University's Slade School of Art. In conjunction with his wife, they produced a biography of James Abbott McNeill Whistler. He won an award from the 1904 Louisiana Purchase Exposition, which also honored a painting by Frank Duveneck of his mother. Pennell is also known for his posters for a Liberty Loans campaign during World War I. Towards the end of the conflict, the Pennells returned to the United States and resided in New York City.

John Singer Sargent (1856-1925), who referred to Frank Duveneck as "the greatest brush" of the generation, was a highly successful and innovative painter. Born in Florence, Italy, to American parents, Sargent took interest early in art and studied in his birth city and in Paris under Carolus-Duran. He was strongly influenced by the Impressionists and cleverly adopted their uses of

314

light. Sargent always regarded himself an American, though he lived most of his life in Europe. His portrait, *Madame X*, exhibited at the Paris Salon of 1884, provoked scandal as it portrayed a woman in a strapless dress. He moved to London and his breakthrough there came with the completion of a masterpiece of Impressionism, *Carnation, Lily, Lily, Rose*, which he painted at the London Royal Academy. Portraiture was his strong suit, however, and he was commissioned frequently to paint socialites in both the United States and Britain. Toward the end of his life Sargent painted murals for the Boston Public Library. In Britain he is also known for *Gassed*, which he completed after visiting the Western Front during World War I as a guest of the British government.

Johann Schmitt (1825-1888), born in Baden, was not formally trained as an artist but learned from Munich artists before emigrating to the United States in 1848. He operated a studio in Melrose, New York, and was hired to paint altarpieces for the Covington Altar Building Stock Company. He operated a studio of his own near the larger studio for religious works. Young Frank Duveneck was apprenticed to Schmitt and to the company director, Cosmas Wolf, O.S.B. From Schmitt Duveneck was said to have learned the basics, such as pigment mixing, cleaning, wood carving, painting and murals. He is buried in Mother of God Cemetery near the Duveneck memorial tomb.

John Henry Twachtman (1853-1902), a leading American Impressionist, was among Duveneck's first students in the United States. He was scarcely five years younger than his teacher, born the son of German immigrants, Frederick Christian and Sophia Droege Twatchtman, in Cincinnati. His initial contact with art came as he followed in his father's footsteps as a decorator of window shades. He began studies at the Ohio Mechanics Institute and transferred to the McMicken School of Design. There he met Duveneck who had just returned from his first tour abroad. He worked with Duveneck at the McMicken School, which later became the Cincinnati Art Academy, and at the studio Duveneck shared with Henry Farny and Francis Dengler. He accompanied

Duveneck on his return to Europe, studied at the Royal Academy of Fine Arts in Munich and followed him to Venice in 1877. His Italian landscapes were a hit at the Society of American Artists. He returned to Cincinnati when Duveneck closed his Florence school in 1881 and married Martha Scudder, daughter of a prominent physician. On a second and longer sojourn to Europe he studied at the Academie Julien in Paris and adopted the style of French Impressionism, applying it to numerous landscapes including works on Niagara Falls and Yellowstone Park. He and his colleagues spent summers in 1900 through 1902 painting at Gloucester, Massachusetts.

James Abbott McNeill Whistler (1834-1908), influenced by multiple sources such as Japanese prints and the works of the Pre-Raphaelite Brotherhood, was America's foremost avant-garde artist. Born in Lowell, Massachusetts, he studied drawing as a youth in St. Petersburg, Russia, where his father, a civil engineer, had been advising the government on railway construction. He was admitted to the U.S. Military Academy at West Point, but was dismissed in 1854 after failing chemistry. Fluent in French, he moved to Paris and closely associated himself with the leading painters of the day including Edouard Manet, Gustave Courbet and Carolus-Duran. He settled in London in 1859 and gained fame with his portrait, *Symphony in White, No. 1–The White Girl* (1862) and the portrait known as *Whistler's Mother*. Known for his etchings and paintings of London and the Thames River at night, he confirmed his status as an avant-garde artist by adopting a style that later became known as Post-Impressionism.

Cosmas Wolf, O.S.B. (1821-1894), an artist and Benedictine who had great influence on Frank Duveneck as the young painter learned his trade, was an important church designer, architect and altar builder. Much like Frank Duveneck, he has left a dual legacy as an artist himself and as one who assembled top-ranked artistic performers, in his case, as church painters and craftsmen. Born in a village in Bavarian Swabia, he studied art in Germany before entering the Benedictine order at Latrobe, Pennsylvania. He became the head of the Covington Altar Stock Building Company, also called the Institute of Catholic Art, in 1862. After the company was closed in 1868 he returned to the Latrobe archabbey and worked as a sculptor and designer.

Constance Fenimore Woolson (1840-1894), a neighbor of the Duvenecks on Bellosguardo hill near Florence, was godmother to Frank and Lizzie Boott Duveneck's son, Frank Jr. She was close to Henry James with whom she shared an odd relationship, frequently the subject of articles and books. A grandniece of James Fenimore Cooper, Woolson started her career as a writer for the *Atlantic Monthly* and *Harper's* magazine. She produced travel articles from visits to the Great Lakes and the Deep South, short stories and several novels, *For the Major*, a highly rated work of fiction of the post-Civil War South. In 1894 while living in an apartment on the Grand Canal in Venice, she died from a fall from a window, whether an accident or suicide, is not known.

Acknowledgements

First on this list of helpful persons is a group referred to in my e-mail account as Duveneck Fans. They are an even dozen who have strong associations with Frank Duveneck. Some are related to him, while others regard themselves—though they are separated from him by time and space—as his students and admirers. Some are Roman Catholic clergy who have heard, as I did early in our lives, that there was amongst us some years ago in Northern Kentucky a great artist and a great man. The Duveneck Fans have been the main source of support for this project. They are Carl Samson, Linda Crank, Michael Hammons, Msgr. William Neuhaus, Msgr. William Cleves, Mrs. Rita Decker Gehring, Carol Osborne, Jim McAllister, Charles Alexander, Kevin Kelly, Paul Tenkotte, and Sister Deborah Harmeling, O.S.B

Hope Duveneck Williams, granddaughter of Frank and Elizabeth Boott Duveneck, and great-grandson, David Duveneck, submitted to interviews and provided valuable information and insights into their ancestors and the family in California. Their distant cousin, Frank Decker III and his sister, Rita Decker Gehring, offered information about the Decker family and prayerful support for the project. The caretaker at Mother of God Cemetery, where Duveneck is buried, Phil Zumdick, was resourceful and knowledgeable about the Duveneck family plot. The staff at the library at the Cincinnati Art Museum was courteous and helpful. Julie Aronson, curator of painting, sculpture and drawings at CAM, suggested a host of revisions, which I took to heart in the realization of her vast knowledge and understanding of art. Tom Ward, archivist for Thomas More College and the Diocese of Covington, was his usual accommodating self.

Elaine Kuhn, who heads the history and genealogy division of the Kenton County Library, was most helpful. Her staff members gave aid as I plumbed the collection of articles in newspapers, magazines and catalogues and many books related to Frank Duveneck.

She also assisted in obtaining census and other data on the Decker and Duveneck families. Two academics also contributed their expertise. Carol Osborne, noted above, has written the most thoughtful and beautifully composed articles on the Duvenecks, chiefly Elizabeth. An art historian and former curator of the Stanford University art gallery, Ms. Osborne provided fresh and illuminating insights into Lizzie's life. Kimberly Allen-Kattus, associate professor of art at Northern Kentucky University, provided a clear assessment of Duveneck's value and neatly demonstrated for me his linkage to Dutch masters. Mary Ran of the Ran Gallery in Cincinnati provided a Duveneck etching for the author to photograph.

As to institutions, I express my gratitude for the availability of Duveneck materials from the Archives of American Art of the Smithsonian Institution, which maintains the Duveneck collection of letters, articles, diaries and photographs. The archive is a wonderful resource. Staff member Elizabeth Christopher was supportive and helpful.

Thanks as usual go to my wife, Charlotte, a former English teacher who accompanied me on a trip to Gloucester and endured the sometimes lengthy commentaries on the artist and his family. She has caught errors and grammatical slips with ease and dispatch. Son, Alec, a lawyer whose love of literature was nurtured in the English departments of Gonzaga College High School in Washington and later at the University of Maryland, performed a copy reading job that would pass muster at the old *New Yorker*.

Sources Consulted

A Guide for the Cathedral, Diocese of Covington, Kentucky, 1947

A Life, James Abbott McNeil Whistler, Gordon Fleming, St. Martin's Press, New York, 1991

The Diary of Alice James, Leon Edel, editor, Northeastern University Press, Boston, 1964

American Painter Abroad, Frank Duveneck's European Years, Michael Quick, Cincinnati Art Museum 1987

Americans in Florence: Sargent and the American Impressionists, edited by Francesca Bardazzi and Carl Sisi, Marsilio, Palazzo Strozzi, Florence, 2012, p.243

Art and Scholasticism, With Other Essays, Jacques Maritain and J.F. Scanlan, originally published by St. Dominic's Press, Ditchling, U.K., 1923, reprint by Kessinger Publishing's Rare Mystical Reprints

Correspondence and Journals of Henry James Jr. and other family papers, 1855-1916, Houghton Library, Harvard University, Cambridge, Massachusetts

Twilight of Painting, an Analysis of Recent Trends to Serve in a Period of Reconstruction, R.H. Ives Gammell, G.P. Putnam's Sons, New York, 1946

The Boston Painters, 1900-1930, R.H. Ives Gammell, Parnassus Imprints, Orleans, Massachusetts, 1986

Life of Johann Schmitt, Diomede Pohlkamp, O.F.M., St. Bonaventure, New York, Franciscan Studies, 1947

Frank and Elizabeth Boott Duveneck papers, 1851-1972, Archives of American Art, Smithsonian Institution, Washington, District of Columbia

Frank Duveneck & Elizabeth Boott Duveneck: An American Romance, essay by Carol M. Osborne for a Duveneck exhibition at Owen Gallery, New York, 1996

"The Underlying Catholicity of Duveneck," Wilde, Mary Leocadia, O.S.B., University of Notre Dame, South Bend, Indiana, 1938

Cathedral Echoes, December, 1926

Br. Cosmas Wolf, monk architect sculpture designer, Br. Nathan Cochran, O.S.B., a catalogue essay for an exhibit at St. Vincent Gallery, Latrobe, Pennsylvania, 2013-2014

Seekers of the Everlasting Kingdom, a Brief History of the Diocese of Covington, James Ott, Editions du Signe, Strasbourg, CEDEX 2, France, 2002

Whistler, A Life for Art's Sake, Daniel E. Sutherland, Yale University Press, New Haven, Connecticut, 2014

Henry James, the Conquest of London: 1870-1881, Leon Edel, a Discus Book, Avon Books, 1962

Henry James, The Middle Years, 1882-1895, Leon Edel, J.B. Lippincott Company, Philadelphia-New York City, 1962

Portrait of a Novel, Henry James and the Making of an American Masterpiece, Michael Gorra, Liveright Publishing Corporation, a division of W.W. Norton & Company, New York, 2012

Italian Hours, Henry James Joseph Pennell, Riverside Press, Houghton Mifflin Company, 1909

The Portrait of a Lady, Henry James

Roderick Hudson, Henry James

The Golden Bowl, Henry James

Sawyier, the Art of Paul Sawyier, Arthur F. Jones, The University of Kentucky Press, 1976

John Twachtman, by Richard Boyle, Watson Guptill Publications, New York, 1988

Gentle Art of Making Enemies, Dover Publications, 1967, William Heinemann, London, 1892, Second Edition.

A Survey of Portraits and Figure Paintings by Frank Duveneck, 1848-1919, by Bill R. Booth 1979, a Ph.D. dissertation, University of Georgia

Beacon Hill, Back Bay and the Builders of Boston's Golden Age, Ted Clark, The History Press, Charleston, SC 29403, 2010

A Short History of Boston, Robert J. Allison, Commonwealth Editions, Beverly, Massachusetts, 2004

The Late George Apley, John Marquand, 1937

Indian Summer, William Dean Howells, 1888

The Essential Transcendentalists, Richard Geldard, Penguin Group, New York

The Proper Bostonians, Cleveland Amory, Parnassus Imprints, Orleans, Massachusetts,, 1947

Last Judgment of Paris The Revolutionary Decade That Gave the World Impressionism, Ross King, Walker & Company, New York, 2006

Life of James McNeill Whistler, E.R. and J. Pennell, J.B. Lippincott Company, London, 1908

Love Well the Hour: Life of Lady Colin Campbell, Anne Jordan, Matador, FEXK /Books Division, London, 2010

Frank Duveneck, Painter-Teacher, Josephine W. Duveneck, John Howell-Books, San Francisco, California, 1970

Recollections of Francis Boott, The Southgate Press—T.W.Ripley Company, 1912, Boston

The Story of Painting, The Evolution of Painting in America, 1907, Charles H. Caffin

My Life on Two Levels, an autobiography, Josephine Whitney Duveneck

Frank Duveneck, His Gloucester Years, Cape Ann Historical Association, April-June, 1987, Volume 7, No. 2

Frank Duveneck, Norbert Heermann, Houghton Mifflin Company, the Riverside Press Cambridge, 1918

Dictionary of American Biography

The Proper Bostonians, Parnasus Imprints, Orleans, Massachusetts, E.P. Dutton & Co., 1947

Venice, City by the Sea, Pennell, Joseph [1857-1926]

William Merritt Chase, A Life in Art, Works from the Collection of the Parrish Art Museum, Alicia G. Longwell, contribution by Maureen C. O'Brien, Parish Art Museum, Water Mill, New York, in association with D Giles Limited, London

Newspapers and Periodicals

Art and Progress

ArtNews

Arts and Decoration

Apollo

Boston Globe

The Cincinnati Commercial Tribune

The Cincinnati Enquirer

Kentucky Post

New York Times

The Boston Sunday Globe

Los Altos Town Crier

Cincinnati Magazine

Cincinnati Times-Star

The Messenger, official newspaper of the Diocese of Covington

Municher Sonntagsblat

American Artist

Apollo

Salon America Journal

Scribner's

The Studio

Institutions

Archives of American Art, Smithsonian Institution, Washington, District of Columbia

Archives, Cincinnati Art Museum

Archives, the Diocese of Covington, Kentucky

Archives, Kenton County Court, Covington, Kentucky

Public Library of Covington and Kenton County, Kentucky

Covington Art Club

Baker-Hunt Foundation, Covington, Kentucky

Encyclopedia Britannica

Xavier University, Cincinnati, Ohio

St. Vincent Archabbey, Latrobe, Pennsylvania

Cathedral Basilica of the Assumption, Covington, Kentucky

James Family Papers, Houghton Library, Harvard University, Cambridge, Massachusetts

Various Publications

The Salon of 1888, Official Exhibit of Academie des Beaux Arts, Societe des Artistes Francais, Eugene von Jagow, September, 1888

American Art at the Nineteenth Century Paris Salons, Lois Marie Fink, National Museum of American Art, Smithsonian Institution, Washington, DC., Cambridge University Press, Cambridge, Massachusetts, 1990

"The Temporary Triumph of Realism," John Canaday, *New York Times*, October 1, 1967

"From Private Grief to Public Monument, The Funerary Effigy of Elizabeth Boott Duveneck," Lois Dinnerstein, *Italian Influence in American Art*, p. 205

American Studio Talk, Charles H. Caffin

Elizabeth Boott Duveneck: Her Life and Times, exhibition catalogue essay by Michel P. Vargas, Triton Museum of Art, Santa Clara, California, p.4

Herman and Bessie Wessel, At Home and Abroad, Carol A. Cyran, Cincinnati Art Club, Cincinnati, Ohio, 1997

Frank Duveneck and Elizabeth Boott Duveneck, An American Romance," Carol M. Osborne, Owen Gallery Exhibition catalogue

"Dear Lizzie: The Life & Loves of Elizabeth Boott Duveneck, Linda Crank, presentation to several organizations

"The Love Affair of Mollie ,Duveneck," James Ott, *Cincinnati Magazine*, January, 1976

"Cincinnati Report: Herman Wessel," Carl Samson and Carol Cyran, *Salon America Journal*, 2004

Br. Cosmas Wolf, monk architect sculpture designer, Br. Nathan Cochran, O.S.B., catalogue essay for an exhibit at St. Vincent Gallery, Latrobe, Pennsylvania, 2013-2014

"Duveneck and Henry James: A Study in Contrasts," Mahonri Sharp Young, *Apollo*, 1970, p. 212

"Duveneck, a Teacher of Artists," L. H. Meakin, *Arts and Decoration*, July, 11911

"The picture season at Villiers-le-Bel, 1876-78, Elizabeth Boott, Thomas Couture, and Henry James," by Carol M. Osborne, *Apollo* 149, no. 447, (May 1999)

German Masters of the Nineteenth Century: paintings and drawings from the Federal Republic of Germany, The Metropolitan Museum of New York, p.32

Jurgen von Jagow, The Salon of 1888, *The Connoisseur*, Vol. 3, No.1, 1888

"The Gloucester Phase of Frank Duveneck," Robert Taylor, *Boston Globe*, Sunday, August, 16, 1987, p.A8

Frank Duveneck: The Gloucester Years, catalogue associated with a 1987 exhibit sponsored by the Cape Ann Historical Association, Martha Oaks, editor

"A Home-Colony of Artists," *The Studio*, Helen M. Knowlton, July 14, 1890, p .326

"The Indian Summer of Frank Duveneck," *ARTnews,* April, 1972, John Asbery

"Frank Duveneck: Artist and Teacher*,"* *Art and Progress*, Anna Seaton-Schmidt, Volume VI, Number 11, September, 1915, pp. 293-394

Persons Interviewed

Orie Ware, former U .S. Congressman, deceased

Aileen McCarthy, former Duveneck student, deceased

William Fay, former Duveneck student, deceased

Hope Duveneck Williams, granddaughter of Frank and Elizabeth Boott Duveneck

David Duveneck, great-grandson of Frank and Elizabeth Boott Duveneck

Gregory Berberich, deceased, former owner of the Duveneck House

Ms. Annette Howell, former owner of the Duveneck House

Carol Osborne, art teacher and writer, former curator of the Stanford University gallery

Frank Decker III, descendant of Duveneck's father's brother, Frank, and his sister, Rita Decker Gehring

Appendix I

[A Sample of Locations of Institutionally Owned
Or on Loan Duveneck Works of Art]

Albright-Knox Art Gallery, Buffalo, NY
Oil on Canvas
Portrait of a Young Man

Allori Cemetery, Florence, Italy
Bronze Sculpture
The Tomb Effigy of Elizabeth Boott Duveneck

Boston Museum of Fine Arts
Sculpture
The Tomb Effigy of Elizabeth Boott Duveneck (marble)
Oils on Canvas
A Girl Reading
A Circassian
The Old Professor
Head of a Child
[A total of 22 items are in the Duveneck collection, including etchings
and sketches]

Cathedral Basilica of the Assumption, Covington, Kentucky
Murals on the theme of the Eucharist dedicated to Katherine Siemers
Duveneck

Cincinnati Art Museum
Oil on Canvas
The Whistling Boy
Guard of the Harem
Beechwoods at Polling, Bavaria

Study of Three Heads with Slaver and Jar
Italian Courtyard
Woman with Forget-Me-Nots
Florentine Flower Girl
Portraits
John White Alexander
Professor Ludwig Loefftz
Elizabeth Boott Duveneck
Francis Duveneck
Sculpture
The first cast of The Tomb Effigy of Elizabeth Boott Duveneck
(The Cincinnati Art Museum's collection includes a total of some 260 of
Duveneck's works, many the gift of the artist in 1915, and extends to
drawings, paintings, and the art of Elizabeth Boott Duveneck.)

Cape Ann Museum, Gloucester
Oil on canvas
Horizon at Gloucester
Study of Braces Rock
Sculpture
Frank Duveneck by Charles Grafley

Carnegie Museum of Art, Pittsburgh
Etching
Desdemona House, Venice
(The Carnegie collection focuses on works by Duveneck Boys Robert
Frederick Blum, Frank Stockton, John Twachtman and John White Al-
exander)

Cleveland Museum of Art
Oil on Canvas
The Venetian Girl
(The collection includes fourteen etchings)

Dallas Museum of Art
Oil on Canvas
Portrait of Old Man
Whistling Boy
Lady in a Red Hat (Portrait of Maggie Wilson)

Detroit Institute of Arts
Seated Nude

DeYoung Museum, San Francisco
Oil on Canvas
Venetian Girl

Harvard University Art Museum
Oil on Canvas
Study of Woman's Head
Henry James, Sr.
Sculpture
Ralph Waldo Emerson
Bust of Charles William Eliot

Indianapolis Museum Art
Oil on Canvas
Henry James, Sr.
Portrait of Squire Duveneck
Nude
Reclining Nude
Self Portrait
Marine
Other modes
The Professor (woodcut)
The Net Mender (sketch)
Memorial to Elizabeth Boott Duveneck (plaster cast)

Joslyn Art Museum, Omaha, Nebraska
Oil on Canvas
Portrait of an Old Actor

Kenton County Public Library
Oil on Canvas
A series of paintings, largely of
Duveneck family members, including
Mollie

Los Angeles County Museum of Art
Female Nude

Lyman Estate, Waltham, Massachusetts
Sculpture of Arthur Lyman, Sr.

Metropolitan Museum of Art, New York
Oil on Canvas
Lady with Fan
Etchings
Bridge of Sighs, Venice
The Realto
View of the Grand Canal, Venice
Piazza San Marco, Venice
(a total of 12 etchings dated 1880-1885)

Milwaukee Art Museum
Oil on Canvas
William Adams
Gratchen
Portrait of Sister Molly (Mollie)

Minneapolis Institute of Art
Etching

National Gallery of Art, Washington, D.C.
Portraits
Leslie Pease Barnum
William Gedney Bunce
(The collection includes four etchings)

Portland Museum of Art
Oil on Canvas
The Carpenter of Polling

Princeton University Art Museum
Oil on Canvas
Portrait of a Woman, 1879

Renwick Gallery, Smithsonian, Washington, D.C.
Oil on Canvas
Head of an Old Man
Portrait of Walter Shirlaw
Water Carriers, Venice
Etchings of the Bridge of Sighs, Venice, and Riva degli Schiavoni

Saint Louis Art Museum
Oil on Canvas
The Bridges, Florence

Saint Vincent Archabbey, Latrobe, Pennsylvania
Oil on Canvas
Our Lady of the Immaculate Conception

Saint Walburg Convent, Villa Hills, Kentucky
Oil on Canvas

Madonna and Child

Taft Museum
Oil on Canvas
The Cobbler's Apprentice

Toledo Museum of Art
Oil on Canvas
Head of an Old Man

Xavier University
Portraits in Oil on Canvas
Mary Poland Verkamp
Mrs. John Henry Twachtman

Appendix II

Dates in the Life of Frank Duveneck

1848 –Born October 9 in Covington, Kentucky, son of Bernard Decker and Katherine Siemers Duveneck. (After the 1849 death of Bernard Decker, Katherine Decker married Squire Joseph Duveneck.)

1862 – Learns painting, modeling and carving as an apprentice with the Altar Building Stock Company, Covington; learns his trade from Brother Cosmas Wolf, O.S.B., and Johann Schmitt.

1867 – Works with Wilhelm Lamprecht, a painter who studied at the Royal Academy of Fine Arts, Munich, and travels to Quebec, Canada. There he worked with Lamprecht on the interior of Saint-Romuald d'Etchemin church.

1870 – Travels to Munich to study at the Royal Academy; he studies under Wilhelm von Diez and is influenced by Wilhelm Leibl.

1872 –wins a top prize in a competition for composition and is granted use of a studio.

1873 –Returns to Cincinnati and works in the church decorating business.

1874 –Exhibits portraits in Cincinnati and wins acclaim for an exhibit at the Boston Art Club.

1875 – Returns to Munich.

1877 – Travels to Venice and exhibits paintings at the National Academy of Design, New York.

1878 – Returns to Munich from Venice and launches school for painters, which attracts a host of followers, the celebrated Duveneck Boys; works are exhibited at the New York Academy of Design and the Kurtz Gallery.

1879 – Elizabeth Boott starts studies with Duveneck in Munich; Duveneck's school moves to Florence for the next two years.
1880 - Begins practice of etching with student Otto Bacher.
1881 - Exhibits his etchings with the Society of Painter-Etchers, London.
1882 – Returns to Venice and exhibits etchings a second time in London.
1885 - Stays in Venice and continues painting and etching, travels to Paris that fall.
1886 – Marries Elizabeth Boott in Paris and moves to Villa Castellani in Florence.
1887 – Son Frank Duveneck, Jr., is born.
1888 – Travels with his family to Paris where wife Elizabeth dies of pneumonia.
1889 - Returns to America and works in Boston and visits Cincinnati.
1890 – Starts teaching painting class organized by Mrs. Bellamy Storer in Cincinnati.
1892 – Travels to Paris and Florence and begins work on the memorial to Elizabeth.
1893 - After travel in Europe, returns to Cincinnati, receives award at the Columbia Exposition in Chicago.
1894 – Spends two months in Spain.
1895 – Receives honorable mention from the Paris Salon for the effigy memorial and family crisis over sister Mollie's indiscretions.
1896 – Elected first president of the Society of Western Artists
1899 - Serves as a juror for paintings at the Paris Exposition of 1900.
1900 - Joins the faculty at the Cincinnati Art Academy.
1902 - Wins silver medal for painting at the Pan-American Exposition.
1904 – Serves on the International Jury for the Louisiana Purchase Exposition.

1905 – Travels to Italy and begins his studies for the murals in the Cathedral Basilica of the Assumption, Covington

1910 – Exhibits works in the Exhibition of American Art, Berlin.

1911 – Exhibits in the International Fine Arts Exposition, Buenos Aires, Argentina; serves as a juror for the Fifteenth Annual International Exhibition of the Carnegie Institute, Pittsburgh.

1915 – Serves on the jury for the Panama-Pacific Exposition in San Francisco and receives a special gold medal of honor.

1917 - Receives LL.D. degree from the University of Cincinnati.

1919 - Dies in Cincinnati on January 3 at age 71 years.

Made in the USA
Lexington, KY
29 April 2016